A TEXTBOOK OF
EUROPEAN MUSICAL
INSTRUMENTS

In the foreground a Positive Organ, Harp, Lute (in case), Long Drum, Kettle-drum, Trombone, and Tricorde. On the table, Viol, Clavichord, Cross-blown Flute, Krumhorn, Recorder, Tabor-pipe and straight Cornett. At the back a Cornett-player. Centre, the young King of Austria, Maximilian I. Instruments characteristic of the late fifteenth century.

THE SKILL OF MUSIC

By HANS BURGKMAIR (*c.* 1500)

A TEXTBOOK OF
EUROPEAN MUSICAL INSTRUMENTS

THEIR ORIGIN, HISTORY, AND CHARACTER

by

FRANCIS W. GALPIN

M.A., Litt.D., F.L.S.
CANON EMERITUS OF CHELMSFORD CATHEDRAL,
HON. FREEMAN OF THE WORSHIPFUL COMPANY OF MUSICIANS

GREENWOOD PRESS, PUBLISHERS
WESTPORT, CONNECTICUT

Library of Congress Cataloging in Publication Data

Galpin, Francis William, 1858-1945.
A textbook of European musical instruments.

Reprint of the 1956 ed. published by E. Benn,
London.
1. Musical instruments—History. I. Title.
ML460.G14T35 1976   781.9'1   75-36509
ISBN 0-8371-8648-X

Reprinted with the permission of B.J.F. Galpin, J.L. Galpin and
R.I. Galpin.

This edition first published in 1956 by Ernest Benn Limited,
London

Reprinted in 1976 by Greenwood Press, Inc.,
51 Riverside Avenue, Westport, CT 06880

Library of Congress catalog card number 75-36509
ISBN 0-8371-8648-X

Printed in the United States of America

10 9 8 7 6 5 4 3 2

TO THE MANY FRIENDS AND FELLOW-WORKERS

AT HOME AND ABROAD

WHO HAVE GAINED INTEREST

AND INSPIRATION FROM

OUR INDEBTEDNESS TO THE PAST

CONTENTS

LIST OF ILLUSTRATIONS

The Skill of Music, by Hans Burgkmair, *c.* 1500   *Frontispiece*

PLATES

DIAGRAMS IN THE TEXT

A PRELUDE

WHEN I was asked to write the history of European musical instruments in a short and compendious form, I was appalled at the audacity of the suggestion. It seemed, as it were, a reversal of the old proverb, and that the mouse was being requested to produce the mountain. As my eyes scanned my bookshelves and, in fancy, those of our great libraries replete with countless volumes, each containing the history of but a small portion of this vast subject, my task appeared like an attempt at the impossible. There was, however, one redeeming feature in the request: it was to be a handbook for students.

Now we students are never content with anything that is put before us. We want to know more, or else we should not be students. I therefore foresaw that, although the production of this little book might be disappointing both to the reader and to the author, it might be at least informative and lead on to a more intensive study of particular details here unavoidably omitted. If it does so, I shall be amply repaid for my efforts by awakening such enquiry.

A desire was also expressed that the subject should be treated in a readable way. How difficult it is to define such an expression! The "popular account" style may while away a leisure moment with a certain amount of amusement and so far satisfy, I trust, author and publisher. But those who are in quest of reliable facts close the book with a sigh. If, therefore, I have combined with my narrative particulars which appear somewhat technical, it is for the purpose of supplying information which I have often been asked to give in connection with this subject. For this reason, too,

I have made mention of some of the "eccentricities" in the construction of musical instruments; the ideas may be absurd, but in these days of unparalleled progress they may nevertheless be stimulating and suggestive.

A new field of research and interest is opening out in the so-called electrophonic music of the present day, to which I have devoted a special chapter. At present the inclination is to compare the musical effects produced by electrical currents with existing sounds to which we are accustomed. But in reality electrophonic or electronic music has a realm of expression peculiarly its own, and one which has yet to make its appeal to the rising generation. On this subject I must express my great indebtedness to that skilled and accomplished electronicist, Mr. Martin Taubmann, and also to my sons, Major Galpin, D.S.O., and Captain S. G. Galpin, R.E., who have furnished me with valuable details of the new art.

In dealing with musical instruments I have taken for granted that the student is well acquainted with their outward appearance as used in the present day; but the more ancient forms and their method of construction may be of fresh interest to him. It is with this object also I have included a list of some of the great public collections of musical instruments in Britain, on the Continent, and even in America, where their past is so closely linked with the history of European progress. It is unfortunate that many of these museums keep their specimens in the still silence of the glass case; and, even if they are liberated from their prison-house, they are forbidden to speak. We should never countenance a picture-gallery in which most of the paintings were hung with their faces to the wall; and, for a display of the works of a sister art, a few of those silent voices, at any rate, might be permitted to let their gentle sounds creep once more into our ears.

With reference to the illustrations given in this book, I am indebted to Messrs. Macmillan for permission to reproduce Plates I–VI, IX and X from Grove's *Dictionary of Music* (third edition), which show old instruments in my own collection, and also to Messrs. Reeves for a similar kindness in connection with Plates VII and VIII, which first appeared in the publication of the Musicians' Company's Exhibition Lectures (1904) entitled *English Music*. For several of the line blocks my thanks are also due to Messrs. Macmillan. Two illustrations, new to English literature, are of particular interest—the one, by leave of the directors of the Silesian Museum, Breslau, of the harpsichord made by Shudi of London and presented by him to King Frederick the Great in 1765; and the other of the chromatic trumpet invented in 1788 by Clagget of London, father of the valve-action instruments, taken from his rare pamphlet in my possession. Diagrams of modern valve-systems for brass instruments have been omitted, as they would have been meaningless unless a complete series were shown. They are given in detail in the late Captain C. R. Day's *Descriptive Catalogue of the Royal Military Exhibition* (1890), and by the late Mr. Victor Mahillon in his *Catalogue analytique du Musée instrumental du Conservatoire Royal de Musique de Bruxelles* (1880–1922). To the friendship and researches of both these writers I am deeply grateful, for they kindled an enthusiasm which has given me a lifelong interest and pleasure.

FRANCIS W. GALPIN

RICHMOND, *1937*

SOME NOTED COLLECTIONS
OF EUROPEAN MUSICAL INSTRUMENTS
IN PUBLIC MUSEUMS AND ACADEMIES

(An asterisk denotes that there is a catalogue of special interest)

AMSTERDAM, Rijks Museum
ANN ARBOR (U.S.A.), *Michigan University Museum
ANTWERP, *Steen Museum
BASLE, *Historisches Museum .
BERGEN, Bergenskes Museum
BERLIN, *Instrumenten Museum (Hochschule für Musik)
BOLOGNA, *Museo Civico
BOSTON (U.S.A.), *Museum of Fine Arts.
BRESLAU, *Schlesisches Museum
BRUNSWICK, *Stadtisches Museum
BRUSSELS, *Musée du Conservatoire de Musique
BUDAPEST, Hungarian National Museum
COPENHAGEN, *Musik-historisk Museum. National Museum
CRACOW, Kunst-historisches Museum
DUBLIN, National Museum
EDINBURGH, National Museum. University Music School
EISENACH, *Bach Museum
FLORENCE, Museo del Instituto Cherubini
FRANKFORT-am-Main, *Historisches Museum
GOTHENBURG, *Museum
THE HAGUE, *Gemeente Museum
HAMBURG, *Museum für Hamburgische Geschichte
INNSBRUCK, *Ferdinandeum
ISTAMBUL, Seraglio Museum
LEIPZIG, *Neues Grassimuseum (University)

B   17

LENINGRAD, *Conservatoire de Musique
LINZ, Museum Francisco-Carolinum
LONDON, *Victoria and Albert Museum. Royal College of Music
MADRID, Nationalmuseum
MANCHESTER, *Royal College of Music
MIDDLEBURG, Staatsmuseum
MILAN, *Conservatoire de Musique
MODENA, Museo Civico
MOSCOW, Conservatoire de Musique
MUNICH, *National Museum. Deutsches Museum
NEWHAVEN (U.S.A.), *University Museum
NEW YORK (U.S.A.), *Metropolitan Museum of Art
NUREMBERG, Germanisches Museum
OSLO, *Norse Folkmuseum
OXFORD, University Museum
PARIS, *Conservatoire de Musique. Hôtel Cluny
PHILADELPHIA (U.S.A.), Pennsylvania University Museum
PRAGUE, National Museum. Konservatorium Mozarteum
ROME, Museum of the Academy of St. Cecilia
SALZBURG, *Museum Carolino-Augusteum
STOCKHOLM, *Musik-historiska Museet. Rijks Museum
TURIN, Museo Civico
VENICE, *Museo Civico
VERONA, Museo Civico
VIENNA, *Gesellschaft der Musikfreunde. *Kunsthistorisches Museum
WASHINGTON (U.S.A.), *National Museum
ZÜRICH, Landes Museum

The catalogues of museums, especially those of Brussels (Mahillon), Berlin (Sachs), Vienna (Schlosser), and the Heyer Collection (Kinsky), now at Leipzig, afford valuable information. Various papers on musical instruments published in the Reports of Societies and in periodicals are mentioned in the text.

BIBLIOGRAPHICAL SUMMARY

i. EARLY WORKS

(Words in brackets denote printed editions or reprints)

Latin Manuscript St. Blaise, thirteenth century (Gerbert, *De Cantu,*
  etc., 1774)   [1932]
Latin Manuscript Arnaut, fifteenth century (Le Cerf et Labande,
VIRDUNG, SEBASTIAN: *Musica getutscht,* 1511 (Eitner, 1882;
  Schrade, 1931)   [(Eitner, 1896)
AGRICOLA, MARTIN: *Musica instrumentalis deudsch* 1528, 1545
GERLE, HANS: *Musica teusch,* 1532
LANFRANCO, GIOVANNI: *Scintille di Musica,* 1533
GANASSI, SYLVESTRO DI: *Regola rubertina,* 1542 (Schneider, 1924).
ZACCONI, LUDOVICO: *Prattica di musica,* 1592
CERRETO, SCIPIONE: *Della prattica musica,* 1601
CERONE, PIETRO: *El Melopeo,* 1613
PRAETORIUS, MICHAEL: *Syntagma musicum,* 1618–20 (Eitner, 1884;
  Gurlitt, 1929)
MERSENNE, MARIN: *Harmonicorum Libri XII,* 1635
MERSENNE, MARIN: *Harmonie universelle,* 1636
KIRCHER, ATHANASIUS: *Musurgia universalis,* 1650
MACE, THOMAS: *Musick's Monument,* 1676
ROUSSEAU, JEAN: *Traité de la viole,* 1687
HOTTETERRE-LE-ROMAIN: *Principes de la Flûte . . . Flûte Douce et
  du Hautbois,* 1707
BONANNI, FILIPPO: *Gabinetto Armonico,* 1722 (Ceruti, 1776)
QUANTZ, JOHANN: *Die Flöte traversiere,* 1752 (Schering, 1906)
ADLUNG, JACOB: *Musica mechanica organoedi,* 1768
BEDOS DE CELLES: *L'art du Facteur d'Orgues,* 1766–78 (Hamel,
  1849)   [1911]
ALTENBURG, JOHANN: *Trompeter- und Pauker-Kunst,* 1795 (Bertling,

ii. RECENT WORKS

a. GENERAL

GROVE: *Dictionary of Music* (3rd ed. by H. C. Colles), London, 1927

LAVIGNAC: *Encyclopedie de la Musique*, Paris, 1931 ff.

SACHS: *Real Lexicon der Musikinstrumente*, Berlin, 1913

NORLIND: *Allmänt Musik Lexicon*, Stockholm, 1913 ff.

BRÜCKER, F.: *Die Blasinstrumente in der altfranzösischen Literatur*, Giessen, 1926

BUHLE, E., *Die Instrumente in den Miniaturen des früher Mittelalters*, Leipzig, 1903

DICK, F., *Die Saiten und Schlaginstrumente in der altfranzösischen Literatur*, Giessen, 1932

FORSYTH, C., *Orchestration*, London, 1922

GALPIN, F. W., *Old English Instruments of Music* (3rd ed.), London, 1932

LAVOIX FILS, *Histoire de l'instrumentation*, Paris, 1878.

PEDRELL, F., *Organografía musical antiqua española*, Barcelona, 1900

RIANO, J. F.: *Early Spanish Music*, London, 1887

RUTH-SOMMER, *Alte Musikinstrumente*, Berlin, 1920

TERRY, C. SANFORD, *Bach's Orchestra*, Oxford Press, 1932

TERSCHAK UND HAUPT: *Musik Instrumenten Kunde in Wort und Bild*, Leipzig, 1910–11

b. AUTOPHONES

NICHOLS, J.: *Bells thro' the Ages*, London, 1928

POHL, C. F.: *Die Geschichte der Glas Harmonica*, Vienna, 1862

c. MEMBRANOPHONES

BERGER, F. R.: *Das Basler Trommeln*, Basle, 1928

KIRBY, P. R.: *The Kettle-Drums*, London, 1930

d. CHORDOPHONES

PANUM, H.: *Middelalderens Strenginstrumente*, Copenhagen, 1915–31
SCHLESINGER, K.: *Precursors of the Violin Family*, London, 1910
GRILLET, L.: *Les Ancêtres du Violon et du Violoncello*, Paris, 1907
ARMSTRONG, R. B.: *Irish and Highland Harps*, Edinburgh, 1904
FLOOD, W. H. G.: *The Story of the Harp*, London, 1905
BIERNATH, E.: *Die Guitare*, Berlin, 1907
RÜHLMANN, J.: *Die Geschichte der Bogeninstrumente*, Brunswick, 1882
ANDERSSON, O.: *The Bowed Harp* (trans. by K. Schlesinger), London, 1930
HAYES, G. R.: *The Viols and Other Bowed Instruments*, Oxford Press, 1930
JAMES, PHILIP: *Early Keyboard Instruments*, London, 1930
HIPKINS, A. J.: *The Pianoforte and Other Instruments*, London, 1896
BLOM, ERIC: *The Romance of the Piano*, London, 1928

e. AEROPHONES

CLAPPÉ, A. A.: *The Wind Band*, London, 1912
DAUBENY, U.: *Orchestral Wind Instruments*, London, 1920
KAPPEY, J. A.: *Military Music*, London, 1890
DAY, C. R.: *Musical Instruments in the Military Exhibition*, London, 1891
BOEHM, T.: *The Flute* (2nd ed. by Dayton Miller), London, 1922
ROCKSTRO, R. S.: *The Flute*, London, 1890
FITZGIBBON, H. M.: *The Story of the Flute*, London, 1928
WELCH, C.: *The Recorder*, London, 1911
VIDAL, F.: *Galoubet et Tambourin*, Aix, 1869
ALTENBURG, W.: *Die Klarinette*, Heilbronn, 1904
ELSENAAR, E.: *De Clarinet*, Hilversum, 1927
KOOL, J.: *Das Saxophon*, Leipzig, 1931
BRIDET, A.: *Aperçu historique du Hautbois*, Lyons, 1927
BLECHER UND RAHM: *Die Oboe*, Leipzig, 1914

HECKEL, W.: *Der Fagott* (2nd ed.), Leipzig, 1931
FLOOD, W. H. G.: *The Bagpipe*, London, 1911
WILLIAMS, C. F. A.: *The Organ*, London, 1903
WEDGWOOD, J. I.: *Dictionary of Organ Stops*, London, 1905
WEDGWOOD, J. I.: *Some Continental Organs*, London, 1906
WHITWORTH, R.: *The Electric Organ*, London, 1936
WHITWORTH, R.: *The Cinema and Theatre Organ*, London, 1936
EICHBORN, H. W.: *Die Trompete*, Leipzig, 1881
EICHBORN, H. W.: *Die alte Clarinblasen*, Leipzig, 1894
MENKE, W.: *History of the Trumpet of Bach and Handel*, London, 1934
MAHILLON, V.: *Le Cor, La Trompette et le Trombone*, Brussels, 1906–7

f. ELECTROPHONES

On this new class many articles have appeared, such as:
"Electrical Music," *World Radio*, February 15, 1935
"Electronic Music in France," *World Radio*, May 10, 1935
"New Developments in Electric Music," *Wireless Magazine*, May 1935
The articles are accompanied by illustrations and diagrams

ORIGINS AND PROTOTYPES

D'ERLANGER, R.: *La Musique et les Instruments Arabes*, Paris, 1930
FARMER, H. G.: *The Organ of the Ancients from Eastern Sources*, London, 1931
GALPIN, F. W.: *The Music of the Sumerians, Babylonians and Assyrians*, Cambridge Press, 1937
SACHS, CURT: *Die Musikinstrumente Indiens und Indonesiens*, Berlin, 1923
SACHS, CURT: *Die Musikinstrumente des alten Aegypten*, Berlin, 1921
KIRBY, P. R.: *The Musical Instruments of the Native Races of South Africa*, Oxford Press, 1934
SCHAEFFNER, A.: *Origine des instruments de musique*, Paris, 1936.

ABBREVIATIONS FOR STAFF NOTATION

Each distinctive sequence begins on the note C and embraces twelve
semitones

THE CLASSIFICATION OF INSTRUMENTS

"NOTHING helps the memory so much as order and classification." So wrote Blackie, sixty years ago, in his work on self-culture. It will therefore be necessary, as a preface to the study of musical instruments and as an aid to recollection, that the subject should be treated on definite and systematic lines. In the great science of Botany, for instance, classification plays an all-important part, whether it is based on the artificial system connected with the name of Linnaeus or on the more recent arrangement of natural order. In dealing, however, with such products of art and man's device as instruments of music a classification on the lines of natural evolution is hardly possible, although, as will be shown later, there are certain affinities between them which suggest a progressive development from a common source. The arrangement must therefore follow an artificial method, as indeed it has from earliest days. The Chinese, through long ages, have classed their instruments according to the material of which they are made. They recognize eight kinds of sonorous bodies—skin, stone, metal, clay, silk, wood, bamboo, and gourd. Though they consider such an arrangement "according to nature," it is, in reality, purely artificial; for the material from which a musical instrument is made plays but a small part in its sound-production. Greek and Roman writers give a three-fold classification, placing the instruments under three *genera*, viz. *pneumaticon* or *inflatile* (wind instruments), *enchordon* or *tensile* (stringed instruments), and *kroustikon* or *pulsatile* (percussion instruments). This tripartite division existed also among the Hebrews and throughout the Middle Ages. It has, in fact, only been superseded by closer study and analysis during the last century. With regard to the third division, that of percussion, it is interesting to note that the authoritative writers on music in the sixteenth century, such as Virdung (1511), Agricola (1528), and Zacconi (1592), did not include drums of any kind in the category of musical instruments. For instance, Sebastian Virdung places as his third class "those made of metal or other resonant material"; whilst Martin Agricola, using practically the same words, mentions the cymbals, the *Strohfiedel* (xylophone), the bells, and others of that sort, including—in honour of Pythagoras— the anvil and hammer, but again, no drums. Virdung, the quiet-loving priest of Arnberg in South Germany, gives us his reasons for their omission. In his opinion they were mere *Rumpelfesser* ("rumbling tubs"). "These are to the taste of such as cause much unrest to pious old people of the earth, to the sick and weakly, the devout in the cloisters, those who have to read, study, and pray. And I verily believe that the Devil must have had the devising and making of them, for there is no pleasure or anything good about them. If hammering and raising a din be music, then coopers and those who make barrels must be musicians; but that is all nonsense." Ludovico Zacconi has a peculiar fourfold division of his own; he groups the instruments he describes into wind, keyed, bowed, and plucked. He does not consider any of the pulsatile class, and, even from the wind class, he excludes the trumpet, as not having a diatonic scale and as being an instrument "*da campi ò da battaglie.*"

When we pass to the seventeenth century, excluding the feeble copy of Zacconi's treatise by Cerone (1613), we find a distinct change of outlook. Michael Praetorius (1618) places in his third or percussion class not only those mentioned above, omitting the anvil, but heads it with the drums (kettledrum and tabor). Marin Mersenne (1636) and Athanasius Kircher (1650) follow in the same way.

Now, if we turn to the East again, we find that the Hindus, in this respect, were in advance of Western nations. From the days of Bhârata (*c.* 50 B.C.) there has been a fourfold division of musical instruments, viz. *Tata-yantra* ("string" instruments), *Sushira-yantra* ("pierced or hollow," i.e. wind instruments), *Ghana-yantra* ("struck" instruments of metal or wood, such as gongs and rattles), and *Ānaddha-yantra* ("tied on" or "bound" instruments, i.e. drums, in allusion to the method of affixing the skin heads). Willard, in his treatise on the Music of Hindoostan (1834), gives these same divisions as *Tut, Sooghur, Ghun,* and *Bitut.*

In 1877, when the Museum of Musical Instruments was formed in connection with the *Conservatoire Royal de Musique* at Brussels, with M. Victor Mahillon as curator and M. Gevaert as director, this fourfold division was adopted; the various sound-producers were classed as *Autophones* or self-vibrators, *Membranophones* or skin-vibrators, *Aerophones* or wind-vibrators, and *Chordophones* or string-vibrators, terms which will be more fully explained later on. These classes were subdivided into branches and sections. In 1914 the late Professor E. von Hornbostel and Dr. Curt Sachs of Berlin still further elaborated this classification, retaining the same system under the titles Class, Sub-class, Order, and Sub-order, but adding yet more minute divisions which may be termed group, genus, and species. In this way they endeavoured to embrace the varying characteristics of all known instruments and even of those not yet invented. In this system each class, order, and division is denoted by a number, and a detailed description of any instrument can be represented, therefore, in a numerical formula; class, sub-class, order, sub-order, etc., follow each other in successive digits from left to right. An instance of this all-in system, as given by the authors, may be quoted. There is an instrument, dating from medieval times, known as the *Glockenspiel*, or in England as the bell-chime. It consists of a graded series of small bells or gongs hung on a frame and struck with a hammer or pair of hammers. The numerical formula for such a simple instrument appears in the Hornbostel–Sachs classification as 111242222. This, in translation from left to right, means that it belongs to the first class (self-vibrators), the first sub-class (struck), the first order (directly), the second sub-order (on the outside), the fourth group (upon a receptacle), the second sub-group (a bell), the second genus (in a series), the second sub-genus (hanging), and the second species (with a hammer)—a very correct analysis of its character and a fine tonic for the memory. Since then Dr. Sachs, in his *Geist und Werden der Musikinstrumente* (1929), has treated the subject in a very interesting and novel way, arranging the instruments of music in *strata* according to human progress and civilization. Beginning with the Stone Age as a main group, he shows the characteristic survivals of that period in North and South America (totem instruments), as well as in Oceania and among Africo-Indian tribes. Taking as his next group of *strata* the Metal Age, he recalls the typical examples found in Egypt and nearer Asia (fourth to second millenniums B.C.), and in the East and West during the first millennium B.C., comparing them with instruments still present amongst primitive peoples in Africa, India, Madagascar, and Indonesia. For the Middle Ages group he deals with Southern Asiatic forms and those found in the East and West during the early centuries of the Christian era. On the lines of this "culture" scheme the late Professor Hornbostel developed the "Ethnology of the African Sound-instruments" in the journal of the Oxford University Press entitled *Africa* (vol. vi, 1933), and Professor Kirby still further in his *Musical Instruments of the Native Races of South Africa* (1934).

In the present textbook, however, such minute or appealing classifications as these will not be attempted, and for the term Order, which seems to belong rather to natural science than to human artifacts, the term Division will be substituted. It will be sufficient, therefore, to place the instruments under the following headings:

CLASS, denoting the type of sound-producer; SUB-CLASS, the principle of sound-production; DIVISION, the manner of application (direct or through mechanism); SUBDIVISION, the particular form of construction employed. If it is necessary, as in the case of stringed and wind instruments, to particularize still further, the terms *section* and *subsection* may be employed. In referring to the above-mentioned systems of general classification, (G-M) will denote the Brussels scheme and (H-S) that of Berlin. The classes, therefore, of our present scheme will be as follows:

I. AUTOPHONIC INSTRUMENTS or self-vibrators, i.e. instruments of solid substance which, owing to their elastic nature, have a sonority of their own, which is emitted in waves when they are struck, plucked, or stimulated by friction or air. The title *Idiophone* (H-S) gives perhaps a more personal meaning, but the prefix *auto* is more generally understood. The term "phonic" (from the Greek *phōnē*, "a voice") is applied, according to Sir Charles Wheatstone, to "the body by which the sound is produced, occasioning in the surrounding air vibrations or oscillations corresponding in number and extent to those which exist in itself."

II. Membranophonic instruments or skin-vibrators, i.e. instruments in which the sound-waves are due to the vibrations of a stretched skin or membrane when struck, plucked, or stroked.

III. Chordophonic instruments or string-vibrators, i.e. instruments in which the sound-waves are dependent upon the vibrations of a stretched string and induced by plucking, striking, or by friction or air.

IV. Aerophonic instruments or wind-vibrators, i.e. instruments in which the sound-waves are produced by the vibrations of a column of air, the pulsations being set in motion by some special device, flue (whistle), reed, or the lips.

V. Electrophonic instruments or electric-vibrators, i.e. instruments in which the sound-waves are formed by oscillations set up in electric valves. This class, sometimes called electronic, is entirely new and included here for the first time. It is only recently that the familiar "howl" of the oscillating valve has been raised to the dignity of musical expression. Electro-magnetism is also used.

In this subjoined scheme the classes are denoted by large Roman numerals; sub-classes by small Roman numerals; divisions by Roman capitals; subdivisions by small Roman letters; and sections by small Arabic numerals. Some typical examples of the instruments listed have been added in the last column; but we may call attention to the following points. In the Membranophonic class, Sub-class iii is termed "by co-vibration"; the principle involved can hardly be included under "sympathetic vibration." In the Aerophonic class the expression "voiced" is taken from a passage in North's *Memoirs of Music* (1728), in which, speaking of the ancient *tibia*, he says, "I guess it was voiced rather by the lipps as a cornett or else by some Reedall [reed.]" The word "flue" is the old English term for "a narrow slit or windway," still used by organ-builders. In Sub-class ii, Subdivisions a and b, the shape of the tubes (cylindrical or conical) precedes the section denoting the form of reed employed. This is the more correct order, for the typical attributes of the instruments depend more on the shape of the tube than on the vibrating reeds, which can be interchanged with but little alteration of tone. In these instruments also the cylindrical shape of the natural reed preceded the conical shape, whereas in the next Subdivision (lip-voiced), the conical form of the natural horn anticipated the cylindrical. Free reeds require no tubes, but simply vibrate through a "frame."

CLASS I.—AUTOPHONIC INSTRUMENTS

Sub-class	Division	Subdivision	Typical examples
i. By striking	A. Direct	a. Clashed	Cymbals, Castanets
		b. Shaken	Ball rattles
		c. Struck	Xylophones, Bells
	B. Indirect	a. With keyboard	Dulcitone, Carillons
		b. Automatic	Clock chimes
ii. By plucking	A. Direct	a. With finger	Jew's harp
		b. With ratchet	Notched rattles
	B. Indirect	a. With keyboard	Claviola
		b. Automatic	Musical box
iii. By friction	A. Direct	a. With finger	Musical glasses
		b. With bow	Nail harmonica
	B. Indirect	a. With keyboard	Clavicylindre
		b. Automatic	Barrel Aiuton
iv. By blowing	A. Direct	a. From mouth	Cracker glass
	B. Indirect	a. With keyboard	Aeolsklavier

CLASS II.—MEMBRANOPHONIC INSTRUMENTS

Sub-class	Division	Subdivision	Typical examples
i. By striking	A. Direct	a. On rim-frame	Timbrel, Tambourine
		b. On cylinder frame	Side and bass drums
		c. On bowl frame	Kettle drum
	B. Indirect	a. With ratchet	Handle drum
		b. With pedal	Pedal drum
		c. Automatic	Barrel drum
ii. By friction	A. Direct	a. With rod	Rommelpot
		b. With cord	Brummtopf
	B. Indirect	a. By whirling	Waldteufel
iii. By co-vibration	A. Direct	a. Vocal	Flute eunuque, Mirliton
	B. Indirect	a. Automatic	Gramophone

c

CLASS III.—CHORDOPHONIC INSTRUMENTS

Sub-class	Division	Subdivision	Section	Typical examples
i. By plucking	A. Direct	a. Without neck	1. Open strings	Musical bow, Harp, Lyre, Psaltery
			2. Fretted strings	Zither
		b. With neck		Lute, Cither, Guitar
	B. Indirect	a. With keyboard		Virginal, Harpsichord
		b. Automatic		Barrel spinet
ii. By striking	A. Direct	a. Without neck		Dulcimer, Tambourine
	B. Direct	a. With keyboard		Clavichord, Piano
		b. Automatic		Pianola
iii. By friction	A. Direct	a. Without neck		Talharpa, Ancient Crwth
		b. With neck		Rebec, Viol, Violin, Trumpet marine
	B. Indirect	a. With keyboard		Nyckelharpa, Hurdy-gurdy
		b. Automatic		Celestina, Violina
iv. By air	A. Direct	a. Without neck		Aeolian harp
	B. Indirect	a. With keyboard		Anémocorde

CLASS IV.—AEROPHONIC INSTRUMENTS

Sub-class	Division	Subdivision	Section	Typical examples
i. Flue-voiced	A. Direct	a. Open tube	1. End blown	Kaval, Giorgi flute
			2. Whistle-blown	Recorder, Flageolet
			3. Side blown	Transverse flute
		b. Closed tube		Ocarina
	B. Indirect	a. With keyboard		Pipe organ
		b. Automatic		Bird organ
ii. Reed-voiced	A. Direct	a. Cylindrical tube	1. Single-beating reed	Clarinet
			2. Double-beating reed	Krumhorn
		b. Conical tube	1. Single-beating reed	Saxophone
			2. Double-beating reed	Oboe, Bassoon
		c. Framed	Free reed	Mouth organ
	B. Indirect	a. With finger-holes		Phagotum, Bagpipe
		b. With keyboard		Regal, Harmonium
		c. Automatic		Barrel-organ
iii. Lip-voiced	A. Direct	a. Conical tube	1. Simple	Natural horn
			2. With holes	Cornetto, Ophicleide
			3. With slide	Slide horn
			4. With valves	Valve horn, Cornet
		b. Cylindrical tube	1. Simple	Natural trumpet
			2. With holes	Keyed trumpet
			3. With slide	Slide trumpet, Trombone
			4. With valves	Valve trumpet and trombone

CLASS V.—ELECTROPHONIC INSTRUMENTS

Sub-class	Division	Subdivision	Typical examples
i. By oscillation	A. Direct	a. Free hand	Aetherophon, Electronde
		b. Graduated	Trautonium, Hellertion
	B. Indirect	a. With keyboard	Givelet-Coupleux Organ, Phototone
ii. Electro-magnetic	A. Direct	(not in use)	
	B. Indirect	a. With keyboard	Hammond Organ
		b. Automatic	Radio-Gramophone
iii. Electro-static	A. Direct	(not in use)	
	B. Indirect	a. With keyboard	Compton Organ and Electrones
		b. Automatic	Bells and Clock Chimes

I

AUTOPHONIC INSTRUMENTS

including

CYMBALS, RATTLES, XYLOPHONES, BELLS, CARILLONS, THE
JEW'S HARP, MUSICAL BOX, MUSICAL GLASSES, NAIL-VIOLIN,
HARMONICAS, WITH THEIR KEYBOARD AND AUTOMATIC
AMPLIFICATIONS

WE stand on the threshold of a wondrous Art. In far-off
prehistoric days man began to realize that, beside his own
voice and the calls of beast and bird, there were other sounds
in Nature which he might harness to his use. As the din of
crashing rocks echoed through the valley, as the wooden logs
clattered whilst he piled them for the hearth-fire, or the
hollow tree boomed to his blows, Nature's own untutored
symphony filled his mind with new ideas. The din was
terrifying; then with it he could strike terror into the hearts
of his foes, whether men or demons. The clitter-clatter of
the logs and the boom of the tree were rhythmical; did they
not bid him and his to the dance? Thus the human mind
awoke to the two ideas which permeated this primitive life
of war and recreation, namely, noise to ward off enemies to
its peace and rhythm to speed the feet in measured steps.
So, with the tap of the hand on the conductor's desk, we are
presented with the world's first overture to music.

i. STRUCK TYPE

CLAPPERS

i.A.a. The instruments which give forth their sound by *clashing* are generally called clappers. In their earliest form they were probably mere sticks of wood or pieces of bone. Known as "dancing-sticks," they appear in Western Asia five thousand years ago, held in the hands and struck together in the same way as in the stave dances of the much later Morrismen. In course of time the clappers were hinged and known to the ancients as *Crotala*—a name also applied to the very similar sound made by the rattling beak of the storks. When the Metal Age appeared the "dancing-sticks" gave place to swords; but the Arabs still use the *Qadib* or wooden wand to accentuate the beats. A refinement is apparent in the flat clappers held between the fingers, and called in France *Tablettes* or *Cliquettes*, and in England popularly known as knicky-knackers or nigger bones. Their early use in Spain is revealed in eleventh- and thirteenth-century manuscripts, and Shakespeare mentions them in *A Midsummer Night's Dream* (IV. i) with approbation: "I have a reasonable good ear in music; let us have the tongs and the bones." To these more rural accompaniments succeeded the square or round castanets, so called from the chestnut (*castanea*) wood from which they were mostly made. Like the Greek *Crembala*, they were suspended from the fingers, and found a place in the ritual of the early Coptic Church, though now more intimately connected with Sicilian and Spanish dances. In Italy at vintage-time a curious little clapper is constructed of two spoons held together in the hand and struck with another spoon. Bonanni (1723) calls it *Cucchiari di legno*.

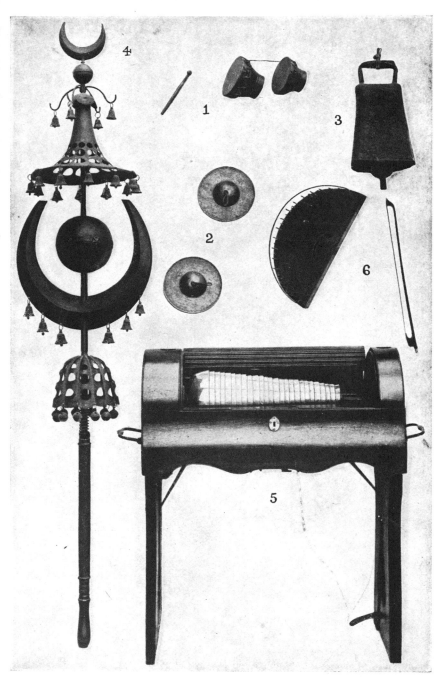

PLATE I.   AUTOPHONES AND MEMBRANOPHONES

PLATE I

1 ARABIAN DRUMS (Naqqareh)

2 ORIENTAL CYMBALS

3 HANDBELL (thirteenth to fourteenth century)

4 TURKISH CRESCENT (*c.* 1810)

5 ENGLISH MUSICAL GLASSES (*c.* 1770)

6 NAIL HARMONICA (*c.* 1800)

As with the wooden sticks, however, these little instruments gave way to the metal cymbals, small at first and known as *Acetabula* ("vinegar-cups"). They are still very popular in Oriental countries and are sometimes attached to wooden rods. In their larger form they were employed by the ancient Babylonians, and probably originated in the orgiastic rites of Western Asia. Accordingly Gluck introduced them for his chorus of Scythians in *Iphigénie en Tauride* (1779). They are frequently shown in the European paintings and illuminations of the eleventh to sixteenth centuries, but the large so-called Turkish cymbals only became fashionable as military instruments in Western Europe with the advent of the "dusky Moors" and the janizary music of the late eighteenth century. The German name *Becken*, like the Greek *Cymbala*, is derived from their cup-like shape (Plate I, 2).

RATTLES

i.A.b. Contemporary with, but probably a little later in origin than, the clashed-sticks are the ball-rattles, which consist of stones, seeds, or other hard pellets within a hollow vessel and are shaken. Amongst the American Indians, as with the ancient Mexicans, they occupy an important place in worship; a similar position was held by the *Sistrum*, with its rings and metal bars, in the cults of Isis and Ishtar. The Cuban *Maraca*—a round rattle—has descended to the ritual of the modern European dance band.

To the same "shaken" group belong the jingles attached to the tambourine or set in a metal ring without a parchment head. They appear in the early centuries of our present era, and Mahomet had a strong aversion to them. Small horse-bells (*Schellen* or *Grelots*) are found amongst some of the earliest civilizations. Another instrument of a rhythmic character, emanating from the East, took its place in the military bands of the eighteenth century under the names *Chapeau Chinois*, Turkish Crescent, or the Jingling Johnny (Plate I, 4). It was in the form of an ornamental standard of pierced brass on a pole and decorated with little bells. The lower portion somewhat resembled the conical hats worn in China, and the top was adorned with the Moslem crescent. Its use in Turkey was known in the sixteenth century. Even the churches could not resist the tinkling sound, and, as an appendage to the organ, the revolving *Cymbelstern's* music went round and round from the little bells hung on its picturesque star-like frame. Similar sounds were heard in the old Russian bands, for a V-shaped instrument of brass with small horse-bells attached accompanied the soldiers of certain cavalry regiments as they sang on the march. The instrument (called *Lojki*) was used in pairs struck together, and the rest of the band consisted of a clarinet, oboe, a pair of cymbals, a tambourine, a *Chapeau Chinois*, and a bass drum.

XYLOPHONES

i.A.c. It is evident, however, that the easiest way in which to produce sound from these sonorous substances was by striking them with a rod or hammer, either from outside or from within. Here at last begins the approach from mere rhythmic noise to tonal appreciation. The simplest forms, however, take us back to earliest days—to the *Tric-trac* or *Troccola*, a wooden board hit with a hammer, either hinged or used separately, employed in the Roman churches for ritual signals; or it may be a metal frame struck with a metal beater as in the triangle, known in medieval France as the

Trepie, and introduced into military bands with other percussion instruments of the eighteenth century. The triangle makes its appearance in Haydn's Military Symphony (1794), and still earlier in France in Grétry's *La Fausse Magie* (1775). A very modern composer has introduced the clicking of the typewriter into the orchestra.

Even resonant stones have played their part, as they have done for many thousand years in China. In 1841 a *Rock Harmonicon*, consisting of sonorous stones, was produced by a Cumberland quarryman. Originally consisting of but ten or twelve stones, its size and compass were ultimately increased to five and a half octaves. A little later appeared Baudre's *Clavier de silex*, with twenty-six stones of flint and two of schist. As the stones were natural pieces it was argued that the instrument was possible in Palaeolithic times! A more artificial instrument was the *Lithokymbalon* of Weber (Vienna, 1837), who employed shaped disks of alabaster.

When such a succession of sounds was recognized, it was discovered that the degrees of the scale could be represented on such materials as these by variation of their length and weight. Hence arose the various forms of *Harmonica*, of which the earliest in Europe appears to have been the *Strohfiedel* ("straw-fiddle"), a series of wooden bars, resting on straw bands and struck with small hammers. Agricola (1528) gives an illustration of such an instrument with a compass of three diatonic octaves. In more recent times it has been dignified by the name *Xylophone* ("sounding wood"), and is known in France as the *Echelette* or *Claquebois*, in Italy as the *Sticcato*. It emanated perhaps from Southern Asia or even Oceania, and spread into Africa as the *Marimba* or Kaffir piano. Introduced by Saint-Saëns into his *Danse Macabre* (1874), it has now become a *virtuoso* instrument.

Akin to it, but later, are the *Metallophone*, wherein metal rods replace the wooden slabs, and the *Tubephone*, with metal tubes. The sound-production of these instruments has been greatly augmented by the additional resonators, though this again is no new idea, for the Javanese *Gendir* is fitted with resonators formed of bamboo tubes and the African *Marimba* has hollow gourds. A popular improvement in the present day is the *Vibraphone*, whereon a small fan is placed over the mouth of each of the resonating tubes beneath the metal bars; the fans are revolved by an electric motor affixed to the end of the stand. The speed can be regulated at the will of the performer, and with it the rapidity of the vibrating effect on the sounds.

The principal instrument, however, in this subdivision is undoubtedly the bell. Originating, it may be, in the *Gong* or *Tamtam*, so commonly found in Asiatic countries and sometimes introduced into European orchestras for special effects, it holds the premier position in the ranks of the *Autophones*.

Early European bells were formed in four-sided shape, with a ring or handle, by folding and riveting iron plates together and then brazing or bronzing them (Plate I, 3). Such a bell is St. Patrick's *Clog* (c. sixth century), six inches high, five inches broad, and four inches deep. It is carefully preserved in a case or shrine of richly ornamented brasswork (c. 1100).

Cast bells, however, were well known to the Assyrians in the first millennium B.C., and in China they were made in bronze from yet earlier times. A large bell hung in a tower at Pekin is reputed to be over four thousand years old; it is still in use for striking the watches of the night. Bells in small form were common to the Greeks and the Romans, and in Hebrew ritual they were hung on the robes of the priests. By Moslem law they are forbidden. It has, however, been suggested that the appearance of the bell in Northern Europe during the early centuries of our era and its use in connection with religious worship was due to old Celtic traditions, brought from Nearer Asia. According to the popular idea, derived from the medieval Latin name for the bell (*Campana*), church bells were first made in the Italian *Campagna* (*c.* A.D. 400) by Bishop Paulinus of Nola. At any rate, *Nola* was a name given to a small bell. Church bells were to be found in France in the middle of the sixth century, and Benedict Biscop brought a bell from Italy in the seventh century for Wearmouth Abbey. Another name given in medieval times to small bells was *Scilla* or *Eschelle*, whence the Italian *Squilla* and the present Latin name for the nodding bluebell (*Scilla nutans*).

Owing to the importance of this instrument of sound-production, and seeing that many musicians, though they are keenly interested in their church organs, ignore the music of the bells, we may well enter more closely into a few details of campanology.

In the old days a large bell was suspended from the cross-piece or "headstock" in the bell-frame by "canons," i.e. metal loops placed upon its crown and cast solid with it. The present method, however, is to cast the bell with a flat boss at the crown and to pass the staple or rod from which the clapper is hung through a hole in the boss, so bolting it on to the headstock. The alloy used in casting a bell is usually about thirteen parts of copper to four parts of tin, the latter giving the tone and the former ensuring solidity. It has been found that the small Nineveh bells, used by the Assyrians, consist of ten parts of copper to one of tin. Bells have also been cast in aluminium, in bronze, and in steel.

Half-way down the bell is the "waist," and the lower end is known as the "lip" or "brim." Within, where the shape curves outward, is the striking-place of the clapper, termed the "sound-bow." The axles or "gudgeons" of the head-stock, to which the bell is attached, rest on roller bearings, and a large grooved wheel is fixed on one side, over which the rope passes and to which it is securely fastened. On the other side of the headstock there is an upright "stay." When the wheel is pulled over, the bell is inverted and this stay catches on a sliding rod in the frame below. By this means the bell is held in poise and remains fixed or "set" with its mouth uppermost. If the rope is again pulled, it comes off its balance and swings right round to a similar position, where the slider catches the stay again. This is technically known as "ringing." In "chiming," on the other hand, the wheel only moves slightly, and by checking the swing by a sharp grip on the "sallie" or worsted holdfast placed on the rope, the moving clapper hits the stationary bell. The strike-note, as is well known, is not a pure sound; with it are heard the overtones or harmonics and also an undertone called the hum-note. In the old method of tuning, if we take c^1 as the strike-note, the harmonics sounded as e^1, g^1, and c^2, and the hum-note was d. Canon Simpson's new tuning, however, is now frequently adopted, in which, on the same note, the harmonics are e^1 flat, g^1, c^2, and the undertone c. The actual note of a large bell is not in reality so deep as it sounds to the ear.

We have mentioned the early hand-bells, and, like them, the first church bells were longer in proportion to their diameter. Some of these twelfth- and thirteenth-century "long-waisted" bells still exist in England. In later times the length was shortened and the crown flattened, thus rendering the bell more convenient for ringing.

The largest bell in Europe is the Great Bell at the Kremlin, Moscow; its weight is estimated at 180 tons and it is over 19 feet in height. Cast in 1734, it was only suspended from a beam, and the clapper pulled backward and forward with ropes by twenty-five men on each side. In 1737 the chamber in which it hung caught on fire, and the monster fell, losing a piece from its rim. It now stands on a raised platform in the courtyard, forming a kind of chapel. In Russia there are other large examples, but they have never been "rung" in the true sense, but either "clocked," with a rope attached to the clapper, or struck from outside with a hammer. The largest "ringable" bell in the world is said to be Great Paul (16¾ tons) in St. Paul's Cathedral, London. "Big Ben" of Westminster is 13½ tons in weight.

The technical term for a number of bells tuned in scale is a "ring," and we speak of a "ring of eight" or a "ring of twelve." Change-ringing, or altering the position of the bells from the regular scale, is a peculiarly English pastime and appeared in the seventeenth century. The order in which these changes are rung if below 5,000 is called a "touch," if above 5,000 a "peal." These changes are regularized in various "methods" composed by expert ringers. "A peal of Treble Bob Major" thus means the ringing of 40,320 changes on eight bells in the Treble Bob method. If only seven bells are rung, the methods are called "triple"—among the most popular being Grandsire and Stedman. The largest bell, called always the "tenor," sometimes keeps its own place throughout, and is then said to "cover" the change. All sorts of devices, known as "hunting" or "dodging," are resorted to in order to vary the changes or groups of changes without repetition. With so many rules and methods to memorize, the success which attends so many village bell-ringers is remarkable and worthy of all praise. "Rope-sight" must be a heaven-sent gift.

In medieval times "chiming" was very popular, and from the ninth century onward we find in the illuminated manuscripts of the period illustrations of small bells suspended on a stand and struck with one or two hammers. This is the *Clokarde* (*Glockenspiel*) or ring of "Chymme Bells." Sometimes, instead of assuming the graceful shape of the ordinary bell, they are in the form of hemispherical gongs. This perhaps explains the Latin name *Cymbalum* given to the ring, and the English word "chime" is probably derived from the anglicized form "Chymbal." St. Dunstan (tenth century) excelled in "touching the Cymbals," and they found their place in the church services with the organ. Theophilus, a monk who lived in the latter part of the eleventh century, has left an interesting treatise on their manufacture, which is printed in full in Rimbault's *History of the Pianoforte* (1860), because, we presume, of the derivation of the old name for the keyboard instruments, *Cymbel* or *Cimbell*, due to their similarity of tone to the chime-bells. They were cast in moulds, the metal being a mixture of tin (one-fifth or one-sixth) and copper. They must not be confused with the modern *Glockenspiel* without a keyboard, consisting of steel bars on a lyre-shaped frame and used sometimes in military bands; Wagner introduced this instrument into the Peasant's Dance of *Die Meistersinger* and the Fire Scene of *Die Walküre*. Handel's "Carillon of Bells" in *Saul* (1740) was probably a set of chime-bells, and the word *carillon* is said to be a corruption of the low Latin *quadrilion-es*, that is, a ring of four bells for marking the quarters of the hour. The tower-carillon, with its modern mechanism, is described in the next division (i.B.a). Two bells were introduced by Bach into his cantata *Schlage doch* (1723–34) under the name *Campanella*.

In the Balearic Isles a small bell is formed of earthenware with a clapper of the same substance, and similar instruments are to be seen at Italian festivals. The sound closely resembles that of metal bells; this shows that the tone-colour is due in greater measure to their shape than to the substance of which they are made.

Wooden bells are also found; and a very ancient form, mentioned in the second century B.C., now finds a place in the dance-band effects of the present day. For the so-called Chinese Temple-Block is the wooden fish or *Mu-yü* of spherical shape which from time immemorial has been used by their Buddhist priests. The fish, which its outline and decoration are supposed to represent, is to the Chinese a symbol of wakeful attention, so necessary at prayers. It must be a constant reminder to weary jazz players, whose "autophonic" duties are so multifarious. It is clapperless and struck, like the ancient bells, on the outside with a wooden hammer.

In 1885 John Hampton of Coventry introduced tubular bells. Though requiring less space and of cheaper construction, they cannot properly take the place of the old tower-bells. For orchestral purposes they are in a way useful, since they combine more effectively with string and wind tone, and the dissonant overtones, present in the true bell, have been eliminated. They are, however, not heavy enough in resonance, and Forsyth (*Instrumentation*, 1922) happily suggests the employment of clockmakers' spring gongs. These, with the modern amplification of tone by electricity, would solve the difficulty, or by *Electrones* (V.iii.B.b.).

The substitution of glass for wood or metal has given us the *Glass Harmonica*, which in its simplest form consists of small plates attached to two suspending tapes. It is sometimes called the *Krystallophone*, to distinguish it from the glass harmonica played by friction and described under Sub-class iii.A.a.

The tuning-fork (*Diapason, Stimmgabel*) was invented about the year 1711 by the English Lutenist and sergeant trumpeter to George I, John Shore. He used it for tuning his lute, "not having [as he was wont to say] a pitch-pipe about him but, what will do as well, a pitch-fork." Clagget, at the close of the same century, elaborated this invention, as detailed in the following division (i.B.a). In 1891 Guerre of Rouen placed the tuning-fork on a sound-box and set it in vibration by an electric current.

HARMONICAS AND CARILLONS

i.B.a. The direct stroke on these sonorous substances which we have hitherto been considering was in later times superseded and simplified by the attachment of mechanical devices which would indirectly produce the same result. This was especially true of the type of *Autophone* known as the *Harmonica* and producing a regular scale of notes. Mersenne (1635) and Kircher (1650) also describe fully the keyboard mechanism used in their day by the Flemish *carilloneurs* for their performances on the bells in the church towers. To an elementary clavier of wooden rods, with a pedal-board of similar construction, ropes were attached which, passing into the belfry overhead, pulled the clapper against the rim of the bell—a system still known as "clocking," and very apt to crack the bell on which it is used. This primitive arrangement, which seems to have been known in the fourteenth century at Bruges and required the use of the fists on the so-called keys, has now been supplanted by much more delicate mechanism which only demands a light touch. The modern *Carillon*, with its chromatic scale, is a very elaborate piece of machinery compared with those early attempts. There should be at least two complete octaves of bells, but a compass of four octaves (forty-nine bells) is more suitable for the due execution of the music now demanded. The carillons of Belgium and Holland are, of course, famous, especially Malines (forty-five bells), Bruges (forty-seven bells), and Ghent (fifty-two bells). The heaviest carillons, however, are to be found in America, that at New York (Riverside), erected by Gillett and Johnson, possessing sixty-four bells, the largest weighing $18\frac{1}{4}$ tons. By the help of electricity the touch is no longer heavy. Wires are run from the console or keyboard to relays, and thence to powerful magnets connected with the clappers. On depressing the keys, electrical force is trans-mitted to the magnets, and they pull the clappers against the bells. The travel of the clapper is about an inch, which is quite sufficient to produce a full tone. Pedals are still employed for the heavier bells, but these are aided by electric motors in the form of pistons which add their force to the blow of the clapper. The oldest carillon in England is that at Cattistock, Dorset, erected in 1882 by Van Aerschodt of Louvain (thirty-five bells). For practice, players use a similar keyboard, by which metal strips, instead of bells, are struck by under-hammers.

The application of a keyboard to the wooden xylophone, under the name *Régale de bois*, and also to the metal-barred *Glockenspiel*, appears in the seventeenth century, the latter reaching its highest achievement with the addition of resonators in Mustel's *Celesta* (1886) with a compass of four octaves from c^1. Two years later M. Mustel produced the *Partition Mustel*, which was contrived as a guide to tuning other keyboard instruments, and consisted of twelve bronze strips (as a chromatic octave) struck by small wooden hammers covered with felt. Some such an instrument, known as the *Stahlklavier*, was introduced by Mozart into *Zauberflöte* (1791) under the title *Strumento d'acciaio*. In 1890 tubular bells appeared with a keyboard in the French Opera House as the *Codophone*. But all these inventions seem to have been anticipated by Charles Clagget, an Irishman living in London, who in 1788 patented his *Aiuton* or ever-tuned organ. Here steel bars, somewhat in the shape of tuning-forks, were struck by small hammers, and an interesting description of the new instrument is given in a rare little treatise written and published by Clagget as No. 1 of *Musical Phaenomena* (1793). On this idea Mustel, in his *Typophone* (1865), and Fischer of Leipzig, in his *Adiaphon* (1882), improved, and its present representative is the *Dulcitone*.

The use of a keyboard for the *Glass Harmonica* was also not overlooked, and in 1752 Leftel of Vienna produced such an instrument, followed by Beyer of Paris with his *Fortepiano à cordes de verre*. To such the name *Glassichord* is generally given; and a somewhat kindred instrument, with two manuals and with porcelain bells, was designed at the Meissen factory, Dresden. In 1816 Day of London patented an addition of musical glasses to the pianoforte so that they could be used conjointly or separately at pleasure; but the most wholesale adaptation is to be found in Whitaker's *Cherubine Minor* (1859), which "combined harp, organ, and glass-bells in one harmonious piano."

CHIMES

i.B.b. Automatic or self-playing mechanism, either by weight, spring, hand, or foot power, has been applied to these instruments. Clock chimes are an instance of this device. Here a revolving barrel, set with pegs or studs as touch-pieces at the required points, actuates levers attached to hammers striking the bells. In this way were some of the best-known quarter-chimes played, such as the Cambridge or Westminster Quarters, said to have been arranged by Dr. Crotch in 1793 for the University Church, and copied at the Royal Exchange, London, in 1845. By their appropriation at the Houses of Parliament (1859) they are generally known by the latter name. The Oxford or Magdalen chimes (1713) are less rhythmical, and the so-called Whittington chimes at Bow Church, London, have been reset in 1905 by Sir Charles Stanford for twelve bells, but on the lines of the old six-bell tune, found in D'Urfey's *Pills to purge Melancholy* (c. 1700). In the fifteenth century a chime-barrel, set with the five-note tune of *Requiem aeternam*, was placed with bells on a frame and wheeled through the streets as a lament for some deceased inhabitant. Kircher (1650) devotes a large section of his *Musurgia Universalis* to this subject, and explains the proper pinning of the barrel. Even the Romans, on their *Clepsydra*, had a method whereby the water-clock periodically sounded a bell. Old St. Paul's Cathedral, London, had "clock-jacks" or "quarter-boys" in 1298, the "jack" being a figure, generally clad in armour, who struck the bell with his javelin. The name was probably given to such figures because they took the place of a boy or helper who would otherwise have been employed for the purpose, as in boot-jack or screw-jack. The Strasbourg clock, with its famous mechanical figures, was erected in 1571; the knights in Wells Cathedral are in fifteenth-century armour; while the "jacks" at St. Dunstan-in-the-West, London (recently restored), date from 1671. The use of electrical power also has not been forgotten; in fact, not merely chiming but even the ringing of bells has been rendered automatic by this means. The French *Auto-sonneur* is provided with a motor which gives a drive to the bell on its upward stroke and, by a reversing gear, alters the motion and brakes the bell on the downward stroke. The 16-ton bell at Sens Cathedral is rung automatically in this way, and it is in use in many continental churches.

In the *Campana mutaphone* Carter of London applied the mechanical principle to change-ringing, but, as far as is known, only in the form of a small model with gongs, now in the Victoria and Albert Museum, Kensington.

Various small percussion instruments have been introduced into barrel-organs, but in 1799 a triangle was added to the pianoforte. Real cymbals have been placed in church organs, and the *Cymbelstern* with its jingling bells, moved by wind-power, has already been mentioned. The Spanish *Matraca*, used in the Roman churches, is also a rotary development of the more primitive *Tric-trac*, as it is of the Neapolitan *Tricca-ballacca* with percussion hammers.

ii. PLUCKED TYPE

JEW'S HARP

ii.A.a. The representative instrument in the plucked type of *Autophones* is the *Crembalum* or Jew's-harp—the *Trumpel* of Virdung (1511) and the *Maultrumpe* or *Maultrommel* of later German literature. In France it was early known as the

Rebute and later as the *Guimbarde*. The English name connects it in our minds with a Jewish origin, like the nickname *Judenharfe* in Germany; but the Dutch title *Jeudgtrompe* suggests that the little sound-producer was so called as being a child's toy. The idea that our English name refers to its being held between the jaws has no foundation. Perhaps it was first imported or supposed to have been imported into this country by Jewish traders. The instrument is found abundantly in Eastern Asia and Oceania, and, though there generally made of bamboo, presents the same principle of intonation. The vibrating tongue within the frame, which is placed between the lips, is plucked by the fingers or jerked by a string, and the overtones can be reinforced at will by altering the size of the cavity of the mouth. This gained for it the epithet "trump," the harmonic series of notes being the same as on the ordinary metal trumpet. By employing two or more vibrating tongues of different fundamental pitch a complete scale may be obtained. Scheibler's *Aura* (1816) had six to ten tongues united in two blocks, and the famous performer Eulenstein (1827) used sixteen vibrators.

NOTCHED RATTLES

ii.A.b. In addition to the bell-rattles (mentioned under i.A.b) there is a closely related subdivision in which a wooden or metal tongue is set in vibration by the cogged teeth of a ratchet-wheel. In England the instrument is generally called the watchman's or policeman's rattle, but it is now, in a smaller form, only a child's toy, and as such was placed by Haydn in the score of his *Toy Symphony* (1788), and by Mendelssohn (1828) in the same way, while Strauss has used it to emphasize the merry pranks of *Til Eulenspiegel* (1896).

It is commonly found in India, and may have been introduced from that country. The ratchet is revolved by whirling the instrument; but Bonanni (1723) gives an illustration of a less portable form in the shape of a box with a turning handle. These and similar rattles are employed in the Roman churches, especially during the Holy Week, and also by the Jews at Purim in their synagogues. In France it appears under the name *Crécelle*, and in Germany as *Schnarre*, which is also the term used for unduly rolling the "r" in affected speech.

CLAVIOLA

ii.B.a. The attachment of a keyboard to this type of instru ment has been attempted with small success. Fischer (1835) made a pianoforte in which the sounds were produced from metal springs instead of strings, and in 1847 appeared Pape-lard's *Claviola*, whereon a plectrum placed at the further end of the key plucked two metal tongues for each note, tuned in octaves. The compass of the instrument ranged from *c* to *c4*. In 1862 Crawford of London conceived the idea of an instrument with metal prongs or vibrators somewhat similar to those used in musical-boxes. On it there was a form of "jack" movement which, after deflecting the vibrator, slipped off and released it.

MUSICAL BOX

ii.B.b. The principal example known of an automatic action, in connection with this type, is the musical-box, the French *Boîte de Musique* and the German *Spieldose*. With its "pinned" barrel it was invented, probably in Switzerland, at the close of the eighteenth century, the motive power being either by weight, turning handle, or, later, by clock-spring. The vibrating tongues are cut out in a steel plate called the "comb," and are heavily loaded with lead for the lower notes. The principle, apart from the automatic attach-ment, is embodied in the popular African *Zansa*. In this little instrument, which enlivens many leisure hours, wooden or, more often, metal tongues are attached to a sound-box and plucked by the thumbs or forefingers of the native performer. It was a Kaffir instrument in the sixteenth century. Clagget (*c.* 1780) is said to have constructed a metal harmonica on these lines with fifty steel tongues, also set in vibration by the fingers.

iii. FRICTIONAL TYPE

MUSICAL GLASSES

iii.A.a. History fails to record the day when man discovered that by friction he could produce sounds from solid sub-stances. It may have had quite a primitive origin, for in the islands of the Pacific, such as those of New Ireland and Dutch New Guinea, the natives use for their purpose a hollow block of wood, called *Kulepa*, partly cut into four unequal sections. These, when rubbed with the palm of the hand, emit four notes of different pitch. In Europe the principle was brought into practice on the Danish *Melk-harmonika* (*Stockspiel*), which consists of eight upright wooden rods of graded length which, when rubbed down by the rosined fingers, vibrate and produce a scale of notes. As many as twenty rods are found in some instruments of this type, which appeared in the eighteenth century. Earlier still, however, the set of drinking-glasses, which had hitherto been struck with little rods as a *Glockenspiel*, were set in vibration by the pressure of the moistened finger on the rim. In 1743 an Irishman, Pockrich, produced his *Angelica* or Musical Glasses, which became the rage in England under the patronage of Gluck, who in 1746 performed a concerto on twenty-six *Verres à boire* accompanied by an orchestra. It is to this instrument Goldsmith alludes in the *Vicar of Wakefield* (1761), coupling its popularity in society circles with pictures and Shakespeare. A more extended form with thirty-eight to forty-six glasses was called the *Mattauphone*. In 1760 Benjamin Franklin improved on this arrangement under the name *Harmonica* or *Armonica* by placing hemispherical glasses of correct pitch on a revolving spindle turned by a treadle, the glasses being kept wet by passing through a trough of water placed beneath them (Plate I, 5). In the *Angelica* the water had been put into the glasses themselves, as a means also of tuning them. Franklin's glasses, thirty-three in number, were coloured in order to show their position in the musical scale, the diatonic notes being red, orange, yellow, green, blue, indigo, and violet, as in the spectrum, and the chromatic notes black. In later examples as many as forty-six glasses are found, with a compass from *c* to a^2, and the chromatic notes have a gold border. The classical composers deigned to write for this instrument. For Marianne Kirchgessner, a noted performer, Mozart composed an *Adagio e Rondo*, with flute, oboe, violin, and violoncello accompaniment. Beethoven's little "melodram" for the same instrument, written in 1814 or 1815, was printed in the earliest edition of Grove's *Dictionary of Music* for the first time. It appears, too, in Berlioz' Fantasia on *The Tempest* (*c.* 1830), and Naumann has left six sonatas for it, he himself being a player. Another famous performer was Miss Marianne Davies (*c.* 1762), for whom Hasse wrote. The popularity of this instrument, so peculiarly trying to the nerves, lasted longer on the Continent than in England; as late as the year 1818 it found a place in the Court orchestra at Darmstadt. The vibration of metal rods under friction was first exploited by the acoustician Chladni, who, in 1790, produced the *Euphone*. The sounds were obtained by rubbing with the fingers small glass tubes attached to steel rods, which thus received the vibrations. Dietz of Emmerich (1806) introduced a somewhat similar instrument.

NAIL HARMONICA

iii.A.b. The principal invention, however, of this type of harmonica was the nail-violin or *Nagel harmonica*, which was also dignified by the name *Chalybs-sonans* or the "sounding steel." It is credited to Wilde, a Bavarian musician attached to the Imperial Orchestra at St. Petersburg (1740). Metal pins, firmly fixed into a semicircular or a round frame, which serves as a sound-box, are set in vibration by a violin bow, and a chromatic compass of two or more octaves can be obtained (Plate I, 6). In later specimens the nails often assume the shape of flat-headed staples, and are placed on a second or upper sound-box. Other examples are fitted internally with sympathetic wires to increase the resonance. This latter type is sometimes called the *Violino-harmonika*.

A novel sound-producer at the present day amongst metal *Autophones* is the *Serrulaphone* or musical saw. For its scale it depends on the varying tension of the steel blade as it is bent over by the player, who grips the handle of the saw firmly between his knees. The greater the curvature the higher is the pitch of the note. By expert performers a well-rosined violin-bow is used and drawn across the plain edge; by others it is struck with a small hammer, and so would be grouped under Sub-class i.A.c. The bow has also been applied to the *Glass Harmonica.*

CLAVI-CYLINDRE

iii.B.a. Many attempts have been made to adapt a keyboard to these frictional harmonicas. In 1786 Cheese of London produced an instrument in which circular plates of glass, varying in size and fitted on a revolving spindle, were brought into contact with cork or leather rubbers fixed on levers connected with the keys. The inventive mind of Clagget (1788) proposed an endless fillet of silk rubbed with resin dissolved in spirits of wine. This, passing across the tuning-forks or metal bars as used in his *Aiuton* (i.B.a), produced and prolonged the tone. The same device was adopted by Träger in his *Nagel Klavier* (1791). Chladni, in his *Clavi-cylindre* (1799), yet further improved on these ideas. By him a graduated series of metal rods were brought into contact with a revolving cylinder, with a frictional surface, by depressing the keys. Amongst the many other forms of the instrument which appeared during the early part of the nineteenth century we may mention the *Melodicon* by Rieffelsen of Copenhagen, who employed tuning-forks, and the *Panmelodikon* by Leppich of Vienna with metal rods. Uthe's *Xylosistron* used wooden rods, as also did Buschmann in his *Uranion* and *Terpodion.*

Even the nail-violin received a keyboard from Brambach of Marting (1888), the metal pins being raised by the keys to meet the bow.

A curious frictional instrument, which should find a place under this sub-class, is the *Violon des Gilles*, made by the Walloons at Binche during carnival-time. A violin-shaped board is fitted with wooden tongues within an opening cut in it, and these are scraped by a notched stick like a bow. The South Italian *Pandola* is somewhat similar.

iii.B.b. The application of an automatic barrel to the *Aiuton* (i.B.a) is provided for by Clagget; but the prolongation of sounds in all these autophonic instruments becomes objectionable owing to the inharmonic overtones produced.

CRACKER-GLASS

iv.A.a. The production of sound from sonorous substances by air pressure is possible. An instance is noted by Dr. Moule in his *Musical Instruments of China* under the name *Ku tang*. It consists of a glass bulb, somewhat like a wine decanter. As the bottom is extremely thin, when the mouth is applied to the open end and the breath drawn quickly in and out, it vibrates with a loud crackling sound. This may be the origin of the Nuremberg *Schall-Glass* or Cracker-glass, though it can scarcely be called a *musical* instrument.

iv. AIR-VIBRATED TYPE

AEOLSKLAVIER

iv.B.a. The use of wind in the vibration of resonating tongues in conjunction with a keyboard was the subject of experiments during the last century. In 1822 Schortmann of Weimar produced the *Aeolsklavier*; light little rods of wood were set in motion by wind from foot-bellows, and it found a place in the concert-room. Baudet of Paris, in the *Piano chanteur* (1878), employed small steel plates. This principle must not be confused with that of the free reed (Aerophones, ii.A.c) as placed in mouth harmonicas and harmoniums (Aerophones, ii.B.b).

the voice of the deity himself, who was enshrined within. The peculiar shape appears to have been evolved from the union of two half-gourds, placed back to back; perhaps in very primitive days the crowns of two human skulls were used, as is still the custom in Tibet. It appears in Spain in the eleventh century of our era in conjunction with sacred emblems, and has been, as usual, attributed to Moorish influence. In the thirteenth century it was held with the waist on the shoulder and tapped with the fingers of one hand only.

As a musical instrument the tambourine is useful to accentuate dance rhythms, and has been successfully introduced in Berlioz' *Carnival Romain* Overture (1843) and Elgar's *Cockaigne* overture (1901), as well as in music of a gipsy or Oriental character, such as the Arab Dance in Tchaikovsky's *Casse-Noisette* Suite (1891).

DRUMS

i.A.b. It was, however, discovered that, by placing the skin-head on a deeper receptacle instead of on the shallow frame, the resonance could be greatly increased. Hence the instrument properly known as the drum, a name appearing in Dutch as *Trom*, in Scandinavian as *Tromme*, and in German as *Trommel*, no doubt derived from its rattling, booming sound. An amusing use of the name appeared in the eighteenth century when the fashionable but noisy parties were called "drums." Lady Mary Montagu in 1753 writes that London was no place for her, "it being impossible to live in a drum." This particular word appears to be confined to the North European languages. Southern linguists use the word *tambour* or *tamburo*, derived from the Greek *tympanon* (something that is "beaten" or "struck"); it is applied to drums in general, the word *timpani* being reserved for the kettledrums.

The association with the North would suggest that the larger and deeper resonating body was due to the warlike propensities of the Nordic and Teutonic peoples, who, with their great horns and trumpets, delighted in the din of battle. Large barrel-shaped drums, however, were well known to the Chinese in their earliest dynasties, and were frequently erected on poles in their temple courts, as they are to-day. In India, too, the use of drums with double heads has been common for ages. Willard, in his treatise on the *Music of Hindoostan* (1834), says: "A drum is an ever-attendant and inseparable companion to Indian songs, whether any other instrument be present or not. Its sound is taken as the key-note, and all other instruments, that may be present, and the voice are regulated to it."

The smallest instrument of this type is known in England as the tabor (Plate VII, 2), the Provençal *Atabor* and old Castilian *Atambor* introduced, probably with the Morris dance and its accompanying pipe, from Spain. So shallow, indeed, is its receptable that it might almost be classed with the timbrels of the previous subdivision. The deeper-bodied drum, called the great tabor, long drum, or, in France, *Tambour de lansquenet* (or pike-man), was a much finer instrument (*Frontispiece*). It is said that it was of English origin and introduced into France by King Edward the Third, when his army entered Calais in 1347. In the sixteenth century it was $2\frac{1}{2}$ feet in depth and 2 feet in diameter. It should not be mistaken for the bass drum, for it was hung at the player's side and struck with two sticks on the upper head; it must have been extremely awkward on the march. It also had the vibrating cords of gut, already mentioned, stretched over the head at one end and called in England "snares." As this drum was frequently used with the Swiss fife it was known in Scotland as the *Swesch*. In Italy its diameter was decreased, and this long drum is often made there without the snares. The use of cords or "braces," attached to the heads, to tighten the parchment when required, is very ancient, being found in Egypt in the second millennium B.C. Another still narrower drum is the *Tambour de Provence*, which is employed in rustic dances with the *Galoubet*, or whistle-headed pipe. The tenor drum (*Caisse roulante* or *Caisse sourde*) is somewhat similar in size to the old side-drum, but is without "snares," and is known in Germany as the *Wirbeltrommel* or tattoo-drum; in England it is now chiefly found in the pipe bands of the Scottish regiments. The more modern side-drum (*Caisse claire, Kleine trommel*), with its snares, is a much sharper-sounding instrument. It was introduced into the British army in 1858. The use of a side-drum in the orchestra was apparently initiated by Marais in the storm scene of his opera *Alcyone* (1706).

In 1859 Rose and Carte of London constructed a side-drum in which the closed receptacle was superseded by open framework, and Sax of Paris in 1862 followed on the same lines with the bass drum and kettledrum. The change had no particular effect on the vibratory power of the instrument, though it affected the tone.

The bass drum, though comparatively a late arrival in Western Europe, has a history reaching back five thousand years. It is figured on some of the earliest monuments of Mesopotamia and of a size over 6 feet in diameter. Whether these huge circular drums had two skin-heads it is difficult to ascertain. From their appearance they look more like the large gong drum, occasionally observed in British orchestras.

These instruments of ancient days had the head fastened to the frame with wooden pegs, the large heads of which, noticeable in the sculptured representations, have been mistaken for little bells. African tribes employ the same device at the present day.

The bass drum, as now used, is associated with Eastern Europe, and formed in the fourteenth century an important item in the janizary regiments of Turkey. It is this instrument which is figured among the fifteenth-century stall carvings in Rouen Cathedral. Across the head is stretched a "snare" hung with little *grelots* or ball-shaped bells. The janizary bands relied greatly on percussion for their martial effect, their constitution being three small oboes, two large oboes, one flute, a large kettledrum, two small kettledrums, three little drums and a large drum, two pairs of small cymbals, one pair of large cymbals, and two triangles. Early in the eighteenth century it became the custom for the leader to march in front bearing a bell-adorned standard with the Turkish crescent (Autophones, i.A.b). Percussion instruments such as these were introduced into Poland, and in 1725 Russia also adopted them; by the end of the century they were to be found in most of the European bands.

KETTLEDRUMS

i.A.c. The kettledrum (*Frontispiece*), in which the skin-head is stretched over a bowl-shaped body, is also of very ancient use. In Asia, from West to East, it was known long before the present era. On an old Babylonian tablet minute instructions are given for re-heading the instrument, which was called *Lilis*, and on another tablet a scribe has presented to us a line drawing of its shape. Allusions to it are found from the fourth millennium B.C. Placed on a foot or pedestal, it was pre-eminently a ritual drum, images of the great gods being deposited within it. Throughout Persia, however, and in China and India, the same type appears in common use. The Egyptian *Daraboukeh*, with an earthenware body, is related to it, though more portable; they are called "footed" drums and have but one skin-head. In our own era we find amongst the Moslems and Saracens various sizes of these drums, though, as a rule, the foot is omitted. The little *Nakers* or *Nacaires* are carried in the hand and used in pairs (Plate I, 1). The larger drums are hung on either side of a camel or horse, the predecessors, in fact, of our cavalry drums. In Europe they appear soon after the days of the Crusades in the fourteenth century and bear the Oriental name. The Bosnian *Daoulbes*, with its leather-covered hemispherical body, represents an early type. In the larger form, as cavalry drums, their use in Hungary in the fifteenth century set the fashion for other European regiments. A trace, too, of their Asiatic origin remains in the German name *Pauken*; for the Indo-European root *puk* provides a drum name amongst several nations, even amongst the Chinese and Koreans, the meaning being to "hit" or "strike." Plutarch informs us that those fine horsemen, the Parthians, frightened their enemies "with hollow vessels covered with skin, on which they beat, making a terrifying noise."

The interesting point, however, in this type is that it has not remained merely rhythmic in its sound, but by alteration of the tension of the head has become one of the tonal members of the orchestra. The stretching of the skin by tightening the cords or braces, either with constricting tabs as on the Chinese "hour-glass" drum, *Chang Ku*, a survival of the ancient Sumerian *Balag*, or by inserting reel-shaped wedges as is the

custom in Africa, is nothing new. In India, too, it is effected
by weighting the parchment with a paste of flour and water,
mixed sometimes with iron filings, and applied to the centre
of the head, as on the *Tabla* and *Mridanga*. The method
adopted in Europe of increasing the tension by side-screws
on the rim, however, is far more efficient, and is displayed
in Virdung's illustration of the *Herpaucken* (1518), that is,
the kettledrums permitted to barons and other high estates
for honourable use. Nevertheless, in Poland the old system
of tuning wedges was retained for nearly a century later.

As is well known, a pair of these drums is used for
ordinary orchestral purposes, and their introduction is attributed in France to Lully (*c.* 1670). They are generally tuned
to the tonic and dominant of the musical key, but a third
drum, as used by Weber in his overture to *Peter Schmoll*
(1807), is often added. But there is no restriction on the
various tunings which may be adopted. Berlioz, for instance,
in the "*Tuba mirum*" of his famous *Requiem* (1837), employed
eight pairs of *Timbales*, tuned respectively in minor thirds,
minor sixths, major thirds (two pair), fourths (two pair), and
fifths (two pair), as well as two long or bass drums, a *Tamtam* (gong), and three pairs of cymbals—another triumph
for the percussion instruments. As the tuning of these drums
for various keys employed in orchestral music requires an
alert tympanist and the rapid alteration of seven to ten screw-
handles a practised hand, methods were adopted to secure
quicker tuning. In 1821 Stumpff invented a revolving frame
which tightened or relaxed the head. Cornelius Ward in 1837
produced a kettledrum with a single central key in the side
which, working on the head-rim by a system of pulleys,
achieved the same result. In 1830 a method of rapid tuning
by means of pedals, at first seven, but later only three, and

now only one, was advocated in France, suggested probably by the action of the pedal harp. The present one-pedal drum gives sure tuning and perfect tone because the action transmits the tension equally to each internal rod. A complete chromatic range of well over an octave is obtainable.

MECHANICAL DRUMS

i.B.a. Some simple devices have also been adopted for striking these instruments of percussion. A small drum on a handle, fitted with a ratchet wheel, when whirled in the hand sounds under the action of the wheel on the ends of two little hammers. The use of a pedal also is common in the dance bands of the present day for the larger drums. In 1799 Joseph Smith introduced into the pianoforte a "falling-off action" for sounding either a drum, tabor, or tambourine.

i.B.b. Automatic action to produce similar effects is described in detail by Kircher in his *Musurgia Universalis* (1650), pins being set in a revolving barrel "to make the hammer or drumstick beat to time." The present century has seen the production by a Saxon maker of an automatic drum, in which a rotating disc, pierced with holes, regulates by a pin and lever action the fall of the hammer on the parchment. It can be affixed to any instrument of the drum type and the rhythm of the beat varied by interchangeable discs.

ii. FRICTIONAL TYPE

FRICTION DRUMS

ii.A.a. The vibration of a stretched membrane by means of friction is a device of long standing. The Indian drummers, by sliding the ball of the thumb across the drum-head with a slight pressure, raise the pitch of their instruments and produce a curious clicking sound. As this is the principle on which the field-cricket makes its peculiar note, and the fact that the name of an ancient Sumerian drum was also given to the insect, it is very probable that this particular stroke, which is still used by tambourine players, was in vogue several thousand years ago. In Spain at the present day the friction-drum is known as the *Chicharra* or cricket.

The first means systematically adopted to produce this particular effect is seen in the stick friction-drum. In the middle of the parchment head, strained over a clay or wooden receptacle, is affixed a short stick, standing erect. The stick is rubbed with wet or rosined fingers, and, as the membrane vibrates under it, a loud sound is heard. This form, which is very popular in Flanders, is described by Mersenne (1635) and is called the *Rommel-pot*, though in this case the rod is placed horizontally on the head instead of vertically. In Spain it is known as the *Zambomba*, and appears at festal rejoicings. In Flanders it is particularly associated with Christmastide; in Italy, as the *Caccarella*, it is more frequently heard at vintage-time. In fact, the little instrument, in one form or another, is widely distributed throughout the world, as Mr. Henry Balfour, in his monograph on *The Friction Drum*, published by the Royal Anthropological Institute, has clearly shown. In some instances the stick is placed through a central hole in the drum-head and pulled to and fro. In African specimens it is put within the resonating chamber or barrel of the drum and vibrated from below. It is also said that, by pressing the finger on the membrane and so raising the pitch of the sound, very simple tunes can be played on it.

.A.b. Another form of the instrument dispenses with the central stick and, instead of it, a waxed or rosined cord, generally of horsehair, is affixed to the centre of the parchment. In England this is popularly known as the "jackdaw," owing to its imitation of the voice of that bird, and is the *Chicharra* of Spain. In France it is rudely termed *Le cri de la belle-mère.* Balfour considers that the origin of the friction-drum is to be found in the simple hand-bellows of the African smith.

ii.B.a. The instrument can also be operated indirectly by whirling. The end of the cord is in that case attached to a stick held in the hand, and the friction is caused as the cord twists round its rosined point. Attempts have been made to show a connection between this form and that of the bull-roarer or *Schwirrholz,* a slip of wood whirled at the end of a string, which is still in use amongst primitive races for ceremonial purposes (Chordophones, iv.A.a). But, according to the evidence adduced, it seems very improbable that this friction-drum was used for any sort of mystical rite, notwithstanding its German name *Waldteufel*; its usual appearance is at merrymakings.

The earliest notice of its presence in Europe comes from the close of the sixteenth century, and the old German name *Brummtopf,* or "growling pot," is now merged into the more dignified *Reibtrommel.* Mersenne, who gives an illustration of the form with the horizontal stick (mentioned under ii.A.a), inclines to consider it as an Indian instrument; but in that country the distribution is very limited, and the type shown is Dutch. In the last century the whirling form became a very popular toy in England and was called in some districts the ho'or or hummer.

iii. CO-VIBRATING TYPE

MIRLITONS

iii.A.a. An instrument of the membranophonic class is the *Kazoo, Zazah,* or *Zobo,* known in France as the *Mirliton.* In its ordinary form the sound is produced by the vibrations of the vocal chords in humming or singing on a stretched skin; it adds a peculiar reediness to the voice, and is more aptly described as co-vibration rather than as sympathetic vibration. This principle has been long recognized, for in China the transverse flute, called *Ti tzu,* for the last six centuries at least, has been played with a thin membrane—generally of rice-paper—placed over a hole in the flute between the embouchure and the uppermost finger-hole. The effect is a reedy tone which is much admired in that country, and was copied by Wigley and McGregor (1810) in England when they produced their *Flauto di voce.* It has been said that the old English recorder had at times the same vibrating membrane; but this is an error which has arisen from the specimen of an eighteenth-century recorder in the Victoria and Albert Museum, London. In this instance a hole has been bored in the side of the cap (i.e. above the whistle), where it cannot affect the tone; the object here was to holdt he instrument sideways like a concert flute.

A medieval development of this principle is seen in the *Chalumeau Eunuque* or onion flute, an onion skin being frequently used for the vibrating membrane. It was made in the shape of a reed-pipe with a large bell, and sometimes, for greater semblance, finger-holes were bored in the tube. They had, of course, no effect upon the pitch of the sounds, which was wholly dependent upon the performer's voice as he sang or hummed into a hole at the side and so set the membrane in vibration. Mersenne (1635) notices with approbation concerts of *Flûtes eunuques* in four or five parts, an *ensemble* reproduced three centuries later in the French *Bigophones*.

That the vibrations of the vocal chords can affect a membrane without singing or humming into the instrument, as in the *Mirlitons*, etc., is shown in the Indian *Nyastaranga* or throat trumpet. In this unique instrument the membrane, usually the outer covering of a spider's cocoon, is placed in the small end of a brass horn. It takes up the vibrations when this end is placed on or near the vocal chords and the performer hums with closed mouth. The principle of the *Mirliton* appears to have been derived from the use by country-folk of a piece of thin bark stretched tightly before the mouth when singing, resembling in its effect the little ribbon-reed used to represent the voice of Punch.

GRAMOPHONE

iii.B.a. That automatic mechanism should be applied to produce the same result may appear strange, but the *Gramophone*, invented by Thomas Edison in 1877 as the *Phonograph*, is practically an adaptation of the vibrating membrane, in this case a metal disc. The latter name is now generally confined to the recording instrument, which receives on a cylinder or disc of wax the impressed vibrations of a membrane under the influence of musical or vocal sounds. Berliner of Washington (1887) developed the reproducing instrument, which, on its discs of hard material, represents the indentations made and transmits them to a vibrating diaphragm; this transforms them into sound waves again, and a large horn, as a resonator, intensifies them. This is the gramophone, an educational instrument of great value, which has been increased by a system of electrical amplification and a closer and truer approximation to sound values.

The various forms of sound-waves produced by different classes of musical instruments and indicative of their peculiar tones have been thoroughly investigated by Dr. Dayton Miller, Professor Emeritus of the School of Applied Science, Cleveland, Ohio, and published in *The Science of Musical Sounds* (Macmillan). His unique collection of flutes, numbering nearly 1,500 specimens, is well known.

III

CHORDOPHONIC INSTRUMENTS

including

HARPS, LYRES, PSALTERIES, ZITHERS, LUTES, CITHERS, GUITARS, DULCIMERS, VIOLS, VIOLINS, AEOLIAN HARP, AND THEIR KEYBOARD AND AUTOMATIC AMPLIFICATIONS SUCH AS VIRGINALS, SPINETS, HARPSICHORDS, CLAVICHORDS, AND PIANOS, ETC.

FOR the two classes of musical instruments already considered, their origin has been traced to the common experiences and requirements of primitive man. The falling stones of the mountain-side, the clattering logs of the firewood pile, the tautly stretched skin of the warrior's shield, have furnished the earliest ideas of musical sounds. This is also true of the important class of stringed instruments which will now demand our attention, and we therefore turn once more to those prehistoric days when the hunter's bow supplied the necessities of life. That this is no mere flight of fancy is shown by the recent researches which have been made into the practice of tribes and peoples still in a primitive state of civilization, and we are indebted to Mr. Henry Balfour, Professor Kirby, and other collaborators for the careful investigations which they have carried out with respect to the use of the hunting-bow as a sound-producer, and generally known as the *Musical Bow*.

It is only natural that the old-world sportsman, as the

arrow sped forth to find its quarry, should not only have noticed the musical twang of the released bow-string, but also that he could reproduce the pleasing sound by twitching it or plucking it with his finger. There is a tradition in Japan that, when the Sun-goddess had hidden herself in the recesses of a cave and men no longer enjoyed the blessings of her light, they met together and entreated her to return. She resisted all their efforts until one of them took six long-bows and, setting them firmly with the back of the staff in the ground, twanged their strings. As he played the fair goddess listened, and, her limbs swaying in cadence with the pleasing rhythm, came forth from her hiding to restore light—with music, dance, and song—to the waiting world. Such is the mythical origin they tell of the invention of their national instrument, the *Koto*, derived in reality from China in long-forgotten ages of the past, but still retaining in its narrow sound-box and its plucked strings traces of some such early parentage.

i. PLUCKED TYPE

HARPS

i.A.a¹. To the hunting-bow, then, we owe the harp with its open strings, that is, without a finger-board to alter their pitch. In its earliest shape it is found in Asia more than five thousand years ago, not merely bespeaking its origin but showing even then an advance upon yet more primitive efforts.

In the well-known form of the bow-shaped harp (*Bogen-harfe*) the combination of many bow-stocks laid side by side is discontinued and the strings are attached to one stock

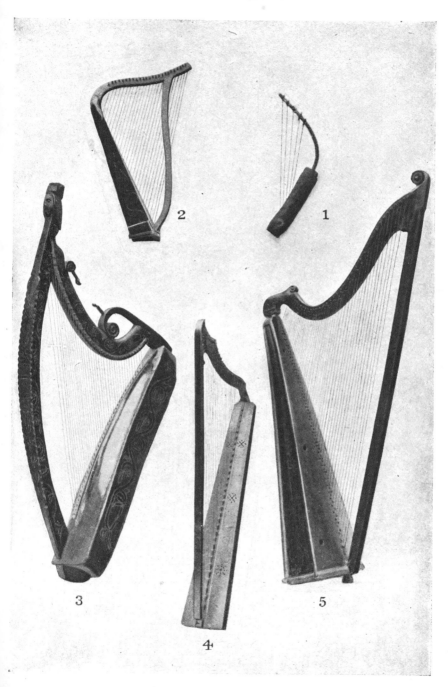

PLATE II.　CHORDOPHONES

PLATE II

(Plate II, 1). At the farther end is added also a resonator, generally a hollow gourd; and in this we note that the incipient musician had already discovered the fact that by placing the end of his bow on a hollow receptacle—whether his own mouth or a common pot—the resonance of his melody was greatly increased. This little harp, with its five, seven, or nine strings, is closely associated in these early times with Central and Western Asia, the probable scene of man's first existence. Thence, in a somewhat altered form, it passed into Egypt during the opening years of the third millennium B.C., and from thence it spread by tribal migration across the breadth of the African continent. In Greece and Asia Minor it was known as the *Nabla*, and is identical with the Hebrew *Nebel*, which by the translators of the Authorized Version of the Bible is variously rendered as a psaltery, viol, lute, or instrument of ten strings. In its more primitive shape it still exists in further India as the *Saun* or *Soung*, the neck, arching as a bow, being without tuning-pegs and the tightly twisted strings simply raised or lowered on it to alter their pitch. Like its descendants on the Asiatic continent, the absence of a pillar or support for the curved neck prevents the use of heavy strings and any strong tension upon them. The tone, though sweet, is therefore weak. Among the Russian Ostyaks, however, who dwell on the confines of Asia and Europe, the first step towards the final perfection of the harp is evident. A rod, often bent by the pressure, is inserted between the two ends of the bow-shaped instrument.

In this form the harp was introduced into Europe by the westward migration of the tribes, and as the northern or Scandinavian harp, with its bent fore-pillar and gut or wire strings, is figured on the medieval monuments of Scotland and Ireland (Plate II, 2).

In the twelfth century we find it under the name *Cithara anglica*. The late Mr. Robert Armstrong, in his *Irish and Highland Harps* (1905), has entered minutely into the structure and stringing of these instruments with their graceful and handsome lines. This ancient type is recalled in the modern "Celtic" harp, a diatonic instrument with loop-stops or hooks to raise the pitch of the strings by a semitone. The large Irish harp, called *Clarseach*, of which several historic specimens are still in existence, had from thirty-five to forty-five wire strings, which were plucked by the finger-nails (Plate II, 3). It was diatonically tuned.

The orchestral harp of to-day, however, is a far more elaborate instrument. It has a stout and straight fore-pillar, gut strings, and a much extended compass. With its double-action pedals for semitonal changes it is the perfected form. It appears to be a South European type, perhaps connected with the classical Trigons of Asia Minor, and coming into use during the fourteenth and fifteenth centuries. Its development into a chromatic instrument is interesting. Praetorius (1618) gives a description and an illustration of the *Arpa doppia* with a semitonal arrangement of strings; and early in the same century the Welsh triple harp appears, an elaborate instrument with thirty-seven strings in the right-hand or bass rank, twenty-seven strings in the left or treble rank—all diatonically tuned—and thirty-four strings in the middle rank for the semitones (Plate II, 5). This instrument is figured by Mersenne (1635), and is still occasionally found in Wales.

In the second half, however, of the seventeenth century the diatonic harp received the "hooks" or "loop-stops" for the fingers. Through them the diatonic strings passed as they left the tuning-pins in the head of the instrument, and, by turning them, each string could be raised by a semitone, the hook nipping it at a lower point. In the Tyrol this type took the name of *Hakenharfe*, and was termed in France *Harpe à crochets*, in Italy *Arpa a nottolini*. About the year 1720 pedals with a single action were added by Hochbrucker in Bavaria, the mechanism being contained within the front pillar, now made hollow. By the pedals placed at the base of the instrument the "hooks" could be turned without removing the player's hands. In 1782 the French makers, Cousineau, father and son, doubled the number of pedals, and in 1819 Sebastian Erard of Paris perfected the double-action harp and made it chromatically complete. By this system the pedal raises the pitch of the string either by a semitone or by a whole tone; and as the instrument is tuned with the pedals half down, the player can either lower or raise each string by a semitone. The eighteenth-century harps are generally decorated in the so-called "Grecian" style, but in 1831 this gave way to the "Gothic" or "Empire" style, and as such they are usually found in the present day. Unfortunately for the designers, the ancient Greeks scorned the harp, preferring the lyre.

During the later half of the last century a curious malformation of the instrument appeared in the *Arpi-guitare*, which, made in the old shape, dispensed once more with the front pillar and substituted a guitar finger-board with seven strings and tuning-pegs in the head; the open strings disappeared. Despite its decorative sound-hole, carved head, and mother-of-pearl inlay, it is happily defunct.

At the beginning of the last century Egan of Dublin produced a very graceful "Royal Portable Irish Harp" on the lines of the Celtic instrument, but with gut strings. On the curved fore-pillar he placed seven stops or "ditals," which, when pressed down by the thumb of the left hand, shortened certain of the strings, so raising them a semitone in pitch to provide accidentals or for change of key. Harps of similar design are met with without the "ditals," but fitted with the old "loop-stops." The medieval minstrel's harp was a small instrument with a shallow sound-box and extremely portable (*Frontispiece* and Plate II, 4).

LYRES

The popular instrument on the shores of the Eastern Mediterranean Sea was, as we have said, the lyre, so different in its construction and origin from the harp. For whereas, in the latter instrument, the sound-chest is below the strings and they pass into it, on the lyre it is behind the strings and they pass over it, supported by a low bridge and fastened beneath it. It is evident that this type originated from a form in which the strings or sinews were stretched over a hollow or concave receptacle—perhaps the traditional tortoise shell— to which were in time added "horns" or upright bars united at the summit by a cross-piece, thus giving greater length and better attachment for the strings. In Central and Eastern Asia the lyre is unknown, and, from its general use by the Jews under the name *Kinnor* (unfortunately translated "harp" in the English Bible) and its becoming their national instrument and emblem, it is most likely of Semitic origin, and passed westward through Phoenician traders, becoming the classical *Cithara* of Greece and Rome. The difference between the *Lyra* (*Chelys*) and the *Cithara* consisted mainly in an alteration of shape and increased resonance. The small round sound-box of the former instrument—in the primitive examples of the present day still frequently a tortoise shell—

was expanded into a carefully constructed body with back, sound-board, and sides. The inserted bars or supports for the cross-piece were made as parts of the instrument, and a system of fine tuning by means of small rods was attached to the "yoke" or cross-piece, although this refinement had been adopted, if not invented, by the Sumerians two thousand years earlier.

Another migration, probably Celtic, carried the lyre before the commencement of our era into Central Europe and Britain, where it was known as the *Crot* or *Cruit*, and in later days as the *Rote* or *Rotte*. In the medieval manuscripts this instrument—either as a lyre or a *Rote*—is depicted in the hands of King David, but how far it was still retained in popular use is uncertain. In contrast to the harp, it was called the *Cithara teutonica*, or "the Rote of Almayne." In the grave of an old Alemannic knight opened in the Black Forest a rote with six strings was discovered of the sixth century A.D., and in Norway a seven-stringed instrument, called the *Straengeleg*, was found, though with the sound-board, which may have been of hide, missing. Though generally made with straight sides, this specimen retained the older shape of the round lyre, a type which maintained its existence in Germany and Scandinavia till the twelfth or thirteenth centuries.

There is no need to dwell on the way in which the lyre and cithara advanced the art of music for one thousand six hundred years by the ordering of the scale with its tetrachordic, hexachordic, and heptachordic systems from Terpander to Guido d'Arezzo. Its later use as a bowed instrument, called the *Crwth* or *Crowd* in Britain, in Finland the *Jouhikantele*, and in Sweden the *Talharpa*, will be explained in a subsequent division (iii.A.a).

PSALTERIES

One other group of these plucked stringed instruments without a neck remains to be considered. Whilst on the harp the frame is open completely, giving the player the use of both hands, and on the lyre partially closed by the sound-box, leaving, however, the left fingers still free to pluck, mute, or stop the strings, in this third form the frame of the instrument is wholly closed and the strings supported by bridges at both ends. It is known as the psaltery type, and was, in its first conception, merely a number of strings stretched over a plain board underneath which a gourd or some similar resonator was attached. In this guise it survives amongst uncivilized races to-day. It must soon have been perceived that, substituting a box-like chest for the simple board, resonator and frame could be combined. In all likelihood this perfected form as it affected Europe was evolved in Asia Minor in the first millennium B.C., though in Eastern Asia the same type of instrument had already existed for thousands of years as the *Kin* of China, and has spread along the Pacific coast. From Asia Minor the many-stringed psaltery passed eastward into Mesopotamia and Persia, as the *Kanûn*, and also westward into Greece, so closely allied to its original home. With the expanding commerce of Byzantium it was carried northwards into Germany and Scandinavia, whilst the Mediterranean traffic landed it in Italy and Spain. In this way we can best account for the widespread character of this type in Europe, where it was recognized in medieval times as the *Cythara barbarica*. Virdung (1511) and Agricola (1528) represent it in a triangular shape with a diatonic compass of over three octaves. Praetorius (1618) shows it in the quadrangular form, and also in the fantastic shape known as the *Stromento da porco* or *Schweinskopf.*

The Western Asiatic *Kanûn,* with its gut strings, also appeared in Europe in the Middle Ages, the name being corrupted into *Canon,* and that of a smaller type into *Mi-canon* (i.e. *Demi-canon*) or *Medi-cinale.* The psaltery in Europe, with wire strings, assumed even the lyre and the harp shape, though always with the closed frame. On some instruments only the fingers were used to pluck the strings, but in others small plectra attached to the finger-tips; from the plucking action its Greek name, *Psalterion,* was derived. Readers of Chaucer's *Canterbury Tales* will remember how the "poore scholar" delighted in its music after his astrological studies. We can picture his little one room with its bed, book-shelves, and curtain-covered cupboard.

> And al above ther lay a gay sawtrie
> On which he made a-nyghtes melodie
> So swetely, that all the chambre rong
> And *Angelus ad Virginem* he song,
> And, after that, he song the Kinges Noote.

We may wonder whether this fourteenth-century student would have been equally refreshed by "turning on the wireless."

The present-day representations of the instrument are the triangular-shaped Russian *Gusli,* with twenty-three to twenty-eight gut strings, and not to be confounded with the Slavonic one-stringed fiddle of the same name, the trapeze-shaped *Kantele* of Finland, a national instrument now disappearing, and *Arpanetta* or *Spitzharfe* of Germany, which assumes the form of a double psaltery and is played vertically, like the harp, and not on the lap or on the breast. Praetorius' *Gross-Doppel-Harff,* already mentioned, is in reality a double psaltery of this kind, for the strings are stretched over bridges on both sides of a sound-board, the bass strings on the left, the treble on the right.

About 1800 Light of London constructed a *Diplo-Kithara* on similar lines, and in Norway the chromatic *Korsharpe* ("cross-harp") attempted a similar arrangement with cross-strung wires. Another form of psaltery was the bell harp introduced (*c.* 1700) by Simcock of Bath, and probably so-called because it was held downwards, the thumbs, capped with small quill or horn plectra, plucking the wire strings, and the whole instrument waved to and fro as a bell. An instrument of the same kind, called the *Schelle-ʒither*, appeared about the same time in Germany. Small and simple psalteries are still to be found as children's toys. A larger kind, known as "the Prince of Wales' Harp" and fitted with special mechanism for playing chords, had, at one time, a considerable vogue. In the illuminations and ecclesiastical sculpture of the Middle Ages the psaltery is frequently depicted in the hands of angelic musicians. Spanish illustrations of many different shapes—even semicircular—are to be seen in the famous Codex of the *Cantigas de Santa Maria* (thirteenth century), reproduced by Riano in his *Notes on Spanish Music* (1887) and in Grove's *Dictionary of Music* (third edition, 1927). They are still to be traced in the Spanish and Italian *Salterio*, which is often highly ornamented. Praetorius affords us an illustration of an instrument which is an adaptation of the lyre or psaltery stringing to the lute, the upper part of the neck being turned at an angle to receive the tuning-pegs for twenty-three open strings.

The description of the dulcimer (Plate IV, 6), which is exactly like the psaltery save in the manner of playing, is placed under sub-class of struck strings (ii.A.a).

ZITHERS

i.A.a². At some period in late medieval days the open-strung psaltery received the addition of a narrow board placed beneath one or more of the strings and furnished with "frets," that is, little cross-bars of wood or metal set on the finger-board at the points where the strings should be stopped by the fingers of the left hand for the tones or semitones of the scale. The thumb of the right hand plucked the strings and the other fingers of that hand swept the remaining open strings as an accompaniment. This type became very popular in Central and Northern Europe, receiving in Germany the name *Zither* or *Schlag-zither*, to distinguish it from the later *Streich-* (or bowed) *zither*. This is one of the several names for stringed instruments derived from the old Greek *Cithara*, and must not be confused with another loan-word from the same source, the *Cither* or *Cistre*, which, as an instrument furnished with a neck, falls under the next subdivision (i.A.b).

The *Scheitholt* ("log of wood"), described by Praetorius (1618), appears to be its earliest form, especially as that writer classes it with the *Lumpen-instrumente* ("beggarly instruments"). It is still in use under the much more graceful name of *Epinette des Vosges*, where it is most popular. Its construction is of the simplest kind, consisting of three or four metal strings, stretched over a long, narrow box, with frets placed beneath them. The strings are swept by the right-hand thumb, and, in earlier days, a small rod, held in the left hand, pressed them down on the finger-board and, by being drawn up and down, varied the sounds. The principle has been more recently resuscitated in the so-called Hawaiian guitar. Praetorius links it also with the *Monochord* used by theoreticians, the frets—so called from the French *ferretté* ("banded with metal")—being substituted for the movable bridges of that scientific instrument. The strings are tuned as unison, fifth, and octave, a relic of the old system of the "organum." Probably the *Clavichord* of the troubadour, Girault de Calanson (1210), was of this kind.

An improvement, however, was effected by extending the narrow sound-box on one side and placing over it open accompaniment strings. This was the *Helm-zither*, after the Salzburg model, with a semicircular extension and four or five melody strings with some twenty strings for accompaniment (Plate IV, 5). The Bavarian zither retains in a greater degree the earlier rectangular shape, while the more symmetrical Mittenwald model adopts the rounded extension on both sides, with two or three melody strings and seven or more strings for accompaniment. A large number of varieties, however, exist, some much greater in length, as the *Elegie-Zither*, or with an increased set of accompaniment strings, as on the concert zither with forty-two strings. In small forms, however, the principal characteristics are retained, the melody strings being of brass or steel and the so-called "harmony strings" of gut or covered silk. The Swedish *Humle* and the Danish *Hommel* or *Noordische Balk* are similar to the Salzburg and Mittelwald models. The Norwegian *Langleik*, however, with its narrow sound-box, represents more closely the original *Scheitholt*; it has but one melody string and six or seven strings for accompaniment. The Icelandic *Langspil*, which is a very near relation, is now played with a bow as described under subdivision iii.A.a. The *Bûche* or *Epinette des Vosges*, previously mentioned, is fitted with a pair of melody strings in unison (tuned to g^1) and three brass strings for accompaniment (tuned to c^1 and g^1g^1). In the late eighteenth century a French rectangular zither, called *Psaltère*, was introduced, with two pairs of melody strings and seven pairs of accompaniment strings, all being in metal.

Here, too, we may place the English harp-lute and its kindred forms. Invented in 1810 by Edward Light of London, it reflects the lyre or rote type in general outline, having a somewhat similar sound-box, though the attached head is harp-shaped. But it has on one side a fretted finger-board, like the zithers, for the left hand, with seven strings for melodic use, while from the arched neck there are four or five open strings, some, as a rule, provided with loop-stops for raising the pitch, as in the *Hakenharfe*. An additional short finger-board was added by Wheatstone, carrying three strings for the highest notes, and further accompaniment strings appear on Light's Regency harp-lute. These instruments were held and played sideways on the lap; but the harp lyre, with an oval-shaped body, has a stand or pedestal and is played vertically; in other respects it resembles the harp-lute. Light's British lute-harp (1816) had cleverly arranged mechanism for altering the pitch of its twelve open strings. This consisted of small studs placed in the head of the instrument and pressed by the left-hand thumb. There was also a small finger-board for three melody strings. In 1819, with fresh improvements, it became the dital harp, and could be played—harpwise—with both hands. It possessed a compass of three octaves. The harp Ventura (1828), so called after the name of its inventor, was very similar, but the "ditals" were placed on the inner side of the finger-board and fitted with lever-action to the head as on the pedal harp; it was named by Ventura the *Imperial Octavino* and made in London. Several continental manufacturers, such as Levien and Pfeiffer of Paris, took Light's models (cf. R. B Armstrong, *Musical Instruments*, Part II. 1908).

During the latter part of the eighteenth century the guitar, too, was made in lyre form, and became very popular with classically minded ladies. The strings passed over a finger-board placed between the upright arms and joining, in most cases, the cross-bar to the body of the instrument. It was generally known as the lyre-guitar. Another yet more fantastical form, with an arched cross-bar, was called the Apollo or French lyre; it appeared at the opening of the last century in Empire style, and, in some cases, had additional open strings for the deeper bass notes.

The *Harpolyre* of Salomons of Paris (1827) resembled a gigantic guitar with three finger-boards, the two outer ones being placed on the arms of the lyre-shaped model. The German *Lyro-harfe* (1837) has but two finger-boards, in this respect following the French *Bissex* of the previous century. All these instruments, which are frequently to be seen in the sale-room, found no place in orchestral music, and, though often artistic in design and decoration, have not outlived the prevailing fashion of their day.

A very up-to-date development of the zither, hailing from America, is displayed in the electric zither (1936), with its companion the electric guitar (i.A.b). In both cases the use of a sound-box is dispensed with, and in its place an electro-magnet is affixed to the frame of the instrument close to the bridge and beneath the strings. When plucked by the fingers or a plectrum in the usual way only a feeble sound is heard; but when an electric current is passed through the magnet, the sound can be amplified and, through a loud-speaker, increased to an unparalleled extent. The zither is held horizontally on the knees, the guitar, as usual, on the arm.

LUTES

i.A.b. Closely allied with the last-mentioned psaltery type but differing from it in one or two important features is the plucked instrument furnished with a narrow neck, on which the pitch of the strings can be altered by the use of the fingers. Here again we revert to man's primitive sound-producer, the musical bow.

The African native has discovered that by pressing his knuckle against the string or by pinching it at one end a note higher in pitch is easily obtained. On the simple harps of the Middle Ages this same device was often adopted to secure a needed semitone. But the aboriginal tribes of India went further, and observed that if a stouter piece of wood was used for the bow-staff, which would not bend under the tension of the string, and a small wedge of hard wood was inserted between the string and the staff at each end, the various notes could be more easily obtained by the fingers as they pressed down the string on the staff. Such a primitive instrument as this is still in use among the Dravidian folk in Chota Nagpur and Orissa, where it is called the *Tuila*. To it is attached an interesting legend which may point to its original source.

A certain hero, by name Lingal, whose fame is celebrated in Ghond epics, came, they say, to their people in far-off days and taught them agriculture and how to make fire. He also constructed from a bamboo stick, inserted in a gourd, and with a string of two twisted hairs, a musical instrument known as the *Jantur*. By its strains he brought peace and unity to those amongst whom he had found a home. He made eleven sounds (*naddang*) to his instrument, and, from the traditional story, it is evident that it was not the first time

that Lingal had contrived this method of making music. To
this day, in connection with their old religious rites, the
Ghonds and the Koles of Central India hold dances in honour
of their ancient hero; for these they use a musical bow called
Pinga, to which is attached a gourd for increased resonance.
These tribes originally inhabited the North-West Province,
but repeated invasions have driven them southward. To reach
their earlier home Lingal must have come from the north
through one of the passes at the western end of the Himalaya
range. That to western Central Asia we owe the particular
type of instrument which we are now considering, and which
permits the use of the fingers on a long neck for obtaining
a musical scale, appears to be borne out by this tradition
and subsequent history.

However that may be, the type became popular in Mesopotamia and Egypt during the opening years of the second
millennium B.C., the gourd resonator being replaced by a
triangular or oval sound-box. Passing westward, it became
the *Balalaika*, a Russian national instrument, which in its
more ancient form, with a long neck and but two strings,
reflects its original model, though it is now made with a
shorter neck and three gut strings, tuned to *e*, *e*, and *a*, the
two first strings being in unison. In Turkey it retains its
Asiatic name, *Tanbûr*, which by a not uncommon interchange
of consonants was also known in Asia Minor and Europe as
the *Pandur* or *Pantur*. In Bulgaria it is also called *Tanboura*,
and has but two pairs of metal strings played with a plectrum.
A larger form is known as the *Balgarina*, and in Bosnia also
the *Saže*, in various sizes, represents the same type, the smaller
being known as the *Bougaria* and *Sargija*. In Southern Italy
the long neck is still retained for the *Colachon* or *Colascione*,
an instrument in its largest form over 6 feet in length with

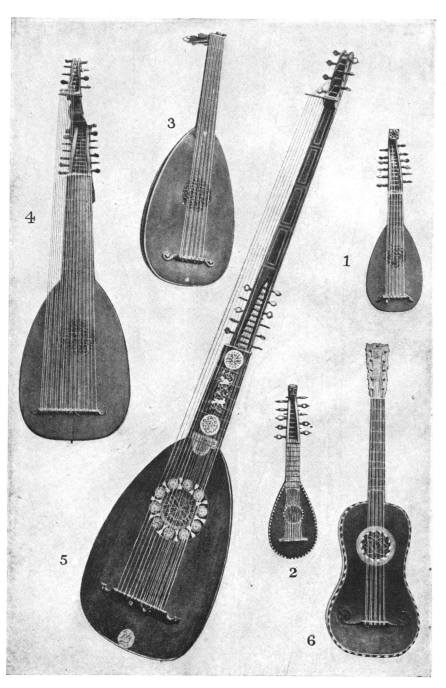

PLATE III. CHORDOPHONES

PLATE III

1 MILANESE MANDOLINE (eighteenth century)

2 PANDURINA (M. A. Bergonzi, 1756)

3 LUTE (Sixtus Rauwolf, 1593)

4 THEORBO (Mathye Hofman the Elder, 1619)

5 ARCHLUTE or CHITARRONE (Italian, seventeenth century)

6 GUITAR (R. Champion, c. 1725)

two or three strings, and described under the first name by
Mersenne (1635). A smaller edition, the *Colasciontino* or
Tanburica, is also found in Italy and in the Danubian pro-
vinces.

Of this Asiatic instrument there are illustrations in the early
years of the Christian era on Roman sepulchral monuments,
and specimens have been discovered at Herculaneum, but it
did not rank with the classical lyre and cithara.

Akin to the *Tanbûr* is the lute (Plate III, 3), the esteemed
accompaniment of song throughout the late Middle Ages.
Taking its name from the Arabic *Al'ûd* (the "wooden" instrument), it has usually been attributed to the Asiatic peoples
of the earlier centuries of our era, but its characteristic form
with a short neck is found in the second millennium B.C., a
Minoan or early Greek statuette unearthed in Egypt displaying
this particular feature. Here, however, the neck and pear-
shaped body seem to be made in one piece, and it is probable
that the substitution of a separate or "grafted" neck, such as
we find in later days, was due to the Persian or Arabian
lutenists of the eighth or ninth centuries. It was in this form
that it entered Europe during the Moorish ascendancy in
Spain and the Crusading wars. The body or "chest" of this
lute still retained its half-pear shape, and in the centre of the
"table" or sound-board a decorative "rose" was cut out as
a sound-hole. The neck of the treble or ordinary lute carried
ten to fourteen strings arranged in pairs, though very often
the highest string was but single. They were attached to a
bridge or holder affixed to the "table." The head, forming
the peg-box, was reflexed almost at a right angle, partly with
the idea of increasing the hold of the strings on the "nut"
or strip of ivory over which they passed, but also in order
to lessen the length of the instrument for the convenience of

the player. The strings were plucked by the fingers. Towards the close of the sixteenth century additional open strings for the lower notes were added, and on the *Theorbo* (Plate III, 4) and Archlute the straight portion of the neck was prolonged and a second peg-box formed to carry the extra strings, which lay by the side of the finger-board as "open" basses. On the Roman *Chitarrone*—the largest form of lute (Plate III, 5)—the length of the neck equalled that of the *Colascione* already mentioned. In the seventeenth and eighteenth centuries a lute called the *Angélique*, with seventeen single diatonic strings, was in use; and in French medieval poems we read of the *Barbot*, a miniature lute with four strings, derived from the Persian and Arabian *Barbat* (the Greek *Barbiton*). In Russia the *Torbane*, popular in the eighteenth century also in Poland, possesses not only the two peg-boxes carrying twelve and four gut strings respectively, but also a set of fourteen diatonic strings (b^1–a^3) attached to the main bridge and carried to little pegs in the side of the body. The *Theorbo* is generally attributed to a certain Signor Tiorba, a mythical Paduan lutenist of the sixteenth century; and in England at the opening of the next century it appears to have been considered a new instrument. But Pedrell (*Organografía musical Antigua Española*, 1901) finds mention of it in the records of the Catholic Queen Isabella in 1498.

All the lutes make use of "frets" (*bunde, tons*), the use of which has already been described (i.A.a²). In their case they greatly facilitated the playing of chords, and, like those used on the viols, were formed of gut and tied on when and where required. On the cithers, mandolines, and guitars they were usually replaced by metal or ivory strips.

We may here add a note on the notation used in medieval days for the lute and other instruments and known as "tablature." It was not a tonal notation, but digital, that is, it showed the fingering for the required notes but not their relative sounds. By a system of signs also, borrowed from the old Church notation, the time value of the notes was represented, strokes with or without one or two crooks to them being employed for the purpose. This system of "tabling" musical sounds appears to have arisen in the fifteenth century from the custom of writing the letters of the alphabet on or by the little bridges of the monochord. Hence arose the clavichord and organ tablatures, the letters being marked on the keys of the instruments and shown in the notation with a time sign above them. By this laborious method chords could be depicted, and Virdung (1511) gives a short ecclesiastical melody with an accompaniment for the clavichord in tablature. Some of the early virginals still bear on their keys the solmization-letters originated by Guido. On wind instruments the tablature denoted, by figures or short lines, which hole in the instrument should be opened to produce the right note. On the lutes, viols, and other instruments of that class the alphabetical letters were set on lines equal in number to the strings, and they showed the player where the finger should be placed to obtain the required sounds. The uppermost line represented the highest string, and the letter "a" stood for the open note to which it was tuned. The letter "b" stood for the first semitonal fret, the "c" for the second, and so on, reaching to "y" ("i") and "k," the eighth and ninth frets. The bass strings, tuned generally to the diatonic scale and not stopped by the fingers, were represented by the letter "a" with one or more strokes attached, the lowest strings of all being marked "4" and "5."

Such was the common tablature used in France, the Netherlands, England, and Germany; but in Italy and Spain the strings and frets were shown by lines and numbers (0, 1, 2, 3, 4, etc.), the lowest line in the tablature denoting, most awkwardly, the highest string of the lute.

A very curious system is described by Virdung, and said by him to have been invented by Paulmann of Nuremberg, a blind lutenist of the fifteenth century. Here each fret for each string is lettered, so that, on the usual lute of the period, the first fret was denoted by a, b, c, d, e for the five pairs of strings, the second by f, g, h, i, k, and so throughout the alphabet. This was a cumbersome method which, in spite of patriotic predilection, disappeared at the close of the sixteenth century in favour of the French practice of lettering the strings.

Of course, for all these lute and viol tablatures the tunings of the open strings had to be known, and one of the most valuable books for the English reader who desires to know what these tunings were (and they were many), as well as all details with reference to the structure and capabilities of the lute, is Thomas Mace's *Musick's Monument* (1676). The author, a clerk of Trinity College, Cambridge, was one of the last of the old school of lutenists, and his affection for his instrument, then passing into oblivion, is only equalled by his perfect knowledge of his art. It is, unfortunately, a rare book, but with the increasing interest now being taken in the old lute music it would certainly deserve a reprint.

Besides the survivals of the older lute already mentioned, there are the North African *Kuitra*, found in Spain, with four pairs of gut strings, the Hungarian and Polish *Kobsa*, with eight or ten strings, and the Russian *Bandurra*, with two peg-boxes. The Swedish *Theorbo*, with eight strings on the finger-board and seven open strings in a second head, is a flat-backed instrument, and more closely resembles the archcither. The Arab lute (*E'oud*) is sometimes seen in Turkey; it has a very deep body and six or seven pairs of double strings. It is common in Egypt.

Another ancient kind of lute is the *Mandore* (*Mandora* or *Mandola*), its name being a corruption of the Asiatic word *Pandur*. It is mentioned by Praetorius (1618), and is now a tenor instrument with four pairs of strings, tuned an octave below the violin. He also describes its treble counterpart, the four-, five- or six-stringed *Pandurina* or *Mandurichen* (Plate III, 2), now, with a deeper body, merged in the mandoline. Of this instrument there are several kinds, differing mainly in their stringing, single or double. The Milanese type has six pairs of gut strings (Plate III, 1), or, sometimes, at the present day, with six single strings. It is often called the *Mandurina*. The Paduan type has a smaller body with five pairs of strings. The well-known Neapolitan *Mandolino* (the Portuguese *Bandolin*) has four pairs of strings in metal, while the Genoese form has five or six single wire strings. All of these are now played with a plectrum. A narrow, lute-shaped instrument, akin to the Moorish *Rebab*, was known in Spain during the fourteenth century as the *Vihuela de péndola* or *de péñola*, as it was played with a plectrum and not with the bow (*Vihuela de arco* or viol).

CITHERS

Beside the round-backed lutes there are also instruments with flat backs called by another name derived from the ancient word *Cithara*, namely, the cither, cistre, citole, or cittern (Plate IV, 1). Citole is a shortened form of *Citharola*, and cittern appears to have been taken from an older form of the name, found as *Guiterne* or *Quiterne* in the fifteenth and sixteenth centuries. These instruments have wire strings plucked with a plectrum, and, as they have distinct "necks," they must not be confused with the zither type just described in i.A.a².

Of the cither there are several forms with four, five, or six pairs of strings, the largest and most elaborate being provided with twelve pairs of strings. The smallest form, with four pairs of strings (tuned *b*, *g*, *d*¹, *e*¹), was known in the sixteenth century as the little English cither (*Klein Englisch Zitterlein*), and Praetorius, who tells us this, also informs us that it produced very delightful harmony.

In that century, as indeed later also, it was the custom to decorate the top of the peg-box with a carved head, generally grotesque. We find an allusion to this in contemporary English literature such as "a citterp-head, an ill-countenanced cur," a term of abuse paralleled by the French *un visage de rebec*.

The *Pandore* (Plate IV, 2) or *Bandoër*, the *Penorcon*, and the *Opheoreon* or *Opharion* (Plate IV, 3) were also instruments of the cither type with *festonné* sides instead of merely a pear-shaped outline. They carried seven to nine pairs of wire strings. In England the *Bandore* became a useful accompaniment to the voice. For some reason, probably for ease of fingering, the bridge on these larger cithers was set aslant and the frets likewise. In Spain a small instrument of this kind, with six pairs of gut strings, is still called the *Bandurria*. The cither with a pear-shaped outline is sometimes known as the Portuguese mandoline. The Hamburg *Citherichen*, with a bell-shaped body and five pairs of strings, used in the late seventeenth century, affords a. picturesque shape. In the eighteenth century the English guitar—a wire-strung cittern with six pairs of strings—was extremely popular, and speci-

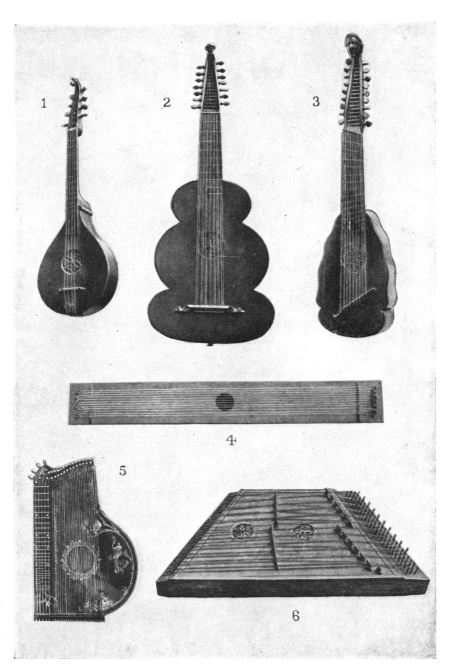

PLATE IV.   CHORDOPHONES

PLATE IV

1 CITOLE or CITHER (P. Wisser, 1708)

2 PANDORE or BANDORA (seventeenth century)

3 ORPHARION (F. Palmer, 1617)

4 AEOLIAN HARP

5 SALZBURG ZITHER (c. 1850)

6 ITALIAN DULCIMER (c. 1700)

mens made towards the close of the century frequently have
a patent tuning mechanism by Preston.

As with the lute, a second peg-box was sometimes added
to the neck, and the *Archi-Cistre* thus had five open bass
strings. There was also an *Archi-Cistre* with two separate
necks and five single strings on the finger-boards, as well as
five open strings from the upper peg-boxes, very similar to
the Thuringian cither, found in the Harz Mountains as a folk
instrument.

GUITARS

We must now turn to another large group of plucked
instruments—the guitars, a name also derived from the
classical *Cithara*. In medieval Spain the *Chitarra*, as it was
called, was represented by two types, viz. the *Chitarra latina*
or *Viola franceʒa*, with the flat peg-head and incurved sides
usually associated with the guitar. If we may trust the illustrations given in the Utrecht Psalter (ninth century), executed
at Rheims, or perhaps at Winchester under Roman monastic
influence, this type was a direct evolution from the old
classical lyre. The other type—*Chitarra moresca* (the medieval
Emmorache)—was a long-necked instrument with an oval-
shaped body which, as its name suggests, was introduced by
the Moors and was a development of the Oriental *Tanbûr*.
In fact, in the thirteenth-century illustrations to the *Cantigas
de S. Maria*, this form of *Chitarra* is shown in the hands of
a dusky Moor; but it seems to have disappeared in favour
of the more convenient small cithers. The *Chitarra latina*
became the guitar (Plate III, 6), or, as it is was known in the
eleventh century in France and England, the *Quiterne* or
gittern. In the early part of the seventeenth century its peg-
box resembled that of the viols instead of being flat, and it

was strung with five pairs of strings; it was used, according to Praetorius, to accompany "the jocular and silly ditties" of Italian singers. But an illustration of an English gittern of the early fourteenth century (British Museum, Arundel, 83) reveals that in earlier days the neck was made one with the body, the depth of which was extended to the peg-box, and a large hole pierced in it beneath the finger-board, through which the player thrust his thumb. Fortunately, an actual specimen of this form survives in the so-called violin preserved at Warwick Castle, and which is said to have been presented to the Earl of Leicester by Queen Elizabeth. As in the earlier illustration, it has but four single strings.

Mersenne (1635) depicts the "Spanish" guitar in its present shape, but with five pairs of strings (tuned g c^1 f^1 a^1 d^2), and the peg-head is flat. He says it was played with the castanets, "refreshing the minds of the hearers with wondrous delight." At the present day the Spaniards have a complete family group of these instruments with six single strings, beginning with the ordinary *Guitarra*, through the *Tenore*, and *Requinto* to the little *Guitarillo* with five strings. The change from the five pairs of strings to the six single strings was coming into vogue in the latter part of the seventeenth century. A small guitar with four gut strings is known in Portugal as the *Cavaco* or *Machête*, which, introduced by the Portuguese into the Sandwich Islands in the last century, has returned to Europe as the *Ukulele*.

The guitar has also been made in lute shape and in that of the lyre, as stated under Subdivision i.A.a². A curious hybrid instrument is the *Chitarra battente* (*Schlag-guitarre*, *Guitare toscane*, or struck guitar), used in the seventeenth and eighteenth centuries in Northern Italy and the Balkan districts. It has the guitar-shaped outline, but a rounded back, and carries seven pairs of wire strings. It received its name from their being "struck" with a plectrum instead of being plucked by the fingers, and was also called the *Guitare en batteau*.

It was only natural that, following again the example of the lute and cither, an attempt should have been made to add additional bass strings to the guitar. Hence arose the French *Bissex* (1773), with six open strings placed at the side of the finger-board, and the *Décacorde* invented by Carulli (1826), with strings in two sets of five each. Here, too, we would place a group of instruments introduced by Light of London (*c.* 1800), with Barry as maker. His harp-guitar (1798) had a sound-box of triangular outline and a rounded back somewhat resembling that of the harp; it carried eight strings. A very similar instrument, called the *Guitare-Harpe*, was produced by Levien of Paris (1825); it has but seven strings and, at the back, three brass stops or "ditals," pressed by the thumb to simplify certain fingerings.

Early in the last century Light invented the harp-lute-guitar, which had a neck with two peg-boxes (like the arch-lute) but a harp-shaped form of body. It had seven strings on the finger-board and four open strings. In 1810 the harp-lute appeared with the same form of body but with a harp-shaped head and supporting pillar as described under Subdivision i.A.a².

The *Banjo*, which reached Europe via America, is said to have been a Negro adaptation of the medieval *Pandore*, the name being written at the close of the eighteenth century as *Banjore*. On the other hand, there is a primitive stringed instrument consisting of a shallow wooden tray, over which strings are stretched, with a short handle, and which the negrotic tribes of the Congo district call the *Bandju*. As a large number of the American negroes came from the hinterland of Western Africa, it may be that they gave their native title to the musical instrument which served their same purpose in the New World.

During the past fifty years the banjo has received many improvements, such as the large resonating back now fixed behind the hoop-shaped body, the use of the plectrum, the replacement of the four or five gut strings by metal strings, and the new method of straining the parchment table. The zither banjo, mandoline banjo with four pairs of strings, the ukulele banjo with four single strings, and the larger banjoline are new types. As for the Hawaiian guitar, it is only the ordinary instrument, strung with steel strings and with a special bridge, played after the manner of the medieval *Scheitholt*. In this case, however, a metal pressure-bar is used on the strings instead of the earlier little wooden rod (i.A.a^2).

A very large bass guitar (*Tambura*) is found in Croatia, over 6 feet in height and strung with four strings. The Russian *Bass Balalaika* is of similar dimensions, but with three strings and a triangular body.

The electric guitar has been already mentioned (i.A.a^2) and its construction explained. As a recommendation it is stated that its amplified power will carry through "a 120-piece military band."

VIRGINALS AND SPINETS

i.B.a. The application of a keyboard to the plucked type of instruments just described has given to Western nations the desired opportunity and means of adding to the art of music that grace of accompaniment and wealth of expression which it lacked under the restricted rules of medieval harmony. Who first designed the predecessor of the harpsichord is not known; but, so far as the keyboard is concerned, this had been used for the *Hydraulus* or Water-organ in later Roman days. Lost apparently to sight and interest, it was rediscovered or, rather, resuscitated about the thirteenth century of our era for the small portative organs. The larger organs, found in the churches, clung for many years longer to the heavy levers, which required the use of the fist to produce the sounds.

The earliest keyboard instrument, of which we find mention in the fourteenth century, is the *Eschiquier* or *Eschaqueil*. It occurs in the writings of the French poets, and in 1360 King Edward III of England presented an *Eschiquier* to his royal prisoner, John of France. In 1385 there is a record of an instrument, *nommé Eschiquier*, being purchased from a monk of Tournay for use in the chapel of Philip, Duke of Burgundy. In 1387 it is described as an instrument similar to an organ which sounds "with strings." In the next century it is correlated with the *Manicordion*, a keyboard instrument of the clavichord type described under the next sub-class (ii.B.a). M. Pirro (*Les Clavecinistes*, Paris, 1925) states that in 1511 the Duke of Lorraine had an instrument which combined an Eschiquier, Organ, Spinet, and Flutes. This implies that the tone-effects of the Eschiquier and the Spinet were not identical.

As for the origin of the *Eschiquier*, discussion ranges over a wide field. On the strength of the word *Schachtbret*, given in a list of instruments used by the Minnesinger (1404), and taken as equivalent, it has been claimed for Germany or for the Netherlands. A suggestion has also been made that its forerunner was the Arabian *Al-shaqira*, a stringed instrument known in Spain in the early part of the thirteenth century. In England it appears under the name *Le chekker* (1392–3). This word, as well as the French and German titles, is usually associated with the meaning "chess-board"; reasons, therefore, have been advanced for considering that its case was decorated in some such manner. Owing to its early date, the reference cannot be to the white and black appearance of the much more modern chromatic keyboard.

Machaut, a French Romance poet (1290–1377), twice refers to this instrument as the *Eschaqueil* (or *Echaqueir*) *d'Angleterre*, and it is interesting to note that the gift of 1360, already mentioned, was made by an English king. There are, therefore, strong reasons for claiming its invention for this country, especially as it is an admitted fact that the earliest music written for this type of instrument originated in England. In describing the Doucemelle (p. 119) a name-clue appears. Still it is true that "chack" or "cheke" was formerly used of a clattering or clicking noise, as noted in the *Oxford Dictionary*. Perhaps this characteristic feature of the virginal and harpsichord may have attracted the notice of the listeners long before Middleton (*c.* 1600), describing frozen Charity, wrote, "Her teeth chattered in her head and leaped up and down like virginal jacks."

Here, however, it will be necessary for us to describe the "chattering" mechanism to which the word "jack" refers. On the end of the balanced key-shaft of the instrument, whether virginal, spinet, or harpsichord, rests an upright narrow strip of wood (J); into the top of it is hinged on a pin a thin slip or tongue carrying a horizontal point or *plectrum* of leather or quill. When the player depresses the key, the strip of wood (called the "jack") rises, and the *plectrum*, passing across the string, plucks it; so long as the key is held down the string is left free to vibrate. When the finger is taken off the key, the "jack" falls back into its original position, but the hinged slip, on which it is fixed, allows the *plectrum* to pass the string without plucking it again, a small spring at the back returning it to its place when at rest. Little pieces of cloth (D D) are inserted in the upper part of the "jack" and act as dampers on the vibrating string when it has returned to its place. In the harpsichord (*Cembalo, Clavecin, Clavicymbel*), which is the highest development of this type of instrument, many improvements have been made to increase and vary the tone and to add expression to the sounds. These will be noted in due course.

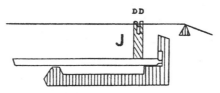

FIG. I.—VIRGINAL OR SPINET ACTION

The earliest recognized name, *Clavicembalum* or *Clavicymbolum,* which appears at the beginning of the fifteenth century in the Minnesingers' Rules, is technically a misnomer. For the word *cymbalum* was applied more particularly to instruments from which the sound was elicited by striking, such as the metal cymbals and also small bells (Autophones, i.A.c). It was also given, owing probably to a similarity of cause and effect, to the dulcimer, its strings struck with small hammers (Chordophones ii.A.a). We know, however, that the common use of a large *plectrum* on the psaltery and the cither has, from ancient times and in many languages, conveyed the idea of a stroke or blow, and this action could easily be attributed to the mechanism of the new keyboard instrument.

During the sixteenth century the *Clavicymbalon* became very popular, assuming various shapes and, unfortunately, diverse names, which we may probably apply in the following ways. The long form, with one straight side like a grand piano, appears to have kept the old name in many countries, being known as the *Cembalo*; but with later improvements it became the harpichord or harpsichord in England, the *Kielflügel* in Germany, and the *Clavecin* or *Clavecin à queue* in France (Plate V, 3). Sometimes the old name is written *Gravicembalo*, it may be owing to its now heavier tone. A smaller form of rectangular shape was known as the virginal (or *Spinetta a tavola*), and is so mentioned by Virdung (1511). This title was probably given to it in England, in Germany, and in the Netherlands because it became the favourite instrument of the maidens, as the lute remained for the use of the men. In *Parthenia* or *The Maydenhead of the first musicke that ever was printed for the Virginalles* (1611) an illustration is given of a lady seated at the instrument. In 1581, too, Vincentio Galilei calls it the *Clavichordium matronale*, using the word "clavichord" in the Italian sense for any keyboard form. Dr. Sachs (*Handbuch der Musikinstrumentenkunde*, 1920) suggests that the name was derived from *virga* ("a rod"), with special reference to the little wooden "jacks." There is an allusion in an old Latin chronicle to a certain Joannes "who took his *Virgella* and began to play sounds of sweet melody." But this might equally well have been some kind of zither or dulcimer. The instrument was frequently termed "a pair of virginals." This did not mean that there were two instruments; but it was used for anything of a complicated or compound unit, such as "a pair of scissors" or "a pair of steps"; so also "a pair of organs" (Aerophones, i.B.a).

A third shape which the virginal assumed was pentagonal (Plate V, 1), and it seems to have been especially popular in

Italy, where it was early known as the *Spinetta*, probably with reference to the little plectra resembling thorns (*spinae*) which plucked the strings. These were made at first of metal or of hard leather, and later of quills. The name appears in the fifteenth century. "Queen Elizabeth's virginal," bearing the royal coat-of-arms, and now in the Victoria and Albert Museum, London, is of this type, and has the usual outer case of Italian workmanship, from which the instrument was withdrawn for performance.

Yet a fourth shape is the *Spinetta traversa*, which apparently first emerged into popularity in Italy in the sixteenth century; it had a triangular or wing-shaped case, placed crosswise, that is, the plank for the tuning-pins was immediately over the keyboard and not at the side, as in the pentagonal form. It was in this shape that the French *Epinette* was made in the second half of the seventeenth century, and became known in England as the spinet, a charming little instrument which disappeared towards the close of the eighteenth century before the small rectangular pianos introduced by German makers.

A final form, yet one of the earliest and still found in the last century, was the vertical clavicymbel called *Clavicytherium* or keyed harp. It is illustrated by Virdung (1511), who says that the strings were of gut. For this a somewhat different mechanism was required in order that the "jack" might pluck the strings, and it does not appear to have been so generally used as the other forms, although, owing to its upright model, it occupied less space. A fine and early specimen of North Italian or Austrian make (fifteenth century) is exhibited in the Donaldson collection at the Royal College of Music, London. A very rare, probably unique, *Clavicytherium* with two keyboards (sixteenth or seventeenth century) and of Italian origin is in the Leipzig University

Instrumentenmuseum. The strings, varying from two to four for each note, are arranged parallel with the keyboards, so that the highest point of the vertical case is on the right hand of the player instead of on the left as usual, the shortest strings being set at the top, with long stickers of wire to reach the action. It was formerly in the Kraus collection, Florence. In the seventeenth and eighteenth centuries the same upright design as the early *Clavicytherium* was adopted for the harpsichord, and both Praetorius and Mersenne call it by the old name. It was, however, generally known in France as the *Clavecin vertical*, or in Italy as the *Cembalo verticale*.

Various instruments of a similar kind have been introduced from time to time, such as Bateman's *Clavilyr* (1813), in which the plectrum plucked the string near the middle with a circular motion resembling that of the finger. The "touch" of the instrument was greatly improved by Dietz of Paris in his *Clavi-Lyra* and *Clavi-Harpe* (1813) by counterpoise weights, and a damping pedal added. Praetorius (1618) mentions an attempt, under the name *Arpichordum*, to give the resonance of the ordinary harp by the use of small brass hooks to pull the strings. The name *Symphony*, given, according to the same writer, to an instrument of the plucked or virginal type, has caused some confusion, because it has also been applied to the ancient *Organistrum* or hurdy-gurdy, and to a sort of drum as well. In Praetorius' day it appears to have represented a *Clavicymbel* with a softer tone, perhaps with gut strings instead of wire. Sebastian Bach owned a *Lauten Werck*, which was probably such a *Lauten Clavicymbel*. Adlung (1768) describes it in his *Musica Mechanica Organoedi* as having a pair of gut strings in unison, with a damper, and giving the perfect effect of a lute. The organ-builder Hildebrand is known to have made such an instrument for Bach about 1740. His Suite in E minor is inscribed *aufs Lauten Werck*, and was apparently written for this lute-harpsichord or lyrichord, as it was called in England. Other authorities consider that the *Symphony* was a true clavichord (ii.B.a), but with wooden, in place of metal, "tangents," or with only a single string to each note.

On the death of Henry VIII, King of England, a complete inventory was made of his musical instruments, and we have given a rescript of it in our *Old English Instruments of Music* (1932, third edition). Some six double virginals, nine single virginals, twelve virginals (either single or double), three virginals "made harp-fashion" (like the *Clavicytherium*), four virginals and regals combined, and one virginal "that goethe with a whele without playinge upon" (i.B.b). As will be explained later under the aerophonic instruments (i.B.a), the words "single" and "double" refer to the compass of the keyboard—either to tenor *c* or to bass *C*—and not to their number. On the other hand, we find a payment made in 1539 for "ii payer of Virginalles in one coffer with iiii stoppes." This appears to denote either an instrument with two keyboards or, more probably, the presence of a little octave or single virginal, included within the larger case, and, in many instances, capable of withdrawal for use. Fine specimens of this twin virginal or *Clavecin-épinette* were frequently made on the Continent in the sixteenth and seventeenth centuries, and can be seen in the Museum of the Conservatoire de Musique at Brussels or in the Musée Plantin at Antwerp. If, however, Henry the Eighth's instrument had two keyboards, it antedated the supposed introduction of the second manual, attributed to Hans Rückers the Elder, by fifty years. The mention of stops, too, is remarkable, for these also have been credited to members of the Rückers family. The stops on these instruments were, at first, in the form of "slides," the ends projecting through the right-hand side of the case, and pulled out or pushed in by the hand. The "slide" moves the "jack" away from the string, so that the plectrum passes without plucking it. Van Blankenburg, in his *Elementa Musica* (1739), tells us that, in these early days, the two keyboards were not tuned in unison, but the lower was a fourth in pitch below the upper. It seems that this arrangement was adopted to render the popular form of transposition in that day more easy.

HARPSICHORD

In the seventeenth century, however, the two manuals became identical in pitch, and, with this, other stops were added to vary or increase the tone of the instrument, then known as the harpsichord. A second string, tuned in unison to the other, not only added volume but, even when unused, vibrated sympathetically with its fellow unison, and, as they said, raised "a sweet and tranquil harmony." Mace (1676) speaks of a theorbo stop, the predecessor probably of the lute stop, by which another row of "jacks" was brought into play and plucked the string nearer the bridge. There was also a buff or harp stop, attached by Plenius in 1745, which muted the string with a leather pad. In some of the French and German instruments there is also a true harp stop—the "jacks" being fitted with broad plectra of leather. Sometimes there is, too, a rank of strings tuned an octave below the unisons. Bach's *Kielflügel*, now in the Instrumenten Museum, Berlin, has this 16-foot or low-pitched stop. Mechanical devices were also employed to perfect the instrument; in 1769 Shudi of

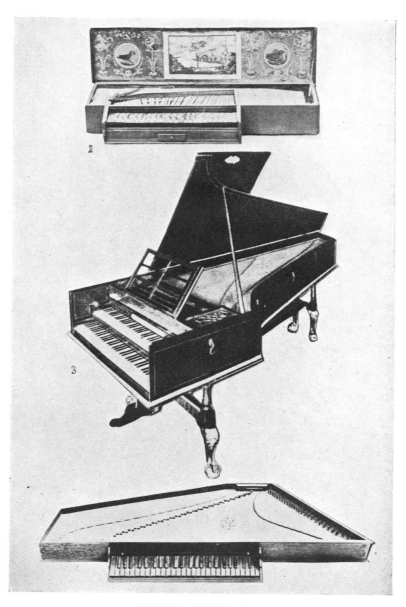

PLATE V.   CHORDOPHONES

PLATE V

1 VIRGINAL or SPINET (Marcus Jadra, 1552)

2 ITALIAN CLAVICHORD (Onesto Tosi, 1568)

3 ENGLISH HARPSICHORD (Burkat Shudi, 1765)
(Made for King Frederick the Great of Prussia)

London added a pedal for the right foot which actuated a set of louvred shutters placed over the strings as a "swell" to increase or diminish the sound, and, a few years earlier, there was set a pedal on the left side, called the "machine," which altered the combinations of the stops. Harpsichords with three manuals have also been made; on these are no stops, but the uppermost keyboard acts on the octave string, the middle keyboard on the unison and octave, and the lowest keyboard on the two unisons only.

The keyboard, too, has been rearranged in its lower octave. In the sixteenth and seventeenth centuries this bottom octave was "short," that is, incomplete. At that time the lowest *G* sharp and *F* sharp were not considered of much use as basses, and their strings were tuned to *E* and *D*, while the lowest string and key, formerly denoted as E natural, took the compass down to *C*. If the instrument were larger and the complete compass extended to *C*, then the *D* sharp and *C* sharp strings were tuned B_I and A_I and the lowest key sounded G_I. Even at the close of the eighteenth century the low *C* sharp was often omitted, especially on the smaller organs. In this century appeared also the "cut" sharps to dispense with this incomplete arrangement. The sharps mentioned above were cut across the middle, and the lower or nearer half raised the "jacks" for the *E* and *D* or the B_I and A_I strings, whilst the upper half gave the normal *G* sharp and *F* sharp or *D* sharp and *C* sharp.

At the opening of the nineteenth century the harpsichord or harpsicon practically disappeared, but the close of the same century saw a reawakening to its useful and peculiar tone-quality. Instead of hand-stops, grouped on each side above the manual, Pleyel of Paris introduced pedals, whereby a *crescendo* effect can easily be obtained. This, however, was no new invention, for John Haward of London invented a pedal harpsichord or harpsicon, as described by Mace, in 1676. Four small "pummels" of wood, touched by the feet, brought into action the various stops. Erard of Paris adapted knee-levers, but Dolmetsch prefers the use of the following pedals: (1) sostenuto, (2) 16-foot tone, (3) 8-foot tone, (4) 4-foot tone, (5) harp lower keyboard, (6) harp upper keyboard, (7) manual coupler, (8) crescendo. The tone of these modern instruments is far heavier and more powerful than that of their predecessors.

An interesting departure from the characteristic "jack and quill" action has been effected by Mr. Dolmetsch. At the end of the key-lever a "jack" with the usual "tongue" is placed, but without a plectrum. The upper edge of the "tongue" presses against a leather pad, attached to a small spring, lying beneath the string. The pad raises the string, but in so doing slips off the edge of the "tongue." By the instantaneous withdrawal of the pressure, the string vibrates and gives its sound. The pluck or "chatter" of the plectrum is, of course, no longer heard.

It is impossible here to do duty or justice to the many makers and composers who have contributed to the development and appreciation of this classic instrument.

Beginning with the Italian makers of the sixteenth century, Basso and Da Pesaro of Venice, we may recall the names of the Rückers family of Antwerp, Hans and his son Johannes or Hans the Younger, Andreas and his son Andreas, whose labours extended from 1550 to over a century. Their productions are works of skill, and the Flemish decoration upon them renders them objects of beauty. A list of their known instruments is given in Grove's *Dictionary of Music* (1927). Amongst German makers were the two Silbermanns, father and son, for another century, and in France Blanchet and Taskin.

In England, Burkat Shudi (the founder of the Broadwood firm) and the Kirkmans became masters of their art. A very handsome two-keyboard harpsichord, made by Shudi in 1765 as a present to Frederick the Great, King of Prussia, and on which Mozart played before it left England, is now preserved in the Schlesisches Museum at Breslau (Plate V, 3). For over a century and a half it had rested in the music-room of the old castle and passed unnoticed by previous writers.

As for the introduction of the harpsichord into the orchestra, Monteverdi is the first to mention it in his score of *Orfeo* (1617), where he has allotted parts to "duoi gravicembali." From that day it took a dominating position in the music of nearly two centuries. At it the composer sat, and from it he conducted his players. In the Italian opera it was used to accompany the recitatives.

A remarkable instance of overgrowth is displayed in the *Arcicembalo* of Vincentio Trasuntino, the Venetian (c. 1561). It was a six-manual instrument with thirty-one subdivisions in the octave on the keyboards, the object being to reproduce the ancient Greek music in its diatonic, chromatic, and enharmonic systems.

Of the seventeenth-century spinet in transverse wing shape there is little more to be said. To its single string another was sometimes added, actuated by a stop or lever. An Italian *Spinetta traversa*, seen in a London sale-room in 1910, had two manuals, the upper sounding a single unison string, the lower an octave string, but also lifting the upper "jacks." Amongst famous English makers were Haward, Keene, and the Hitchcocks, while as makers of the decorative rectangular virginals were the Whites, Loosemore, and Leversidge. So

H

popular, indeed, was the instrument that Marius of Paris (1700) introduced a *Clavecin brisé* or *Clavecin de voyage*, which closed up like a box. It had a compass of nearly five octaves.

The combination of the virginal or harpsichord with the organ was known in the sixteenth century. Henry the Eighth possessed examples of a single virginal and a single regal (a small organ) with a stop of wooden pipes. Also he had a double virginal with a double regal with three stops of pipes on a wainscot base containing the bellows. In the Victoria and Albert Museum, London, there is a *Claviorganum* (as the instrument was also called) consisting of a harpsichord by Threwes of Antwerp (1579) and an organ of five stops, wood and metal. A fine eighteenth-century example by Crang (1745), combining a two-manual harpsichord with an organ of six stops, is now in the Nettlefold collection at Wrotham, Kent. As a rule these united forms are not very successful, owing to the difficulty of keeping the two instruments in tune with each other. In 1792 Geib of London introduced a two-manual combination of the spinet and the piano, the latter played by the upper keyboard.

BARREL SPINET

i.B.b. The earliest instance we have of automatic mechanism being applied to this type of instrument in Europe is King Henry's instrument "that goeth with a whele without playinge upon." In his collection (1547) it is classed with the virginals, and in the Kunsthistorisches Museum at Vienna there is a rectangular spinet or virginal by Bidermann of Augsburg (c. 1575) with such an automatic attachment, as well as with a four-octave keyboard. A pinned barrel, turned by a handle, depresses small touch-pieces which move the "jacks." The compass is diatonic (F to d^2). Kircher, in his *Musurgia* (1650), alludes to a simple method advocated by a London physician, Thomas Fludd, some thirty years earlier. Small toys have also been made with a central shaft set with quills, which plucked stretched wires as it revolved. Some of the modern forms of piano-players might, of course, be easily adapted to virginals and harpsichords, if it were thought at all desirable.

ii. STRUCK TYPE

ii.A. If the hunting-bow has been, as we have seen, responsible for some of the early types of stringed instruments plucked by the fingers or with a plectrum, it is also closely associated with the sub-class which will now occupy our attention, wherein the string is struck with a rod or hammer and the sound waves produced by its percussion. The traditional story of the invention of the Eastern Asiatic psalteries, represented by the Chinese *Kin* and the Japanese *Koto*, which we related at the commencement of the preceding subdivision, would suggest that the instruments with plucked strings were more generally popular in that continent than the struck strings. On the other hand, investigations into the use made of the musical bow on the African continent tend to show that there the method of the striking stick was more usual than that of the fingers or the plectrum. It is true that the strings of one form of Chinese *Kin* are sometimes sounded by blows from a short bamboo stick, and also that the *Santir*, the old Persian psaltery, is played with two little beating-rods as a dulcimer. But both of these appear to be methods introduced at a later

date. If we turn to Africa, however, the evidence from primitive custom points entirely in the opposite direction. The
Bushman, for instance, has made a kill, and as he rests and
awaits his companions he taps the bow-string with the shaft
of his arrow. An old rock-painting by the Bushmen in
Basutoland shows this action continued in the after-dance of
triumph. The seven bows of the hunting-party have been
collected and placed on the ground, with the strings uppermost, in front of a musician, who plays upon them by striking
them with a stick. A reproduction of this interesting scene is
given by Professor Kirby as the frontispiece to *The Musical
Instruments of the Native Races of South Africa*. This music,
we are told, is still to be heard at the present day, and it
distinctly shows the origin of the dulcimer type of instrument,
which is characteristic of one important section of this class.
The string must be struck sharply, and by pressing the
knuckles against it the note can be varied. Overtones are
heard, and if the bow is placed over the mouth they are
reinforced by the native players in the same way as those of
the Jew's harp (Autophones, ii.A.a).

DULCIMER

ii.A.a. We have, however, placed the struck-string type as
the second sub-class of chordophonic instruments because, in
Europe at any rate, it did not rise to popularity so early as
the plucked string. There are also traces of its use which
more closely associate its method of sound-production with
the autophonic substances and the stretched membranes of
the drums. For in the Basque provinces and in the French
district of Béarn a little whistle, called the *Galoubet*, is accompanied by a stringed instrument called the *Tambourin*,

apparently identical with one form of the medieval *Chorus*. It consists of a long sound-box over which seven strings are drawn, which are struck with a short stick. The strings are tuned to the tonic and dominant of the *Galoubet*, and the *Tambourin* is held on the right arm, the right hand fingering the whistle and the left hand wielding the drum-stick. Here we find, then, a close connection between the chordophonic and the membranophonic instruments.

For more modern requirements this principle has been elaborated in the form of the bell machine, which was especially introduced for use in Wagner's *Parsifal*. Four sounds are required by the composer, and they are obtained from four ranks of heavy piano-strings, six to a rank and three in each rank tuned to the octave. They are struck with a broad-headed hammer.

The chief representative of direct action in this class, however, is the dulcimer (Plate IV, 6)—the French *Tympanon*, the Irish *Tiompan*, the German *Hackbrett*, and the Hungarian *Cimbalon*. It is also mentioned under the name *Doucemelle* (*Dulce-melos*, "sweet music") in the old Romance chansons and as the *Dowcemere* by English poets of the fifteenth century. In this instrument the resonance-case is rectangular or of trapezoid form, and the strings are arranged in ranks of two or more for each note. It has a close resemblance to the ancient *Psalterium*, plucked by the fingers or with a plectrum, and the Persian dulcimer, the *Santir*, shows that this was its origin.

In China, where, as we have said, the psaltery form and plucked string are more prevalent, the dulcimer is known as the *Yang-kin* or foreign psaltery; but the statement, supported if not originated by Engel, that the Assyrians invented and used the dulcimer is an error based on a much-damaged representation of a ten-stringed harp (*Eshirtu*) on a slab of the Sennacherib era (seventh century B.C.) in the British Museum. It appears to have been known in Europe by the twelfth century of our era, as evidenced in a Byzantine ivory-carving of that period. But its popular use by the gipsy bands of Hungary would suggest a Slav influence for its introduction. About 1690 a Prussian musician named Pantaleon Hebenstreit became distinguished as a performer, and his instrument, which had two sound-boards, was strung with quadruple strings of gut and wire. It is said that his instrument, called the *Pantaleon*, and the effect of the music played suggested the invention of the pianoforte, which is but a keyboard dulcimer. The fact that one of the earliest forms of the piano bore the name of Hebenstreit's instrument appears to corroborate this statement.

We may remark that the direct use of the hammer on instruments having a fretted neck, like the guitar, is unknown in Europe; the so-called *Chitarra battente* of Italy and Spain is played with a plectrum.

CLAVICHORD

ii.B.a. On the other hand, the indirect use of the hammer action on instruments of the guitar type is shown in its simplest form on the keyed cither, an instrument with a fretted neck but fitted with a small mechanical box containing six finger-keys. The box is fastened over the six strings close to the bridge, and the hammers strike the respective strings beneath them. Clauss of London (1783) patented this invention for use on the popular English guitar or cittern of that day. A very similar device was adopted in Bachmann's *Tastenguitarre* (*c.* 1795).

The type of stringed instrument with a keyboard and played by percussion has given to the world of music two very important representatives, viz. the clavichord and the pianoforte. It is ascertained from the old Latin treatise by Henri Arnaut (*d.* 1466) that one form of the *Doucemelle* had a strip of wood, weighted with lead, standing on the key-shaft; the key-end, on rising, struck a buffer; the sudden check threw the strip up to hit the pair of strings and rebound after the blow. The twelve pairs of strings were divided by long bridges into three segments, tuned respectively to unison, octave, and super-octave pitch, and providing almost a three-octave compass (B–a^2). Surely in this "check" action we must see the *Chekker* or *Eschiquier*. It was of the clavichord and not of the virginal type.

Now it is a well-known fact that if a taut string is struck sharply by the thin edge of a piece of wood or metal, it will vibrate, even though the edge remains in contact with the string or wire; and, if the finger is placed on the string at one end to act as a damper, the free end will yield a distinct note of musical pitch; and the nearer the striking-point is brought to the free end the higher will be the pitch of the note, the other portion of the string being muted by the damper. This was the "simple action" of the clavichord (*Frontispiece* and Plate V, 2), which appeared in the eleventh or twelfth century. It was the successor of the ancient Greek monochord used by Pythagoras and subsequent theoreticians to define the vibrations of the notes of the scale. They used movable bridges which, changed from point to point, produced the required sound when the string was plucked. But the single string of the monochord gradually gave place to a more convenient form with four, eight, or even twenty strings, and it was then, about the fourteenth century, that a key mechanism was introduced to supersede the constant alteration of the little bridges.

On the clavichord the striking edge consists of a "tangent" of brass (T) placed at the further end of the key, and the damping of the unrequired length of the string is effected by interwoven strips of woollen material (D). In the earliest instruments the use of several tangents for one string or pair of strings was adopted on the principle already indicated; but with the growth of polyphony this was found awkward, as

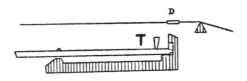

FIG. 2.—CLAVICHORD ACTION

it rendered any other note on the same string impossible in conjunction with an acting tangent. So, when two to five chromatic notes had been obtained from one string, tangents were arranged to strike other strings in the same way. This instrument, with its crude attempt at harmony, received the name of the *Gebundenes-Klavier* or fretted clavichord, and was in use with various modifications till the opening of the eighteenth century. The Italian instruments, too, retained four or five of the straight little bridges over which the strings still passed, as shown by Mersenne (1635); but in Germany one long bridge carried them all. In order to give absolute freedom for musical expression, the *Bundfreies-Klavier*, or fret-free clavichord, was introduced, probably by Faber of Crailsheim (c. 1720). Here each note was provided with its own string, as on the *Doucemelle*. For this perfected instrument Bach wrote his first series of twenty-four Preludes and Fugues (1722) as a series of studies for his own children. It has been argued that the title, *Das Wohltemperirtes Klavier*, might equally well be applied to the harpsichord. But the recognized names for that instrument were *Klavicymbel* or *Kielflügel*; *Klavier* was reserved for the clavichord. Moreover, if the title was intended merely to express the tuning of the keyboard on the equal temperament system for all keys, the word *Klaviatur* and not *Klavier* would have been used. It is needless to say that, at this early time, the pianoforte was only in its infancy. One of the inventions of John Geib of London (1792) combined the clavichord with the piano by means of two keyboards, the uppermost for the clavichord. They could be played together.

The tone of the clavichord is soft and sensitive but somewhat weak, owing to the fact that the "tangent" must remain pressed against the string to give the required pitch of the note, and does not fall away after the stroke as the piano hammer. But, in the opportunities afforded for delicate expression and sympathetic nuance, it surpasses all other keyboard instruments. Even the *bebung*, or "close-shake," is available. For use in the home or in the musician's study it is unsurpassed, and in Germany and the Scandinavian countries it held its own till the close of the eighteenth century.

In Italy, France, and England the *Clavecin* and spinet occupied the field; but, after the lapse of over a century, the present day has witnessed a great revival of interest in its quiet, old-world strains. About 1760 a marked extension of the instrument was made in Saxony by Gerstenberg, of which a specimen is now at the University Instrumentenmuseum, Leipzig. It has two manuals of 4-foot (octave) pitch and a pedal-board (anticipated by Virdung in 1511) of 8-foot and 16-foot pitch. As for compass, a *Gebundenes* instrument by

Domenico da Pesaro (1543) is limited to four octaves, the lowest being incomplete, whereas a Swedish *Bundfreies* instrument by Rackwitz (1796) in the writer's collection has the complete compass of five and a half octaves. Mersenne, in the seventeenth century, applies the name *Manichorde* to the instrument. This word, which may be a corruption of the earlier title *Monochorde* or *Monochordion*, is correlated by medieval scribes with the *Eschiquier* (i.B.a).

PIANOFORTE

The pianoforte or forte-piano, as it was at first called, is a direct outcome of the dulcimer, and, as has been said, was probably suggested by the popularity of the *Pantaleon* at the close of the seventeenth century (ii.A.a). There is, however, a curious entry in the Inventory of Musical Instruments belonging to the ducal house of Este of Ferrara and Modena in the sixteenth century in the following words: "*Clavicembalo 3 registri col suo Organo sotto, Instrumento Piano e forte lauto tutto a rabeschi,*" that is, "A clavicymbel of three stops with its organ underneath, an instrument soft and loud, all finely decorated with arabesques." Attempts have been made to show that the latter part suggests an early piano, but, from letters of the period relating to this instrument discovered by Valdrighi at Modena, it is evident that the whole description refers to a single instrument, viz. a *Claviorganum* with a "swell" attachment.

The recognized claimants, therefore, for the honour of inventing the pianoforte are three in number: Bartolommeo Cristofori, the famous harpsichord-maker of Florence; Marius of Paris, the originator of the *Clavecin brisé* (i.B.a); and Schröter, an eminent organist and theoretician of Saxony.

To the first named is the award rightly given, as his model of the *Gravicembalo col piano e forte* was minutely described in a Venetian journal of the year 1711, and the invention had been already recognized in 1709. Marius submitted his design for a *Clavecin à maillets* to the French Royal Academy of Science in 1716; while Gottlieb Schröter constructed a *Klavier* with hammers, "upon which one at pleasure might play loudly or softly," when a teacher at Dresden (1717–21).

Of the three inventions the most elaborate and effective

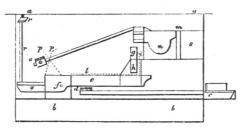

Fig. 3.—PIANO ACTION (CRISTOFORI)

was that of Cristofori. The end of the key lifted a second lever (*e*), which by a movable tongue (*g*), known as the *linguetta mobile* or "hopper," forced the butt (*n*) of the hinged hammer (*o*) upwards to strike the string above it. The "hopper," being loose, allowed the hammer to fall back after the blow, and, when the pressure of the finger on the key was released, a wire spring brought the "hopper" back into its original position. The hammers on their recoil fell on fine strings of crossed silk (*p*) to prevent any noise, and cloth dampers (*r*) were lifted off the strings by a row of wooden rods ("stickers") placed at the farther end of the key-shaft.

In Marius's mechanical movement the hammers were simply formed by an angle-piece of wood at the end of the key. When the key was depressed sharply by the player's finger, the upturned angle, like a balanced hammer, struck the string, and recoiled under its own weight. Schröter's "over-striking" action for his first instrument, called *Pantaleon*, after Hebenstreit's dulcimer, is not known; but, upon its failure, his "under-striking" mechanism showed a more delicate adjustment in that the hammer was pivoted on a back-rail and lifted by a sharp blow from a leather-headed pin placed immediately beneath it near the pivoted end. Falling back on the pin, it left the string free to vibrate. A similar device was afterwards adopted for the keyed harmonicas.

A marked advantage in Cristofori's design was the second lever, now known as the "under-hammer," which provides an "escapement," that is, a space between the hammer and its string, after the blow is struck, necessary for its due vibration, thus preventing "blocking." The first step towards the "double escapement"—an important improvement, which enables the blow of the hammer to be repeated without its falling back into the original position—was made by Sebastian Erard in 1808.

Two pianofortes by Cristofori survive: one, dated 1720, is in the Metropolitan Museum of Art, New York; the other, dated 1726, was formerly in the Kraus collection at Florence, and is now in the University Instrumentenmuseum, Leipzig. The writer is well acquainted with both instruments, and the last mentioned maintains more of its original condition. Made in the long harpsichord shape (*Kielflügel*), its small-gauge strings and little hammers with thin felt heads give forth a sound very similar to that of the Italian virginals with leather plectra. The action, which is light and easy, has been slightly altered by the maker from his first design, the "second lever" being transformed into an "under-hammer," which forces up the striking hammer; a rest or "check," too, is placed at the end of the key to receive the recoil of the hammer in place of the silk strings. In Germany this design was adopted by Gottfried Silbermann in 1726, but Bach condemned his pianos for their heavy touch and their weak tone in the upper octaves.

About 1750, however, Silbermann achieved success, gaining both the full approval of Bach and the patronage of King Frederick the Great. About the same time Friederici of Gera in Saxony is believed to have made the first rectangular-shaped instrument, similar in outward appearance to the clavi-

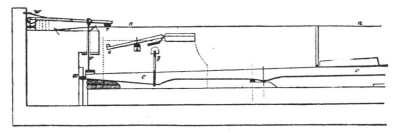

FIG. 4.—PIANO ACTION (ZUMPE)

chord. He called it the *Forte-bien*, a play upon the earlier name. He also constructed pianos in the triangular spinet-shape. Schröter's designs, however, were not overlooked, and were incorporated in what is known as the "Zumpe-action," being the method claimed for Mason and used in the little rectangular pianos made by German workmen in England (c. 1760). Zumpe with eleven compatriots settled in this country and were nicknamed "the twelve apostles"; their instruments were very popular also in Germany and France. In a piano made by Jesse of Halberstatt (1765) we observed the same action, but the little wooden hammers were made in the shape of the clavichord "tangents," alternately felted and feltless, which by a shifting lever produced a change of tone. For forty years the so-called square pianos, introduced into France in 1777 by Sebastian Erard of Paris, were constructed on almost identical lines, and lever-stops were added to lift the dampers for loud *sostenuto* effects or to press a bar of felted wood against the strings for softening the sound. A foot-pedal was substituted by John Broadwood for the former purpose. In 1786 Geib used the "hopper and under-hammer actions" of Cristofori's later model in the square piano (*Piano carré, Tafelflügel*), which only disappeared with the arrival of the upright instrument at the opening of the nineteenth century. Schäffer of Cologne (1793) gave the instrument four pedals, one for a lute effect with a tissue-paper strip resting on the strings, another for a soft effect with a leather strip, and two foot-pedals for bass and treble respectively.

The "grand piano" (*Hammerflügel, Piano à queue*), which was Cristofori's original shape, became popular during the latter half of the eighteenth century, principally through the ingenious workmanship of a Dutchman, Americus Backers, associated with John Broadwood, who thus became the pioneers of the so-called "English action," based on Cristofori's first design for a direct action. As developed by Messrs. Broadwood & Sons, this has provided instruments for Beethoven, Chopin, and many of the most famous modern composers.

On the Continent, however, a rival action held the field, called the Viennese action, from its popularity in Austria, where Stein of Augsburg invented or developed the design about 1773; for it is possible that, in a rudimentary form, it was due to Friederici. There is here no movable hopper or under-hammer, but the striking hammer (*o*) is centred with a projecting butt or tail at the back which, when the key is depressed, catches in the notch of a wooden block (*g*) placed behind it, and so jerks the hammer on to the string. Mozart was charmed with the evenness and lightness of touch obtained in this way, and in 1794, owing to the ability of Stein's son-in-law, Andreas Streicher, and his wife Nanette, maker and pianiste, it was brought to its highest perfection. To these instruments a knee-lever (*genouillère*) was attached for a "forte" effect. At the beginning of the nineteenth century this action was adopted by Sebastian Erard, and in 1821 Pierre Erard patented his "repetition action," which,

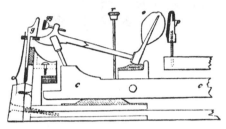

FIG. 5.—PIANO ACTION (VIENNESE)

under various forms and at the hands of the most famous makers, has given to the performer the power of repeating the sound by a very small movement of the key itself through the "double escapement."

A word must be said about the upright piano. Suggested by Marius in his patents of 1716, the vertical form was early adopted. An upright grand piano seen at Pistoia bore the label "Domenico del Mela, 1739"; but such instruments were chiefly adaptations of the horizontal piano action. Many small alterations, claimed as original, were tried, and the designs assumed various names, such as the *Pyramiden Klavier* of Friederici (1745) and the *Giraffen Klavier* of Seuffert (1804). It was made also in lyre-shape, and even circular, the strings being stretched over a body shaped as a kettledrum. Stodart,

in 1795, produced his "newly invented upright grand pianoforte" in the form of a bookcase; but Isaac Hawkins, in 1800,
was the first to design an upright instrument with a special
action of its own. Here the strings were carried down to the
bottom of the tall case and long rods or "stickers," placed
on the end of the key-levers, struck the butts of the hammers.

The cabinet piano was introduced by Southwell of Fleet
Street, London, in 1807, but Müller's *Ditanaklasis* had pre-
ceded it at Vienna in 1800. The cottage piano, with its own
special action, was produced by Wornum of Store Street,
London, in 1811, followed by his piccolo piano in 1829.
Both these models, becoming popular in France through
Pleyel of Paris, became known as the "French action."

Iron bars to resist the tension of the strings were tried by
Broadwood as early as 1808. Tubes were substituted by Allen
(1820), and Erard in 1822 employed nine tension bars; but
the complete iron frame was due to Babcock of Boston,
U.S.A. (1825), as well as the cross- or over-stringing (1830),
though almost similar suggestions appear to have been made
by Theobald Boehm, the father of the modern flute.

Some more recent makers have drawn from the unused
lengths of the wires sympathetic vibrations to increase the
resonance, and, with the same idea, a "free" octave-string
has been added for each note; but this principle had already
been recognized by Silbermann in his *Cembal d'Amour* (1768),
a clavichord with the tangents placed at the half of the
vibrating length of the strings, and even in the *Doucemelle*
of the fifteenth century. With all these improvements in the
framework the tension of the strings has risen from 16 tons
in 1862 to over 30 tons at the present time for a full concert
grand piano.

Among acoustical variations we may mention Steward's

Euphonicon (*c.* 1841), which, rising like a harp, has behind the strings three separate sound-boxes, for treble, mean, and bass, similar in shape to those of the violin, viola, and violoncello; a specimen of this interesting design is in the Victoria and Albert Museum, London. The use of pedals for the piano has already been noted; but in 1788 Clagget of London, on his *Telio-chordon*, introduced two pedals to overcome the lack of "equal temperament" in tuning the instrument; the pedals pressed subsidiary bridges on the strings, thus shortening them to the required sounding-length. By this means, he assures us, every octave can be divided into thirty-nine gradations of sound and "what is called the wolfe is entirely done away with."

In Austria and Germany pedals for the variation of tone were very popular, such as (1) piano (one string only), (2) bassoon (parchment strip on strings), (3) forte (dampers raised), (4) celeste (mute of thin cloth), (5) drum (striking under-side of sound-board), (6) triangle, (7) bells, etc. Combination instruments are also found such as piano and organ, as designed by Longman and Broderip of London at the close of the eighteenth century, or Merlin's combined piano and harpsichord (1774).

A very portable form of instrument was Rollig's *Orphica* (1795), in the shape of a recumbent harp with a string for each note and a compass of four octaves. It was carried by a strap over the shoulder and was sufficient for soft accompaniments.

SOSTINENTE PIANO

Many efforts have been made from time to time to prolong the sound of the piano. Isaac Hawkins in 1800 added to his upright model a roller with pin-projections which, when

I

turned rapidly, vibrated the hammers on the strings so long as the keys were depressed. A similar device was adopted by Caldera in his *Melo-Piano* (*c.* 1870), small hammers being set above the ordinary hammers. An instrument, called the *Choralcelo* (Boston, U.S.A., 1909), employed electro-magnets for setting the strings in vibration, even the striking hammers being dispensed with. But the latest and most effective is the Neo-Bechstein electric piano (1936). It is based on an entirely new principle evolved by Professor Nernst of Berlin, and dispenses with the iron frame, sound-board, and trichord strings. The fundamental tone is designedly soft but very pure, as it is only produced from a single string or, at the most, a pair of strings. Over each group of five strings there is a magnetic microphone which, when the strings vibrate under the touch of the hammers, sets up an electrical current of corresponding frequency. This is amplified, as in radio sets, by valves fitted into the case of the instrument, and the electric waves are passed on to a loud-speaker which converts them back into audible sounds; the electrical power is supplied from the mains. There are two pedals; that on the right raises, as usual, the dampers, but that on the left increases the amplification of the tone from the fundamental whisper to the fullest, almost overpowering, volume. This system opens out a new field of possibilities to the composer and pianist; for sustained chords can not only be held for a much longer period, but will answer to a *crescendo* by the use of the left pedal. The touch is necessarily light, for the blow required is but one-twentieth of that given on an ordinary piano. The *pianissimo* effect is more akin to that of the clavichord in its refined beauty. Notwithstanding the necessary fittings the instrument is more portable than the concert grand piano owing to the absence of some of the heaviest parts.

AUTOMATIC PIANO

ii.B.b. The invention of automatic "piano-players" is comparatively recent, and naturally followed on the late Dr. Gauntlett's advocacy for the instantaneous transmission of the movement of the key to the action of the hammer by electricity. But the idea of automatic mechanism was applied in the eighteenth century to the *Saitenspielwerke,* which in the German and Swiss clocks made melody every hour. In the Austrian Tyrol small instruments of the dulcimer type are sounded by means of a pinned barrel turned by a handle. Messrs. Clementi and Collard in the early years of the last century produced a self-acting piano, the barrel being kept in motion by a steel clock-spring.

In France the little cabinet *Pianette* appeared without a keyboard and affixed to a pole, two thin wires to each note emitting a correspondingly thin sound. Quaint and reminiscent of a bygone day, they were succeeded by the well-known strident and assertive piano-organs with more of the machine than the organ. These probably came from Italy, and, as each hammer was furnished with a stout steel spring, the sound of its rebound, when the barrel-pin "let fly," was sufficient to drown the ordinary traffic noise. Debain of Paris, in his *Piano mécanique* (c. 1850), introduced a system of wooden slabs, set with pins, on a chain, which, passing over a plate, depressed the ends of the special hammer-levers. In 1866 Mennons patented in London an apparatus for the automatic performance of music on keyboard instruments by means of electricity and magnets combined with a perforated sheet of music, in which the notes were "cut out in the form of slots to allow the contact at the required points." This was the beginning of the perforated rolls of paper advocated by

Corteuil under the name *Musique perforée* (1852). In 1897
they were used with pneumatic tubes and bellows attached
to each "striker," the mechanical player being placed in front
of the keyboard, an idea more fully developed by an American
maker named Votey. Since then these "players," generally
included under the name *Pianola*, have dispensed with the
foot-bellows and have been included in the instrument itself
with electrical motive power. Before the gramophone reached
its present-day perfection of recording music, they were useful
for reproducing—as on the *Duo-art* instruments—the actual
time and phrasing of the original player. There was a certain
responsibility in placing the roll on the instrument in the
proper way. On one occasion a well-known musician, now
deceased, was asked to name the classical composition which
was being played. Failing to do so, he discovered that it was
one of Bach's Preludes played "upside down"!

iii. BOWED TYPE

iii.A. The use of the musical bow as a sound-producer has
already been described; plucked by the fingers or struck with
a short stick it is the prototype of the harp and lute class,
and of the dulcimer also. But we are now to deal with a
refinement in method which has given to us the greatest of
all solo and orchestral instruments—the violin. It is difficult
to ascertain how far primitive man employed friction as an
aid to music; but in the friction drums of certain Pacific
islands the principle is present, as already shown (Autophones,
I. iii.A.a). The application of it, however, to the stringed
instruments seems to have been only recognized in our own

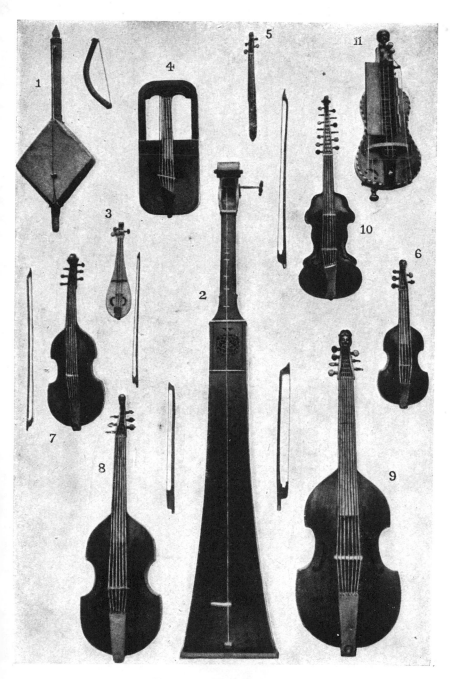

PLATE VI. CHORDOPHONES

PLATE VI

1 ARABIAN REBAB

2 TRUMPET MARINE (French, seventeenth century)

3 REBEC (fourteenth to sixteenth century)

4 CRWTH (Owain Tudwr, nineteenth century)

5 SORDINO or KIT (French, seventeenth century)

6 QUINTON VIOL (Fleury, Paris, 1764)

7 TREBLE VIOL (Henry Jaye, 1632)

8 LYRO VIOL (W. Addison, 1665)

9 BASS VIOL (C. Pierray, 1764)

10 VIOLA D'AMORE (G. Grancino, 1696)

11 VIELLE or HURDY-GURDY (French, nineteenth century)

era, for the musicians of ancient Babylonia, Egypt, and of classical Greece and Rome apparently knew it not.

THE BOW

The invention of the violin bow has been claimed for the Germanic peoples, but the general opinion now is that it emanated from Asia, and more particularly from India. Under Subdivision A.b we alluded to the use in that country of a primitive lute, consisting of a half-gourd or coco-nut with a skin table or cover, and fitted to a bamboo stick furnished with a string of twisted hairs, which rests on a little bridge placed upon the cover. This is the Indian *Ektara* or "one-string" lute, which with its relative, the *Dvitara*, or "two-string," is still in use amongst the native tribes. They are evidently products of the hunting-bow. There is, however, also in India the musical bow, with a peculiarity which has only been noticed in Africa, and especially on the east coast, whither it may have been brought by immigrants from Malabar. On the side of the arched bow-staff are cut little notches, and if a small stick is passed rapidly over them backward and forward the bow-string is put into vibration, with the result that a musical note is obtained. Now it must soon have occurred to the player that, if he notched the little stick and rubbed it across the plain bow-staff, he could as easily produce the same effect; nay, still more easily if he rubbed the string itself with his notched stick. Here is the first idea, then, of the violin bow, and it is interesting to note that in the *Bum-bass* of medieval Europe, only just disappearing, this simple device still obtains. The instrument, used as a drone-accompaniment to a little pipe, consists of a long pole furnished with one string, which, passing over a bladder placed at the lower end and combining bridge and sound-chest, is "bowed" with a strip of wood, notched like a saw. In olden days it was known in France as the *Basse de Flandres*, and in England as the bladder-and-string. In the seventeenth century a somewhat similar instrument, called the *Bumba*, with two bladders and strings, was employed in Iceland.

But further proof of this origin of the violin bow is forthcoming. When the *Hsi Ch'in*, a tribal form of the two-stringed *Hu Ch'in* or Chinese fiddle, was introduced into that country towards the end of the Tang Dynasty (A.D. 618–907), as we are informed by a Chinese encyclopedia compiled *c.* A.D. 1300, "the two strings between [them] used a slip of bamboo to sound them." Professor Moule of Cambridge, who has kindly brought this extract to our notice, adds that the Chinese character used for the words "to sound" (*ya*) appears to denote the production of sound by rasping or rubbing, i.e. friction. Now, although the Chinese have, since the Yuan Dynasty (A.D. 1264–1368), employed a hair-strung bow for the purpose, the hair is still passed "between the strings." In the orchestra of the Tang Dynasty there was also a form of psaltery called the *Ya-ch'in*, which was played by rubbing the strings with a slip of bamboo; in later times this was replaced by a stick, but now a hair-strung bow is used. It was during this dynasty that many foreign instruments were brought into China through Tibet, and the title *Hu*, given by them to this little fiddle, is applied by the old writers to natives of India and other non-Mongol foreigners. As the Indians in remote districts still have this simple type of stringed instrument and, moreover, employ a bow for one particular form, called the *Behala*, we may infer that to their country we, as well as the Chinese, owe the earliest bowed instrument. How it reached Europe is uncertain. It may have been carried from the south-west coast of India by Arab traders, first of all to their own country and to Persia in the seventh and eighth centuries of our era, and there applied, as we find it to-day, to the small lutes already in use. Thence, by commercial routes, it would seem to have passed to Byzantium, for the first-known European example of the bow is found on an ivory casket of Italo-Byzantine workmanship (eighth or ninth century). At a later date, again, it was diffused throughout Europe by the Moorish occupation of Spain, where in the thirteenth century we find it in full popularity.

CRWTH

iii.A.a. In Europe, however, the bow was applied to two widely different types of instruments. Through Byzantine influence and the extensive trade connection with Scandinavia and England in the tenth century which emanated from that important centre, the bow was applied to the lyre-shaped *Cruit* or *Rote* (i.A.a¹), and produced the bowed *Cruit* or *Crwth*, which, as a musical instrument, has only disappeared in Wales during the last century. This Welsh form (Plate VI, 4) shows a finger-board placed beneath the four higher strings, while the two lower strings remain free to be played as drones. In England, where it was called the *Crowd*, and also in Ireland very early representations of the eleventh century show the instrument without a finger-board. In Scandinavia it is still played by rustic musicians, and Dr. Otto Andersson, in his work on *The Bowed Harp* (1930), has collected all possible details about its use. The earliest forms show only an oblong sound-board, across which and over a bridge two or three strings are stretched. It is called the *Sträkharpa* or *Jouhi-Kantele*, and in the left-hand side of the upper part a slit is cut in the wood through which the fingers are passed for stopping the strings. This is done in a peculiar way, still found, however, in the Wendish fiddle called *Husla*: the finger-nails are pressed against the uppermost or melody string, while the others vibrate freely as drones. This method of stopping with the nail at the side of the string was probably derived from the classical lyre, where it was used to alter the pitch of the open strings. On later specimens of the *Sträkharpa* a hole is cut on the right-hand side also, giving a nearer resemblance to a finger-board. Another type of the instrument is known as the *Talharpa* or *Tannenharfe* ("pinewood" harp), and more closely resembles the lyre or the rote. Both forms are dealt with in detail by Dr. Andersson in his interesting monograph; but his patriotic effort to prove that Northern Europe is indebted to Sweden and Finland for its knowledge of the bow is not convincing, for by the ninth and tenth centuries Scandinavia was in close touch with the monastic schools of France and Germany, established under strong Italian influence, as well as in trade communication with Byzantium. In the sixteenth century the name *Crowd* was loosely applied to any bowed instrument.

REBEC

iii.A.b. The lute-shaped form of stringed instrument received, as already stated, the use of the bow in Arabia and Persia in the seventh century; as the *Lyra*, it is mentioned in German literature of the eighth century. In the tenth century an illustration shows it with only a single string, as we find it in the Balkan *Gusla* of the present day; but in the following century it appears with three strings or with a pair of double strings. The name *Lyra* suggests that it came first into South-Eastern Europe, for to this same type of instrument the name is still given in Greece, where its three strings are tuned with a fourth and a third (d^1, g^1, b^1). Its counterpart in the South Slavonic countries, where it is called the *Vijalo*, is tuned peculiarly (d^2, a^1, e^2). Its later name, *Rebec*, appears to have arisen from the fact that in the eleventh or twelfth centuries a larger instrument, called *Rubebe*, was in use in South-Western Europe, introduced through North African influence. The *Rubecchino*, *Rebechino*, *Rebec*, or *Rabé morisco* (Plate VI, 3) was of high pitch and made in one piece, neck and body. The *Rubebe*, at any rate in later days, had an oval or oblong body with a separate neck grafted on. Jerome of Moravia, in the thirteenth century, tells us that it had two pairs of double strings tuned in fifths (c, g) and the compass of an octave and one note. It was evidently evolved from the flat-chested *Rebab esh-shaer* or *Kemangeh a-gouz* (Plate VI, 1), as it is now called, which was in use amongst the Arabs, as well as the boat-shaped form preserved in the *Rebec*. This latter instrument, known also as the *Rubelle* or *Ribible*, and in Germany as the *Geige*, in France as the *Gigue* or *Marionetta* (fifteenth century), was a very popular accompaniment for the country dances. In the thirteenth-century romance, *Cléomades*, the *Viella*, *Gigue*, and *Rubebe* are all mentioned together. In the Castle Ambras Inventory (1596), given by Schlosser in his *Catalogue of the Musical Instruments in the Kunsthistorisches Museum* at Vienna, it is called the *Viole de praz* ("for the banquet or revelling"), and was made in various sizes for bass, mean, discant, and high discant. The *Geige* had no frets on the finger-board, and the three strings were tuned in fifths; a rustic form of it still exists in the Swedish *Traesko Fiol* ("shoe-fiddle"), though with four strings. In the seventeenth century the *Pochette* (*Taschengeige*) or *Kit* (Plate VI, 5) took its place as a small fiddle. Of the *Geige* or *Rebec* the Russian *Gudok* with three strings, the uppermost providing the melody, seems to be an elaboration, whilst the old Dorset Humstrum, with four wire strings and a tin canister as a sound-chest and bridge, looks like a poor brother.

VIOLS

The *Rubebe*, at an early date, yielded to the more conveniently shaped *Fiedel* or *Vielle*, with which it was often associated. It is difficult to determine the earliest date for the appearance of this type with incurved sides. It is mentioned, at any rate, in the Romance poems of the twelfth century. We know, however, that the incurvation of the sides on such stringed instruments as these was not due, as has been imagined, to the exigencies of the bow. In Hittite sculpture of a thousand years before our era this particular trait is displayed on a long-necked lute. The illustrations in the Utrecht Psalter of the ninth century A.D. suggest that the *Vielle* emanated from the application of an extended finger-board to the *Cithara* or lyre, which certainly produced the *Guitarra latina*, as shown by Miss Schlesinger in her exhaustive treatise on the *Precursors of the Violin Family* (1910). But whether the long stick depicted in one of the illustrations is intended for a bow is doubtful. The details of a drawing by Theodorus of Caesarea in a Greek psalter of the eleventh century present clearer features; but the six pegs placed sideways into a peg-box, instead of vertically into a flat head, together with the form of the bow, are more generally associated with instruments of a period several centuries later, and the illustration may be by another hand. However, at the beginning of the twelfth century, there are reliable representations, and, in many cases, the narrow waist and the rounded "bouts" of the sound-chest are fully developed.

The name *Fiedel*, which also appears as *Fidula*, *Fithele*, *Videl*, *Vielle*, *Fithiole*, *Vihuela*, and *Viola*, is connected etymologically with the late Latin *Fidicula*, a small *Fides* or lyre; the outlines of many of the early illustrated forms show a distinct likeness to those of the *Rote* or medieval lyre (i.A.a¹), with the addition, however, of the extended finger-board. Were it not for the absence of this latter feature we might claim the representations of bowed rotes of various sizes given in the Prayer Book of Archduke Leopold of Austria (*c.* 1100) as definite predecessors of the violin.

For these early instruments the bow was naturally of the simplest construction, a curved stick keeping the horse-hair in tension. In the twelfth or thirteenth centuries the "spring" of the stick was restricted to the upper end away from the hand, and the fingers, placed between the hair and stick, assisted the tension. In the fifteenth century a series of notches (*crémaillère*) cut in the stick or on a small metal ratchet enabled the hair to be tightened by slipping the looped end from notch to notch. At length the nut, moved by a screw-thread within the bow-stick, perfected the mechanism, an improvement which is generally attributed to the elder Tourte in the first half of the eighteenth century, and was further extended by his famous son, François, of Paris (1747–1835).

By the close of the fifteenth century the *Vielle* or viol had assumed the prominence which ultimately placed it in the forefront of all musical expression. The earliest music at present known for viols in parts dates from that period, and the combination or "consort" of viols was considered "verie swete"; though their strange shapes, given in the musical treatises of the sixteenth century, may be partly due to difficulties of delineation. The *Gros Geigen* and *Alte Fiedel*, with fantastic corners, a large ornamental sound-hole or "rose," a recurved peg-box like the lute, and two C-shaped sound-holes in the uppermost part of the table, strike us as cumbersome, if not comic. Except for certain Italian viols of the *Lira* type, to be explained presently, the flat head (as on the guitar) had given way to the box and side-pegs in the fourteenth century. The number of strings was now usually five or six, and the tunings were in fourths, except between the third and fourth strings, where it was a major third. The finger-board was "fretted," giving better resonance and the easier production of chords. In the "chest" or "sette" of viols there were usually six instruments, two each for discant, mean, and bass. When played "in consort" they were all held downwards, either between the knees or on the lap, whence they were known as viols *da gamba* (Plate VI, 7, 9), as distinct from the instruments played at the shoulder or on the arm *da braccio*, whence the German name *Bratsche* for the viola at the present day. During the sixteenth century the viols *da gamba* were ranged in the following sizes: the discant (lowest note *d*), the mean (lowest note *A*), and the bass (lowest note *D*); but in the seventeenth century these descriptive titles were altered into: small discant (lowest note *d*), ordinary discant (lowest note *A*), tenor or mean (lowest note *D*), small bass (lowest note G_1), large bass (lowest note E_1). For this reason the bass *Viola da gamba*, as it was in the first instance, is by some writers called the tenor *Viola da gamba*, according to the later reckoning. We are now again privileged to hear the music of the viols; and although, partly owing to the flat back of the instrument, the resonance is not so strong as in the later violin type with moulded back, yet it is remarkably "carrying" and melodious, with a slightly

reedy timbre absent from the tone of the violin and violon-
cello. As Mace (1676) truly remarks of the "generous viol,"
the music thereof "disposes us to Solidity, Gravity and a
Good Temper, making us capable of Heavenly and Divine
Influences. 'Tis Great Pity Few believe thus Much; but, Far
Greater, that so Few know It."

Besides the ordinary set of viols *da gamba* there were other
forms which could be used with them or in solo work. Mace
recommends for his proposed "chest" three full-sized lyro-
viols (*Viola bastarda*). This instrument (Plate VI, 8), for
which the English musician, Daniel Farrant (*c.* 1606), appears
to have been responsible, was smaller than the bass viol and
used for playing "lyra-wise," that is, with the strings tuned
as on the pandore or lute. They were also convenient for
"divisions" or variations on a ground-bass. Sometimes they
had metal strings running beneath the finger-board and tuned
to vibrate in sympathy with the fingered strings. This device
was characteristic of the *Viola d'amore*, the *Violetta marina*,
and the English Violet (Plate VI, 10), which became popular
at the close of the seventeenth century. It was also found on
the *Baryton*, beloved of Prince Esterhazy, for whom Haydn
wrote some one hundred and seventy-five compositions. Here,
however, the wire strings were exposed at the back of the
neck and could be plucked by the fingers. Sympathetic strings,
four in number, are still employed on the Norwegian
Hardanzer Geige. The *Viola da spalla* was a small bass instrument which could be played in processions by a carrying-
strap over the shoulder. If the strings were overspun with
wire, they tended to produce a rattling sound something like
a reed-pipe; hence it was called the *Viola di fagotto, Fagott-
geige*, or bassoon-viol.

A small French *Viole*, very popular in the eighteenth

century, and fitted with only five strings, was known as the *Quinton* (Plate VI, 6), though that name is sometimes given to an alto-tenor instrument with five strings.

The Italian *Lira da braccio* and *Lira da gamba* were somewhat similar in purpose to the lyro-viol, but they had no sympathetic strings. With their flat head-pieces and many strings they bore a close resemblance to types of an early period, and maintained their popularity till the beginning of the seventeenth century. In addition to the strings on the finger-board, they had two or more Bourdon strings by the side to act as drones or basses, like the large lutes. A still larger instrument of this kind was the *Lironi perfetto* or *Arciviola di Lira*, with twelve to fourteen strings on the finger-board arranged in pairs and tuned in fifths (consecutively) with two open strings. The guitar form was more closely perpetuated in the *Arpeggione* of the early nineteenth century with six strings. Franz Schubert wrote for it a very effective sonata, and it was sometimes called the guitar-violoncello. Violins, in similar outline but with moulded backs, have been made by Stradivari, Staufer, Banks, Chanot, and others.

BOWED ZITHER

In Northern and Central Europe there is the application of the bow to the psaltery type of instrument. The German *Streich-Zither* is comparatively a recent example, having been evolved in Munich by Petzmayer in 1823. It takes the form of a small heart-shaped instrument with metal strings and a fretted finger-board. When made in England in violin or viol shape, it took the name of the Psaltery-viol (in Germany *Philomela*), and was provided with short legs at the back to raise it off the table, on which it was laid when played. But the Scandinavian forms are more interesting and appear to represent an early use. Not only was there a two-stringed *Fiedel* or *Fidla* in Iceland (now extinct), but there is still an instrument called the *Langspil*, which has three metal strings stretched over a long and narrow sound-box, the melody string being placed over a fretted keyboard. There is no separate bridge and it is played with a primitive kind of bow. The Norwegian and Swedish *Psalmodikon*, of somewhat the same outline, was introduced by Dillner (*c.* 1810) for accompanying the Church hymn-singing; it has one melody string of gut and eight sympáthetic strings of metal. The Finnish *Streich-Kantele* is a combination of two such instruments for the same purpose, each with its own performer.

TRUMPET MARINE

Before passing to the true violin type, another old-world stringed instrument claims a notice. It is the *Trumscheit, Tromba Marina*, or Trumpet Marine (Plate VI, 2). Originally it was a simple bowed monochord used as a drone-bass; to this one or more strings were added, and they became *Dicordes* or *Tricordes* (*Frontispiece*). Their shape was that of a long, narrow, triangular box, the string or strings being played with a bow and stopped by the fingers or the nails, or even by the knuckles, as in a somewhat similar form of the Iceland *Fidla*. Towards the close of the fifteenth century, however, an alteration took place. The instrument still retained its shape and length, though the latter was frequently increased to 6 feet and the open end rested on the ground. But the bridge for the string, instead of being of the usual form, was cut in heart-shape with a curved arm on one side. The point of the heart-shaped bridge stood on the sound-board, but the long arm or leg only touched lightly upon it so that, when the string vibrated under the action of the bow, it rattled. The bow was drawn across the string just below the top nut and peg-box, and the fingers of the player touched the string lightly at certain points, so as to produce the usual harmonic series of overtones. The result was that the sounds of the harmonics were reinforced by the "brazen rattle" of the bridge-arm and a trumpet effect was produced. It was used to replace that instrument in the convents, and so is said to have received the name *Nonnengeige*. Why it was called *Marina* is uncertain. Some tell us it was in honour of the Blessed Virgin (*Marientrompete*); others that it was used at sea for signalling! Probably it was named after a famous French trumpeter, Marin or Maurin, of the latter half of the fifteenth century, who may have invented the peculiar bridge. Certainly the new title for the instrument appears about that period. The strange name *Tympanischiza*, given to it by Glareanus (1547), was an attempt to render *Trumscheit* into Latin, the translator deriving the syllable *trum* from *Tromme* (a drum) and not from *Trombe* (a trumpet). The greatest virtuoso on the trumpet-marine was Monsieur Prin, a French musician of the latter part of the seventeenth century and opening of the eighteenth century. He added to it sympathetic strings, placed within the long sound-box, to increase the resonance and give the effect of sustained chords. It thus became a *Trompette Marine organisée*. He also inserted a small peg into the head by which, through a fine cord attached to the bridge, he could alter the extent of vibration and so procure echo effects. Sonatas were written for this unique instrument, and it had its own notation in a special tablature. Lully introduced it into his opera *Xerxes* (1660) with an accompaniment for strings, giving it the melody in an interlude *pour les matelots*. In 1674 a concert of four trumpets-marine was heard in London, where it was popularly called the "mock trumpet." Mr. Pepys, too, passed his approval on it and on Prin's performance in 1667, as described in an article by the writer in *Music and Letters*, vol. xiv.

VIOLIN

From this array of bowed instruments grouped under such names as *Lyra, Rebec, Rubebe, Vielle, Fiedel, Lira*, etc., so varied in shape and circumstance, arose in the early years of the sixteenth century the violin, which was destined to eclipse them all. Probably the name of its inventor or even of its first maker will never be known, though from time to time various claims have been put forward. It is now generally assumed that it appeared in its earliest use first in Italy, either as a product of the Neapolitan School, as stated by Vincentio Galilei in his *Dialogues* (1568), or of the North Italian School, of which Kerlino (fifteenth century) and also Duiffoprugar, a Tyrolese, Linarolli, a famous *Lira*-maker, and Gaspar da Salo, of the sixteenth century, were foremost representatives. In the well-known engraving of Duiffoprugar at the age of forty-eight, and dated 1562, a four-stringed instrument of the violin type certainly is shown; the portrait, however, has also been claimed as that of an Italian sculptor of the same period.

If we consider the principal characteristics of the novel instrument, we can hardly consider the violin as an absolutely new invention. It was the happy combination of all the best points found in the earlier instruments we have already mentioned. For instance, the peg-box, instead of the flat guitar-like head, had been known and used for two or three centuries on the *Rebec*: on it too, as on the Polish or Wendish

K

Husla, the frets, if ever employed, had been abandoned. The rounded bridge, for melodic rather than for chordal playing, had appeared on the *Rubebe* and the *Fiedel*. The *f*-shaped sound-holes or something like them had been adopted by the *Vielle* instead of the more common C-shape. On the *Fiedel* corners to the "bouts" were much in evidence, and the string-holder, formerly attached to the table like that on the guitar, had been replaced by the tail-piece since the twelfth century. Even the tuning of the strings in fifths, instead of in fourths and a third, was the practice on the *Rebecs* and *Geigen*. Wherein, then, did the novelty of the violin consist? In two main points, and these derived from an instrument which had become popular during the late fifteenth century—the *Lira da braccio* (iii.A.a.). The body of the *Lira* was shallow; on the viols the sound-chest was deep. The back of the *Lira* was moulded or arched, neither flat as on the *Fiedel* and viol nor round as on the *Rebec* and *Geige*. The embodiment of these two important factors gave to the violin its brilliancy of tone, without the harshness of the *Rebec* or the heaviness of the viol, although to such an ardent viol-player as Mace it sounded "scolding" even in 1676. Still, he was open-minded about it and acknowledged its suitability "for any extraordinary jolly or jocund consort occasion."

The earliest notice we have found of the orchestral use of the violin appears in the *Tragedy of Gorbudoc* performed before Queen Elizabeth of England in 1561: here "the Musicke of Violenze" preceded the first act, in which "wild men clad in leaves" graced the scene. At the burial of King Henry the Eighth six Italian musicians from Venice, Cremona, Milan, and Vicenza played their "Vyolls" (as distinct from the "Vialls") in the orchestra (1548); but these same performers are described in 1555 as playing "Violons," again distinct from the "Viall" players. Monteverdi, in his score of *Orfeo* (1607), names *Violini ordinari da braccio* and also *Violini piccoli alla francese*, and it has generally been thought that under the latter title he alludes to the French *Pochette*, a little violin used for dance music. But the *Violino ordinario* was at that day identical with the viola or *Bratsche*, and the *Violino piccolo* was the modern violin. It may have become popular at any early date in France through the close connection which Gaspar da Salo had with that country.

It is needless for us to recall the names of the many famous makers who since the sixteenth century have contributed to the ultimate perfection of the violin, culminating in the magnificent work of Antonio Stradivari of Cremona (1649–1737): but the various attempts to develop the viola as the tenor instrument of the string quartette are interesting, especially as it has been condemned to play a part which is not its true place, for, as Monteverdi's *Violino ordinario*, it is an alto instrument. Bach's *Viola pomposa* was a large five-stringed viola with a string length of about 17 inches from bridge to neck. It was tuned in fourths and fifths (d,g, d^1,g^1,c^2), as shown by the extant music of Telemann and Lidarti written for it. Specimens by J. C. Hoffmann of Leipzig, the inventor, are to be seen in the museums at Brussels, Leipzig, and Eisenach. Hillmer's *Violalin* (1800) and Ritter's *Viola alta* were also alto instruments of increased size with a violin e^2 string above the usual viola *accordatura*. Stelzner of Dresden on his *Violotta* (1891), one of a complete family of stringed instruments built on parabolic lines, and Zorzi of Florence (1900) on his *Contra-Violino* strung their large violas on tenor lines (G, d, a, e^1) with heavy strings, from which, however, it is difficult to produce full resonance. On the other hand a true tenor violin has been approached from the other side in

Bach's *Violoncello piccolo* (with four or five strings (G, d, a, e^1 or C, G, d, a, e^1) and a vibrating length of about 24 inches). Similar instruments were produced by Snoeck of Brussels in the early eighteenth century. Such smaller models are still made, though nominally for 'cellists of tender age; if, however, they were strung an octave below the violin, the missing part would be replaced.

The *Violone*, or double-bass member of the violin group, retained its flat viol-like back and was bowed in the viol style till the close of the last century: even its frets lasted till about 1800. The mechanical tuning apparatus was developed by Bachmann of Berlin (*c.* 1778) following Praetorius' illustrations. The double bass is now, however, constructed on similar lines to those of its own group. A fine Italian specimen, formerly belonging to the virtuoso Dragonetti (1763–1846) and 8 feet 7 inches in height, is preserved in the Victoria and Albert Museum, London. Bottesini (1822–89), another virtuoso, used a *Basso da Camera* strung with three rather fine strings, which enabled him to obtain his marvellous control of the harmonic notes. In size Vuillaume's three-stringed *Octo-Bass* (1851) exceeds them, being 13 feet in height, with key-levers moved by hand and foot to depress the strings; its lowest note is 16 feet C_1. Even this, however, was eclipsed in 1889 by an American *Grand Bass* nearly 15 feet in height.

As is well known the secret of the vibratory system of the violin and its fellows lies very largely in the "sound-post" and the "bass-bar," for neither of these important parts are placed within the instrument merely as a means of support. The sound-post is necessary in order to transmit the vibrations of the table to the whole sound-chest and to keep them similar throughout. It is required in the bowed instruments because the vibrations are to be sustained, whereas in the plucked instruments they are momentary only. In fact a sound-post in a lute or a guitar would be a hindrance, as shown by the *pizzicato* notes of the violin. It is impossible to say when the sound-post (*Stimmstock*, *L'âme*) was introduced. The modern Greek *Lyra* shows a very primitive method, the post in the upper part being halved and laid against the bridge-foot which rests in the notch as the post passes through the sound-hole. On an eighteenth-century Italian *Rebec* it is placed within the instrument, the end being fitted into a small hole in the back. The bridge of the Welsh *Crwth* has a long left leg, which is passed through the circular sound-hole and rests on the flat back. The three-stringed Finnish bowed harp (*Jouhi Kantele*) had the sound-post in the last century, but in the earlier forms of the instrument it would have been difficult to insert it after the instrument was made. Oriental members of this sub-class are usually without posts. The bass-bar running under the left foot of the bridge transmits the long vibrations necessary for the production of the deeper sounds, while the sound-post would naturally reinforce the shorter vibrations for the higher notes. In fifteenth- and sixteenth-century instruments still preserved both of these details are found.

Notwithstanding the skill of Stradivari many improvements on the violin have been suggested and tried. We have already alluded to Chanot's guitar-shaped instrument (1818), with the string-holder attached once more to the table. Savart's trapezoid violin or Box-fiddle (1817) was built up on thoroughly scientific lines and was pronounced superior to the productions of the Italian makers; probably its unattractive appearance told against it. In Collin's *Echolin* (1879) the body was made circular; inside it was a domed case on which the legs of the bridge, passing through a circular hole in the table, rested. A more drastic experiment was made by Stroh of London at the close of the last century. In his instrument the usual resonating body was dispensed with, and the bridge rested upon a bar-like extension of the neck. To one side of the bridge was attached a short arm, which through the vibrations produced by the bow actuated a diaphragm similar to that of the phonograph or gramophone, and the sounds were amplified by a conical horn. It was played in the usual way and was pronounced quite free of any "wolf" notes. When used in a quartette ensemble, the two violins and viola made on Stroh's system required two ordinary violoncellos for the bass in order to procure due balance. We had the opportunity of hearing a performance of Mendelssohn's Violin Concerto with orchestra and Stroh violin. The effect was pleasing, as its full-bodied notes of semi-viola timbre gave it a peculiar prominence; but the horn attachment sealed its fate.

The latest invention, however, is the application in Germany of electricity and its amplification to the violin and violoncello. Here, too, the instruments are without any sound-chest, but beneath the strings and close to the bridge is a magnetic microphone, which, taking up the sound vibrations, transmits them to the air through an amplifier and loud-speaker. By the use of a foot-switch the volume of sound can be raised from a fundamental whisper to magnificent proportions without any further effort on the part of the performer. A simpler device, adaptable to any ordinary stringed instrument deficient in resonance for a large hall or the open air, is a "pad-microphone," which affixed by suction to the sound-chest conveys the sound to an adjacent loud-speaker.

KEYED VIOLS

iii.B.a. The application of finger-keys to the bowed instruments dates back many centuries. In its simplest form it is shown by Agricola (1528) under the name of *Schlüssel Fidel*. The shape is like that of the old bowed *Fiedel*, but instead of the fingers pressing the strings, small tangents attached to key-rods serve the same purpose. The four- or six-stringed instrument was held on the lap with the key-ends downwards, so that the tangents might drop away from the strings when released. It was sounded by means of a stout bow. The keyed fiddle still exists in the Swedish folk instrument, the *Nyckel harpa* or *Nyckelfiol*, which plays an important part in all the merrymakings. It had originally only two or three gut strings, but the number has now been increased to four or five strings, and the keys are arranged in two rows to include all the semitones. Drones and sympathetic strings are also added. A somewhat similar instrument, introduced by Poussot (1886) and called the *Monocorde à clavier*, has a small keyboard of nineteen keys placed over the single string. They are held off by springs, but when depressed stop it at the required point. An ordinary bow is used in the right hand. The longer form, as a double bass, stands on four legs. Similar methods have been applied to the viola and violoncello under the name *Mélotetraphone* (1892) and a compass of two chromatic octaves obtained.

The principle, however, is of a much earlier date than even the sixteenth century, for this same key mechanism is embodied in the *Organistrum* (*Drehleier*, *Radleier*) of the tenth century, when a treatise on its construction was written by Odo of Cluny. Here, however, the strings are vibrated by a rosined wheel turned by a small handle at the end of the instrument; whence it was termed by monastic Latinists the *Rota*. It was an ecclesiastical perquisite and, as the *Organistrum*, provided a useful accompaniment to the plain-song. At times, owing to its length, it required two performers. In the French romances of the twelfth to thirteenth centuries it appears under the title the *Symphonie* or, later, the *Chifonie*. In Germany, at a later time too, it received the name *Lyra rusticana* or *pagana* and, discarded by the Church authorities, ultimately became the *Lyra mendicorum* or Beggars' Lyre and the English hurdy-gurdy (Plate VI, 11). The popular name in France was the *Vielle à roue*, or the viol with a wheel, for in its early days the sound-chest took the viol shape. Afterwards it was some-times rectangular, but generally in the lute shape. Though the scale was originally diatonic, it became, like the *Nyckei-harpa* with extra keys, chromatic. The names *Weiber-leier* (women's lyre) or *Bauren-leier* (peasants' lyre) have also been bestowed on it. It is now provided with "bourdon" or "drone" strings, and has even been given an organ attachment con-sisting of a few wooden pipes with the bellows inside the sound-chest. This is the *Vielle organisée*. It must have been originally derived from the monochord with its movable bridges, and the little tangents striking the strings may have suggested in the eleventh or twelfth century the similar action of the clavichord (ii.B.a.).

It was only natural that, as complete keyboards had been applied to the plucked and the struck stringed instruments, a similar attachment to the bowed instruments was desired. In the late fifteenth century the first attempt appears to have been made by Leonardo da Vinci, who constructed a *Geigen-werk*, in which the strings were drawn down by the keys upon parchment-covered wheels. Praetorius (1618) describes and illustrates the recently introduced *Geigen Clavicymbel* of Hans

Hayden of Nuremberg, which worked on the same principle. A like specimen by Truchado (1625) is now in the Museum of the Conservatoire de Musique, Brussels; its compass is four octaves. In 1664 Pepys inspected the "arched viall" in London; here the strings were vibrated by a continuous parchment band, but "so basely and so harshly that it will never do." Such, we fear, has been the verdict on most of these ingenious inventions, and they have been many—over fifty, Dr. Sachs tell us, since Hayden's attempt in the early seventeenth century. Here are some of them.

In 1717 Marius of Paris produced the *Clavecin-Vielle*, in which the tangents touched the strings from beneath instead of at the side as in the ordinary *Vielle à roue*, and the wheel was turned by a foot-treadle. The *Lyrichord* of Plenius (1741) had gut and wire strings sounded by rosined wheels: in Le Voir's instrument (1742) a horsehair bow, moving backward and forward by a foot-treadle, was raised by small hooks against the strings. Walker of London, in his *Celestina* (1772), sometimes attributed to Mason, used "the movement of one or more threads or bands of silk, flax, wire, gut, leather, etc." to produce the sound when the strings were pulled against them. In 1809 appeared from Dresden Kaufmann's *Harmonicorde*, in shape like an upright piano. A large wooden cylinder was placed just behind the keyboard and set in rotation by two treadles. When the key was depressed a little tongue of wood, one end of which touched the string, was pressed against the revolving cylinder and the vibrations produced by its friction were transmitted to the string and reinforced by the sound-board. The compass was from C to f^3, and in 1811 Weber wrote an *Adagio* and *Rondo* with orchestra for this instrument. In 1817 Mott of Brighton patented the *Sostenente Pianoforte*, with silk threads attached to the strings and passing over a rosined cylinder; the key action tightened the thread on the revolving cylinder. In 1822 appeared the *Violicembalo*, devised by a Milanese named Trentin. The bow, consisting of woollen and silk material, was drawn backward and forward by two cylinders moved by the feet: the key-levers raised the strings to meet the bow.

Dietz of Paris in his *Polyplectron* (1827), like Röllig of Vienna in his *Xänorphica* (1800), employed separate bows for each note, making them work perpendicularly instead of crosswise. The bows were formed of thin strips of leather passing over a revolving cylinder. The key placed the bow-leather in contact with the string, and it was said that the effect was so immediate that refined execution was possible while the volume of sound could be increased or diminished at will.

In the Great Exhibition of London (1851) an American invention was shown, and a writer of the day described it as "a violin connected by mechanism with a row of keys, which played a dismal unison with the right hand of the performer and put every listener out of spirits for the rest of the day."

In 1865 Baudet of Paris produced the *Piano-Violon*, or *Piano-Quatuor*: here the vertical wire strings had a stout piece of vegetable fibre projecting from the nodal point, which was brought into contact with the revolving cylinder, and communicated the vibrations to the string.

In the Vienna Exhibition (1892) Kuhmayer's *Electric Piano* by a system of magnets drew down an endless band of fine leather on the required string. A simple instrument of the nineteenth century was the *Claviola*, invented by Hawkins of New Jersey, U.S.A. It had twenty-five strings stretched vertically over a viol-shaped sound-chest. A frame holding an ordinary violin bow was moved across them by hand, and the keys with a compass of two octaves brought the strings up to meet the bow-hair.

Like the bowed harmonicas (Autophones, iii.B.a.), no mechanism has yet been devised which can approach to the touch of the bow-hand of a skilled violinist.

AUTOMATIC VIOLS

iii.B.b. Walker of London, in his *Celestina*, not only substituted springs or weights instead of a treadle as a motive power for his endless bow, but also provided for its being played by a "pricked barrel," sometimes within and sometimes without the case of the instrument. Another automatic instrument of this type, called the *Violina*, was produced at the beginning of this century and adapted for use with perforated paper rolls. Three violins of the ordinary model were employed, one string on each instrument being fitted with small levers which pressed the string on the finger-board. An endless circular bow passed across the violins, and as the notes were required a lever brought the particular instrument into contact with the bow. The *Violina* was incorporated in a pneumatic piano-player, electrically controlled, with the addition of a keyboard. It is said that all the delicacies and peculiarities of the most artistic playing were reproduced with staccato, glissando, and vibrato as required. Unfortunately, with all these superior qualities, it has disappeared with the rest of the *Geigen-werk*.

iv. AIR-VIBRATED TYPE

AEOLIAN HARP

iv.A.a. In the previous sub-classes of the *Chordophones* we have been dealing with the production of sound by human agency, but in this sub-class we pass to Nature's own music— the music of the air as played by the aeolian harp (Plate IV, 4). The principle is simple and definitely prehistoric. A gust of wind passing over a stretched cord or tendon sets it in vibration. By increasing its vibratory length and varying the pressure of the wind the series of harmonic overtones will naturally be produced. It was by this means that David's harp (or rather lyre) sang in the breeze as it hung suspended in his tent; and Archbishop Dunstan, too, produced his magic music with the help of the wind through a crevice in the wall. In the sixteenth and seventeenth centuries both Porta and Kircher discussed this subject, and to the latter is accredited the first attempt to bring the aeolian harp into practical use. By the attachment of six to twelve gut strings to a long open frame and directing the force of the wind upon them by sloping catch-boards a succession of harmonic sounds was produced of higher or lower pitch according to the wind's pressure upon them. When sash-framed windows were introduced the "harp" was made with a sloping cover and could be inserted beneath the slightly opened sash. Sometimes it is found in triangular form or with two ranks of strings.

Although Kircher in 1650 considered it a new discovery, the Chinese have had from time immemorial their music in the air, produced either by long bows with a thin bamboo strip or a ribbon for the cord and attached to the head of their paper kites, or else stretched across a small frame and hung on the kite-string. The aeolian harp is now obsolete in Europe; but when the strings are properly tuned in unison the pleasing harmonies which rise from its gentle murmurings under the frictional "flutter" of the breeze on its cords cannot fail to captivate the imagination. In the last century an ingenious mechanic in Basle constructed with iron wires a large instrument which he called the weather harp. He asserted that by "terrestrial magnetism" it sounded when the weather changed. The scientists disproved his theory, and suggested that it changed its tune when the wind—and, we trust, the weather too—changed.

The bull-roarer, used by Australian natives and European children, is also air-vibrated. The weight at the end of the whirling string increases its tension the faster it is turned, thus raising the pitch of the sound as the air strikes it.

ANÉMOCORDE

iv.B.a. It may appear strange that so elusive a means of sound production could be harnessed to a keyboard. In 1789, however, Schnell of Paris exhibited his *Anémocorde*, or *Aeroclavicorde*. It was triple-strung and had a compass of five octaves. A jet of wind from foot-bellows played over each set of strings by the opening of a valve when the key was depressed. The tone, we are told, was very tender but required some length of time to produce, which would be fatal to its popularity in the present age. Isouard of Paris, in his *Piano éolien* (1837), to which Herz added improvements, tried a similar method for eliciting the bashful sound.

As for "automatic action" applied to this type of instrument, none is so simple or so ancient as that of the old wind harp.

IV

AEROPHONIC INSTRUMENTS

including

FLUTES, RECORDERS, CLARINETS, SAXOPHONES, OBOES,
BASSOONS, HORNS, TRUMPETS, TROMBONES, ETC., AND
THEIR KEYBOARD AND AUTOMATIC AMPLIFICATIONS SUCH
AS PIPE AND REED ORGANS AND BARREL ORGANS

OUR consideration of the origins of the three classes of
musical instruments hitherto described has taken us to the
falling rocks, the forest trees, and the hunter's bow. In the
class of aerophones or wind instruments, which in their many
forms we shall now review, we are directed for their inception
to the riverside and the grain-sown fields, or to the sports of
the chase if not to the battlefield.

i. FLUE-VOICED TYPE

i.A. Two thousand years ago the poet Lucretius embodied in
verse the age-long tradition that the whistling of the wind
over the hollow river reeds first taught man to construct a
flute. In order to elicit sound from a tube, whether open or
closed at one end, it is necessary to create within it sound-
waves, and the simplest way of so doing is by blowing across
its open end. If the lips are slightly compressed, a narrow
windway or "flue" is formed, and by directing the little
stream of air against the sharp edge a "flutter" is produced

of a rhythmic character; for all friction is rhythmic. From this flutter the tube selects a special pulsation and raises it by resonance to a musical sound, the pitch depending on the length and size of the tube or resonating chamber. The gas-flame organ, Kastner's *Pyrophone* (1873), is a well-known instance of this action, for which neither breath nor bellows are needed. The jet of gas-flame within the lower end of each open tube is sufficient to cause the indrawn air to "flutter," and so the pipe sounds its fundamental note, while by lowering the size of the flame the harmonic overtones are heard. For all wind instruments, whether the "flutter" is produced by a "flue" windway, by the heating of a reed-tongue, or by the vibration of the lips, the same principle obtains.

We see in the Arab *Nay* or vertical flute (Plate VII, 1), in the ubiquitous panpipes and in the egg-shaped *Hsüan* or Chinese *Ocarina* the "flue" method in its earliest form. When such an instrument on this principle first appeared in Europe is beyond reckoning. Dr. Karl Absolon, during his recent investigations into vast palaeolithic settlements in Moravia, has found whistles and flutes of reindeer joints, swan and goose bones, even of a lion's tooth made by the ancient mammoth hunters, who in quest of their quarry roamed the wide plains of Central Europe. He dates these musical instruments—for such they certainly are—to a time some thirty thousand years ago. They may be so remote; but they are associated with conditions prevalent at the very close of the palaeolithic period and just before the neolithic age of about six thousand years ago. A discussion of archaic dates need not, however, detain us; but it is interesting to note that in the cliff dwellings of Colorado and the ancient graves of California exactly similar bone flutes and whistles have been discovered. In the caves, too, of France, Belgium, and Sweden

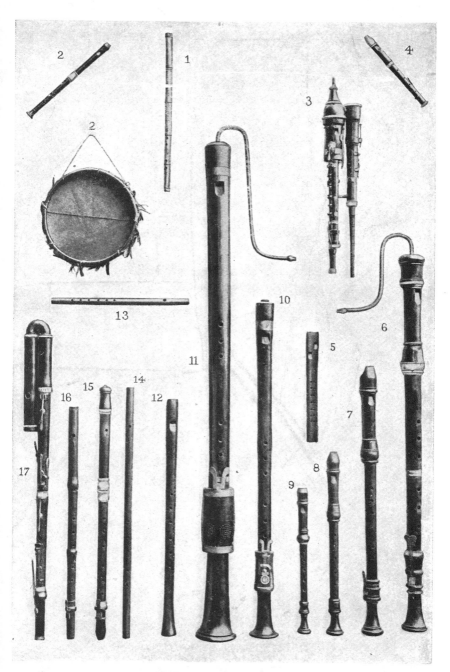

PLATE VII.   AEROPHONES

PLATE VII

1   Egyptian Flute (Náy)

2   Pipe and Tabor (English, eighteenth century)

3   Triple Flageolet (W. Bainbridge, c. 1820)

4   French Flageolet (eighteenth century)

5   Akkordflöte (German, c. 1720)

6–9   English Recorders (Stanesby, eighteenth century)

10–12   Recorders (as used c. 1600)

13   Military Fife (c. 1800)

14   Flute (as used c. 1600)

15   Flute (Chevalier, c. 1670)

16   Flute (F. Boie, c. 1724; formerly Quantz's)

17   Bass Flute (Wigley and McGregor, c. 1810)

horns of animals and bones of birds, made to serve the same purpose, have been found.

VERTICAL FLUTES

A.a¹. The simple vertical flute, however, is not so easy to sound as might be supposed, and even in Dr. Absolon's archaic specimens we find the first step towards improvement. The end of the tube is notched on one side, and the embouchure thereby greatly assisted. It is the beginning of the whistle-head, which we shall consider in the next section. This notch is found on the ancient Chinese *Hsiao* and the yet older *Ti*, as also on some of the bone and reed whistles of African tribes. On the Slovakian *Kaval*, used by the peasants in Albania and Southern Russia, as well as on the modern Greek *Souravlia* and *Floyera*, it is however absent, as it is also on the Persian type of vertical flute. The piercing of holes in the tube, for closing or opening by the fingers, is thought to have given primitive man the first idea of a "scale" of notes. Certainly on such instruments, pierced with three equidistant holes, we have the foundation of the seven-note scale, popular throughout Central Asia in very early times. Blown in the range of the first and second overtones, as we are informed by a medieval antiquary it was, the recognized diatonic scale with a sharp fourth is easily produced. On the long Greek vertical flute (*Darvyra*) of the present day the same method is adopted; but there are six holes instead of only three, and a chromatic scale is the result.

Whether the familiar pentatonic scale was developed from a two-holed flute, or through the inability or unwillingness of bygone musicians to master a semitonal interval, is uncertain; but this scale belongs to a different culture, viz. that

of the Erythraean or South Asiatic and Oceanic peoples. To
this latter culture, too, belong the panpipes, a combination of
simple vertical flutes, either wholly open or, more generally,
stopped at one end, bound together in a continuous line.
Though credited by the Greeks as the invention of their own
rustic deity it undoubtedly came from yet farther eastward
through Mediterranean traders, though in ancient Mesopotamia
and Egypt the panpipes were unknown. In the Pyrenees, as
the *Fieould*, it is particularly popular; in France and Italy it
is called the *Organino* or the *Siringa* (the Greek *Syrinx*). In
a curved shape it is represented by the Rumanian *Muscal*.

The single vertical flute, still (as the *Nay*) popular in the
East, has received among some of the Bulgarian nomads a
double form. A curious reversion to the old type was produced
in 1889 by Winnenberg of Cologne and elaborated by a
Florentine maker named Giorgi (1896). This keyless instrument possessed eleven finger-holes (semitonal), two being
closed by the first finger of the left hand. The embouchure was
placed at the end of the tube, and consisted of a rounded plate
with a lip-hole somewhat similar to that of the cross-blown
flute. This rendered the blowing easy, and as the tube was of
large cylindrical bore the tone was full and rich. Probably
the unusual fingering militated against its wide adoption. At
a little later date it appeared with a unique arrangement of
plate-like keys on Schaffner's system; placed in a straight line
they covered fifteen semitonic holes.

A yet closer return to the primitive embouchure is found on
the *Okraulo*, a vertical flute just introduced by Baron Okura.
It is made in a complete set, the tenor (in *g*) and the bass
(in *c*) yielding a stringy tone. The Boehm system of fingering
is employed.

Another strange version of the vertical flute is found in

the piston flute, or *Sifflet Trombone*, which can easily be constructed from a bicycle pump by removing the nozzle end. Here the scale is formed, as on the trombone, by the use of the piston-slide, every gradation of pitch between two or three octaves being obtainable and the *glissando* perfect. This type with an ordinary whistle-head is generally called the Swanee flute.

A.a². The very ancient vertical flutes of Moravia reveal another step also in history and development. Not only is there the primitive "notch," but there is also the narrow windway ("languid") and the sharpened edge ("lip") of the whistle. These early musicians discovered that, by partially closing the upper part of the tube with pitch or some similar substance and placing a hole just at the end of the stopping, a stream of air could be directed upon the thin edge of the hole without the use of the lips. Here is the parent of the whistle-head, which we find on the recorder and flageolet as well as in the flue-pipes of the organ. This early device is also noticeable on some of the prehistoric American bone whistles; in fact, among many of the Indian tribes it is still in use, though it is often varied by binding a strip of bark, cloth, or metal or a piece of wood over the upper side of the hole to render the air-stream more direct.

RECORDERS

There is therefore no need to relegate to later days the invention of the whistle-head. It was known to such ancient peoples as the Assyrians and Egyptians, the Greeks and the Romans. Amongst the Peruvian Incas and Mexican Aztecs it was fully developed, and in Europe, until the arrival of the cross-blown or transverse flute, provided that popular instrument of the Middle Ages, the recorder (Plate VII, 10–12). In Germany it bears the characteristic names of *Block-flöte* or, from its beak-shaped mouthpiece, *Schnabel-flöte*. In France it is the *Flûte douce* from its sweet tone, whilst the Spanish name *Ajabeba* is probably derived from the Arabic equivalent *Shabbaba*. In the twelfth century it is illustrated in manuscripts of English workmanship, and in the fourteenth century its peculiar name "Recorder" appears. This was probably taken from the similarity of its sound to the low warbling of a bird, called "recording," with the idea, too, of an oft-repeated strain. In the fifteenth century these whistle-flutes or fipple-flutes were made in various sizes to suit the polyphonic needs of the period, and the lowest hole was made in duplicate for the accommodation of right- or left-handed players. Virdung (1511) illustrates four sizes of flutes for a quartette; but Praetorius (1618) describes eight sizes, from the *Klein Flötlein* under 5½ inches in length to the *Gross-Bassflöte* nearly 6 feet 6 inches in height, without the long crooked tube required for conveying the air from the mouth of the performer to the whistle-head. But they were made even larger, for a contra-bass recorder in the Musée Stein at Antwerp is 8 feet 6 inches in height with a volume of sound entirely disproportionate to its size. Praetorius also informs us that the full recorder consort included one contra-bass, two bass, four bassett or baritone, four tenor, four alto, four treble, and two high treble flutes—twenty-one instruments in all. A fantastic form is sometimes found called the *Flûte à colonne*; it is made in the shape of a small pillar with capital and base.

The recorder possesses an inverted conical bore and seven finger-holes in front with one at the back for the thumb; it must not be confused with a six-holed instrument commonly called the penny whistle. The French name *Flûte à neuf trous,* used in the seventeenth century, refers to the use of the duplicate hole already mentioned. Praetorius's high treble flute, however, had but three holes in front, while on it the lower portion of the scale was produced by partially closing the open end with the finger: and consequent on the wonderful performances, through three octaves, upon this little instrument by a blind Italian peasant named Picco in the early nineteenth century, it is sometimes known as the Picco pipe. Owing to the persistency with which the English clung to their recorder throughout the seventeenth and early eighteenth centuries it received the honourable title of the English flute (Plate VII, 6–9), though at last called the common flute in contradistinction to the German or transverse flute. But in those days the deeper-pitched instruments had fallen into disuse, and the bass recorder descended only to tenor *f*. Famous makers of the time were the Stanesbys and Bressan. King Henry VIII possessed flutes called "Pilgrims' staves"; these may have been similar to the Bohemian *Czakan* and the walking-stick flutes, so popular in the early decades of the last century. The recorder, or whistle-flute, was employed by Bach in six of his cantatas, in the Easter oratorio, St.Matthew's Passion, three orchestral concertos, and in the pastoral *Was mir behagt*. Handel included it in his score of *Acis and Galatea*, and a trio for two recorders and a bass recorder appears in his opera *Giustino* (1736). For the aria in *Acis*, "Hush ye pretty warbling choirs," it is peculiarly appropriate. Mozart and Gluck also had a place for it in their works, but, like Bach, only as a treble instrument. During the past decade, however, the interest in the English recorder has been re-awakened, and many efficient makers and players are to be found both in this country and on the Continent. Special compositions, too, have been written for it, both as a solo instrument and in combination with other representatives of its family.

FLAGEOLETS

In the early part of the nineteenth century a simplified and keyed recorder appeared under the name of the English flageolet. It was also made in double form, two tubes being united under a common mouthpiece. This was, however, no new idea. The *Flûte harmonique* (Plate VII, 5), or *Akkordflöte*, was constructed in earlier centuries out of one block of wood, the scale progressions on the two tubes bored in it being generally in thirds. In Bosnia and Dalmatia, where it is called the *Zampogna* and *Dvojnica*, the tubes are separated at the lower end, and it is there still found as a pastoral instrument. In Russia it appears as the *Zalejka*, and in Lithuania as the *Lumʒdʒe*. Pepys, in his diary (1668), mentions that Dumbleby, the pipe-maker, showed him a fashion of having two pipes of the same note fastened together, "so as I can play on one and then echo it upon the other; which is mighty pretty." About 1819 Bainbridge of London introduced a system of keys for simplifying execution, and also for silencing either tube at will. Soon afterwards he produced a triple flageolet (Plate VII, 3), the third tube, with four or five keys, being added to the mouthpiece and manipulated by the player's right-hand thumb. These instruments—pretty in their way— failed to find any definite place in the orchestra, though Sullivan introduced the single English flageolet in the *Sorcerer* (1877). A *Flûte polyphonique*, now in the Liceo Musicale at Bologna and described by Kircher in 1650, possesses five tubes, which are inserted into a transverse stock as windway; the principal flute has eight finger-holes; others act as "drones," supplying sustained sounds.

A different type of instrument, so far as its fingering is concerned, is the French flageolet (Plate VII, 4), known formerly as the *Arigot, Flageol,* or *Flûtet.* Pepys speaks of it also with affection, and used to carry about a small edition of it for his delight on all possible occasions. The instrument has but four finger-holes in front with two thumb-holes at the back. It was popularized by a Frenchman named Juvigny towards the close of the sixteenth century, and was an improvement on the earlier forms. Mersenne (1635) describes it under the name *Tibia minor* or *Flageollet,* and says that it was used in ballets and vaudeville. He even gives a quartette with alto, tenor, and bass flageolets. It is said that the "Flauto piccolo" *obbligato,* allotted by Handel to his famous aria "O ruddier than the cherry," was originally intended for this instrument. The French flageolet is often called the quadrille flageolet and, fitted with keys, was popular among the dance bands of the last century. A small and delicately made form is known as the bird flageolet (*Flautillo*), and employed by bird fanciers to train canaries and linnets in singing. Sometimes these little pipes were made on recorder lines.

Another type of whistle-flute is the three-hole pipe with a cylindrical bore, called the *Schwegel, Galoubet,* or *Chirola.* It could be played with one hand, there being but two holes in front and one at the back. The other hand meanwhile provided an accompaniment upon a small drum suspended from the right arm or shoulder. In England it was known as the tabor pipe (Plate VII, 2), and supplied the music for the Morris and other rustic dances. In the South of France it was also used with the *Tambourin de Béarn,* described under the Chordophones (ii.A.a). This little instrument had also its tenor and bass counterparts, and the name *Stamentienpfeife* given to them by Praetorius (1618) is supposed by Dr. Sachs to be another rendering of the word *Tämerlinpfeife*, or drum-pipe. In Russia it assumes a double form as the *Geleika* or *Sipouka*. It is impossible, however, to describe in detail the many ways in which whistle-pipes have been constructed. Even the simple panpipes had succumbed in the fifteenth century to the whistle-head, and the walking-stick flute has already been mentioned. With many African tribes it is customary to blow across the open end of an animal's horn, with a few finger-holes pierced in it. The medieval *Gemshorn* closely resembled such attempts, being but a chamois horn plugged at the larger end, in order to construct the "fipple" or windway, and provided with three to six finger-holes. It has given its name to a sixteenth-century organ-stop, the pipes of which taper in form and have a pleasing stringed tone. In a similar way the old flageolet, called *Arigot*, has provided the title *Larigot* for a shrill mixture-stop.

TRANSVERSE FLUTES

i.A.a3. The cross-blown or transverse flute, though now found amongst primitive African tribes, cannot vie with the vertical flute in antiquity. So far as is recorded, it appears to have been evolved in Eastern Asia as an improvement on the ancient Chinese *Hsüan* or *Ocarina*, a half-egg-shaped instrument of the resonator type to be considered under our next subdivision. The improved form was called the *Ch'ih*, and was tubular; both ends of the tube were closed with plugs and a mouth-hole placed in the side at the middle point of its length. On the opposite side were pierced six finger-holes, three to the right and three to the left of the central hole. On this strange instrument a diatonic scale of ten notes can be produced. In the first century B.C. Buddhism reached

China, and was soon accepted as one of the State religions. The *Ch'ih*, which was used in the State ritual, was therefore transplanted to other countries, and reaching India, the cradle of Buddhism, became the transverse flute. The mouth-hole, or embouchure, was moved from the centre of the tube to the left end, and the six finger-holes were arranged consecutively between it and the right end, which, being now unblocked, altered the instrument from the resonator type to that of the ordinary flute. On ancient Buddhist carvings this new flute is frequently depicted, and it still exists as the *Murali* or *Pillagovi* of India, beloved of Krishna. In this more acceptable form it returned to China as the *Ti-tzu*, the "foreign" flute. East Turkestan provides a fifth-century illustration of it *en route*. In the early centuries of our present era we find that it had also spread westward to Asia Minor, a late Graeco-Roman specimen having been discovered at Halicarnassus. In the eighth and ninth centuries—with the extension of Arab domination—this instrument of the East was carried into Europe and is figured in Byzantine wall-paintings. In the eleventh century it is portrayed in Russia in the sculpture of Kiev Cathedral. The following century found it well established in Germany.

It is important that this side-blown instrument should be carefully distinguished from two other types which somewhat resemble it. The long Egyptian flute, figured on wall-paintings from the third millennium B.C., is held sideways. This is owing to its abnormal length, 3 feet or more; but it is in reality an end-blown flute, like its vertically held counterpart. The Greek *Plagiaulos*, too, was held aslant; yet it was not a flute but a reed-pipe; existing specimens, which have an apparent mouth-hole at the side, show also that, as the hole is barely ⅛ inch across, it would be unsuitable as an embouchure but well adapted for the insertion of a small beating-reed. The appearance of the *Plagiaulos* in the third century B.C. was evidently due to some freak of fashion.

The cross-blown flute, known in the fourteenth century in France as the *Fleuthe traversaine* and in Germany as the *Querpfeife*, becoming popular in the latter country, also received in the fifteenth century the title *Flauto alemano*, or *Flûte allemande*, i.e. German flute, in contradistinction to the whistle-headed flute already described. In a small form, used with the drum, it became the fife (Plate VII, 13), a shortening of the German name *Zwerchpfeife* ("cross-pipe"). As it was especially adopted by Swiss infantry regiments it obtained also the title *Schweitzer Pfeife*, or *Feldpfeife*, and as such it is described and illustrated by Agricola (1528) in three sizes of purely cylindrical bore with six finger-holes. Shakespeare, noting the way of holding it, fitly terms it the "wry-necked" fife, and remarks on its ear-piercing quality of tone. It retained this keyless cylindrical form till the middle of the last century, when an inverted conical bore was substituted with keys. This was called in England the military fife, and was afterwards adopted on the Continent.

The early history of the flute is difficult to separate from that of the fife. It, too, had a cylindrical bore (Plate VII, 14), though it was generally made in much larger sizes, the length of the bass transverse flute in the sixteenth century being more than 3 feet 6 inches with a compass from tenor *d*. At the end of that century one key was added, probably to enable the performer to reach the lowest note with greater ease. At the opening of the seventeenth century a consort of these flutes consisted of two treble, four alto or tenor, and two bass instruments, and it had already taken its place in the orchestra. About the middle of that century a distinct alteration was made in its construction. Although the cylindrical bore was retained for the upper part, an inverted conical bore was adopted for the rest of the instrument, thereby partly reducing its length and at the same time rendering the higher notes more correctly in tune (Plate VII, 15).

In the last half of the seventeenth century the first semitonal key was added for the production of d^1 sharp, and the footjoint was made separate from the body of the instrument (Plate VII, 16). The body, too, was divided, and sections of tube varying in length could be inserted to accommodate the flute to the various pitches then in use. We sometimes do an injustice to these old-world performers by attributing to them an indifference to true intonation. What shall we say when we find that the next improvement—made by the celebrated player Quantz in 1726—was the addition of a second key to correct the difference between d^1 sharp and e^1 flat! The lengthening of the foot-joint shortly afterwards provided space for the new keys c^1 sharp and c^1 natural; but they were not considered an advantage. The application of a tuning-slide to the head-joint seems to have also been suggested by Quantz about 1752 by the use of a similar slide on the foot-joint in order to correct the intonation when the additional tubes or *corps de réchange* were inserted in the body of the instrument. To him also is attributed the screw-button, the regulation of the position of the cork at the upper end being of great importance. Later in the eighteenth century appeared f^1, g^1 sharp and b^1 flat keys. The long f^1 natural key was first employed by Tromlitz (1786), who also added a long c^2 natural key. The reintroduction of the low c^1 and c^1 sharp keys was due to two London flautists, Tacet and Florio, and improved mechanism was adopted by Potter. In Italy a chromatic extension downwards to g was advocated, but the difficulty of closing so many keys successfully with the little fingers of both hands could not be overcome. In 1808 Nolan of Stratford invented the double-action key, which has now become so general. Attempts, too, were made to perfect the bass flute by Lot of Paris and Macgregor of London: in these instruments the head-joint was reflexed on the body of the instrument. But the early part of the last century saw the greatest improvements which have rendered the flute so perfect for its purpose. To the researches of Theobald Boehm of Munich (1793–1881) must the highest tribute of praise be given, both for the return to the old cylindrical bore (but with a parabolic bore for the head-joint) and for the skilful mechanism for additional keys which now allow the holes to be placed in their true positions. Into the question whether in some of these improvements he was anticipated by Gordon we need not enter, nor into the controversy of the "open" or "closed" key systems. Many other familiar names are connected with this advance, such as those of Nicholson with his large holes, Buffet with his needle-springs, Siccama, Rockstro, Rudall, and Carte with others of the present century. In recent years the thinning of the head-joint has greatly contributed to the increased power and sweetness of the instrument.

Besides the so-called concert flute, of which we have given a brief account, the alto flute in the key of *A*, known as the *Flûte d'amour*, has received attention and been perfected by Heckel of Biebrich-am-Rhein. Handel employed the alto flute in *Ricardo* (1729) under the name *Traversa bassa*. In 1810 Wigley and Macgregor of London produced an alto or tenor instrument, which they called the voice flute (*Flauto di voce*). It had a reflexed head and long "open" keys to reduce the stretch of the fingers. But its peculiarity consisted in the fact that over a large opening in the side between the embouchure and the first finger-hole a thin membrane was stretched, which vibrated as the instrument was played and imparted a reedy tone to the sounds, somewhat resembling that of the oboe. We have already dealt with this principle under the membranophonic class (iii.A.a.). The bass flute (Plate VII, 17) has also been rendered more effective by Moritz and Messrs. Rudall and Carte. In the model produced by Albisi of Milan the transverse head of the Giorgi flute (i.A.a¹.) has been combined with the body of the old vertical flute.

The piccolo flute, as now known, was introduced by Tromlitz (1791): the old *Flauto piccolo* was the flageolet as previously noted.

OCARINA

i.A.b. The application of the whistle principle to closed tubes or resonators is also found. The best-known example is the stopt organ pipe, which in former days so frequently served as a pitch-pipe (*Corista, Stimmpfeife*). Some of the earliest whistles were of this type, a hole bored in the side of one of the joints of a reindeer's foot being sufficient for the purpose; while the *Ocarina* is probably its latest representative. Very often these whistles were made in the shape of birds, with the mouthpiece in the tail. This was the origin of the name *Ocarina*, viz. "little goose," and the instrument was evolved in 1865 by the Italians, Mezzetti and Donati. In France it is called *Coucou*, from the notes given by the finger-holes. The ocarina, as now improved, has the whistle placed at the side, and there are nine or ten finger-holes. It has a compass of over an octave, and has been made in various sizes for concerted use. Pottery whistles in bird or animal shapes are constantly found amongst archaic remains in Mexico and Peru; they have also been unearthed in the prehistoric sites of Europe. In the ancient Indus civilization of the third millennium B.C. they were also known. Their present name in Russia is *Swistalka*, in Spain *Silbato*, and in the Balearic Isles *Siurell*; some of these forms are blown with water in the resonator. The Chinese *Hsüan*, or goose egg, with five or six finger-holes is a very early and highly prized form, made of black clay and decorated in scarlet and gold. It is still employed in the State services and is blown across a hole in the small end like a vertical flute.

An interesting development of the resonator principle is to be seen in the German *Nasenflöte*, which, however, has nothing in common with the nose-flutes of Oceania. It is a tin apparatus with tubes leading from the nose of the performer and directing a current of air against a sharp edge, thus producing a "flutter." The lower part of the instrument covers the chin and the partially open mouth, which acts as a resonator. The more the mouth is closed the deeper the sound of the whistle. With a good ear and a capacious mouth the compass of about two and a half octaves is obtainable.

ORGANS

i.B.a. Suggested probably by the row of vertical flutes as grouped together in the panpipes, efforts were made to apply mechanical means for the production of their music even before our present era. Such was the primary step towards the evolution of the organ. As this instrument, whose very name presupposes machinery, was at its inception only furnished with "flue" or whistle-headed pipes and not with reed-pipes, which were added at a much later date so far as Europe at any rate is concerned, it will be convenient to recall the main points in its history under the present section.

The first consideration, if the necessary wind was not to be drawn from the mouth of the player, would be the means to be adopted to secure a sufficient and steady supply. For

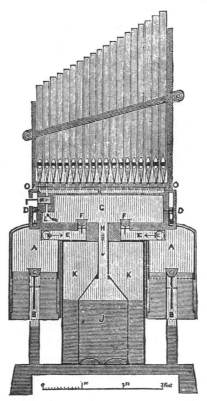

FIG. 6.—HYDRAULUS ACTION

the former requirement the metalworker's bellows, long in use, provided a solution simple and effective, for if two bellows were insufficient they could be multiplied indefinitely. Although the earliest pneumatic organs were quite small and portable, if we may judge by their representations on coins of the Roman period and from remains found at Pompeii, this method of multiplying the number of "feeding" bellows obtained till the seventeenth century and even later. For the large German organs described by Praetorius (1618) twenty to twenty-four bellows, depressed and raised alternately in pairs by ten or twelve men, were required. Sometimes inclined planks were used. But for steadiness of wind the invention of the Alexandrian scientist Ctesibius (third century B.C.), as elaborated by his pupil Hero and the Roman Vitruvius, far surpassed in efficiency this cumbersome device.

The *Hydraulus* or water-organ, as it was called, employed but two or four "feeding" bellows (A) by which the air was pumped into the upper part of a dome-shaped retainer (J) inverted in a cistern containing water (K). The incoming air, forcing the water out of the bottom of the retainer, raised its level in the cistern and so supplied a constant pressure. This organ became the recognized accompaniment at the public games and entertainments. In A.D. 826 an *Hydraulus* "made in the Greek manner" was installed in the palace of Louis the Pious at Aix-la-Chapelle; but, owing to its pagan associations, the instrument was not in general favour with ecclesiastical authorities.

The next consideration was the admission of the wind thus compressed into the rows or ranks of pipes. This was effected by sliding strips of metal pierced with holes corresponding to similar passages in the wind-chest and the sound-board on which the organ pipes stood. By drawing out the sliders the holes coincided and a free passage was provided for the air to the foot of the pipes; by pushing the sliders in again the passage was closed. At the beginning of our era levers were attached to the ends of the sliders and a keyboard was thus formed, superseding the action of the hand. A terracotta figure, found at Carthage, of the second century A.D. displays an organist playing on the *Hydraulus;* the instrument has nineteen keys with three stops and ranks of pipes. A full description of this organ together with details of the working reproduction, made by the present writer, will be found in Grove's *Dictionary of Music,* vol. ii, p. 690. The remains of an organ discovered in 1931 at the Roman Station Aquincum, near Budapest, and dated in the consulate of Modestus and Probus (A.D. 228), shows thirteen similar sliders with portions of the lever-keys and four chromatic ranks of flue-pipes, three of the ranks stopt, and from their measurements sounding a unison, fifth, and octave (which also had a rank of open pipes). It is believed that the instrument was rescued in Roman times from a fire which consumed an adjoining hall. No trace of the blowing apparatus was found, but in the inscription it is called an *Hydraula.* Probably the weight of the lower part prevented its removal to a place of safety A description of this very interesting relic has been written in German and Magyar by Nagy Lajos (Budapest, 1934). It confirms the details given by Hero and Vitruvius.

By the close of the sixth century pagan rites had ceased, and the pneumatic organ soon began to take its rightful place in the Church services. Bishop Aldhelm (*d.* 709) refers to the enormous instruments "with a thousand blasts," to the "windy bellows," and to the "golden pipes." The lever-keys were large and heavy, requiring the use of the fists; hence the performer was called *pulsator organorum.* This was very different from the "light touch" and "flying fingers" described by the later Latin poets as characteristic of the *Hydraulus.* Stops, too, were not in use on these medieval organs, but all the ranks of pipes, ten to each key in the Winchester organ (951), sounded together. There were on that instrument forty sliders or keys, requiring two organists and seventy strong

M

men to blow the twenty-six bellows. In the early years of the fifteenth century the "spring-box," by which any rank of pipes could be silenced at will, was invented in the Netherlands. This was largely superseded by a slider-action, which, placed immediately below the pipes, cut off the wind supply. In the same century additional keyboards and a rudimentary pedal-board were added with independent pedal-pipes. The keys, too, which had replaced the original sliders labelled with the letters of the alphabet, were made smaller and the compass of a fifth could be struck with one hand. In 1499 Crantz of Brunswick so reduced their dimension that an octave could be reached; earlier in that century the semitones, which had hitherto formed a separate manual, were inserted between the natural keys. On the fifteenth-century positive organ, shown in the frontispiece, these semitonal keys are to be seen in their due order as required for the *Musica ficta*, or false music. The older keyboards had only the monochord *B* flat. Variety of tone, too, appeared through the use of various forms of reed-pipes and by string-toned pipes of small diameter and tapering form. In the sixteenth century the tremulant and couplers show themselves. But one of the most important improvements was in connection with the bellows. Intonation had already been made more satisfactory in the pneumatic organs by a steadier wind supply—lead or stone weights having been substituted for that of human beings, so that when lifted the bellows fell of their own accord. Now the old form of bellows with a diagonally rising reservoir above, as in smiths' bellows, was superseded by a larger horizontal-rising reservoir, invented by Green and Cuming in the latter part of the eighteenth century. In many instruments the "feeding" bellows are at the present time made quite distinct from the reservoirs, and where hydraulic or gas engines or the electric fan-motors are employed this is always the case. The key action, too, is on a totally different principle. As the rope-action of early days, required for pulling down the valve or "pallet" with its stiff spring, gave way to the "tracker" action with its light rods and rollers, so this has disappeared before the "pneumatic" action (Barker, 1841) or the "tubular pneumatic" (Moitessier, 1850), with tiny bellows as motors, which have again been surpassed by the "electro-pneumatic" action (Barker, 1868), with highly sensitive magnets actuating the little motor bellows. The number of keyboards has also been increased. In a large instrument there may be as many as five or six, and these manuals are known as the great organ (*Hauptwerk*), the choir organ (*Brust Positif* or *Rück Positif*—if the pipes are behind the player), the swell organ (*Ober-werk*), the solo organ (with imitative orchestral stops), and the echo organ (of soft-toned stops). Sometimes there is also a tuba organ (of pipes sounding on very heavy pressure).

The pipes of the solo and echo organs are, like those of the swell organ, enclosed within louvred shutters (eighteenth century), and very often the pipes of the choir organ also. Even the whole instrument has been so treated, which in our opinion is a mistake and comparable with the unfortunate practice of installing it within a confined organ chamber. Variety of tone is obtained from the flue-pipes in many ways, but chiefly by altering their shape and diameter. The wider the diameter or "scale" the fuller the tone. In the reed-pipes, however, which are considered under Subdivision ii.B.a[2] the tone depends on the thickness of the vibrating tongues and the shape of the resonator attached to them. Full-scale pipes of metal are used for providing the "foundation work," such as the open diapason, principal (a name given on the Continent to all diapasons), and similar ranks. Small-scale pipes include those of stringed tone, such as the viola da gamba, muted viol, etc. Inverted conical pipes are found in the ranks of the gemshorn, spitzflute, etc. Wooden pipes are used for the stopt diapason and bourdon and, as open pipes, for the clarabella, hohl-flüte, etc. A half-stopt pipe (i.e. with an open tube inserted in the stopper) is the distinguishing mark of the rohr-flute. Mixtures, which are not now so frequently found, are made up of ranks of pipes giving the various overtones; of this class was the old cornett used as a solo stop in special compositions, and intended to be imitative of the lip-voiced instrument (iii.A.a²).

As the organ is now employed not only in churches and halls but in the cinemas also, to replace the orchestra, a somewhat new type of instrument is being evolved to meet this special requirement. Space has been economized by the "extension" or "unit" system, advocated by some for churches also. In a properly constituted instrument each stop or register has its full complement of pipes in its particular rank, so that when used with other registers the added effect is distributed throughout the whole compass. Under the "extension" system, however, a rank of pipes, say of 8-foot tone, is given an additional octave of pipes at the bottom of its compass and two octaves at the upper end; this forms the "unit." By using portions of this "unit" a 16-foot stop, a 4-foot stop, and a 2-foot stop can be obtained as well as the original 8-foot tone; but in combination, although the octaves at each end are an addition to the general effect, the middle portion of the compass is merely a make-up of sounds already in use. It is, of course, a subterfuge like the old octave and sub-octave couplers, useful enough on the pedal-organ where chords are out of place, but on the manuals a sacrifice of fullness for the sake of brilliancy.

On continental organs, even in churches, stops are found for effects other than organ-like, such as thunder, drums, chimes, etc. In the modern cinema organ these are greatly in evidence, and xylophones, triangles, castanets, and many other devices for illustrating the scenic effects of the films are incorporated, while the whole is brought under the sentimental sway of an all-pervading "tremolo." A useful addition to the manuals, however, is the "double-touch," made possible by electrical transmission. In ordinary playing a contact is made with a current, which affects the pallets of certain ranks of pipes giving the general tone of the instrument; but with a slight additional pressure on the key a second circuit is touched, which brings into play one or more powerful ranks of pipes. Thus a melody can be emphasized on one and the same keyboard with a softer accompaniment; or a sudden *fortissimo* effect can be produced without change of manual or the use of composition pedals or switches. The opportunity, too, of making various ranks of pipes available for use on any manual is a valuable addition to the resources of the organist. While such improvements may readily be welcomed for church organs, we are in hearty agreement with Dr. Harvey Grace, organist of Chichester Cathedral, that the tendency to exaggerate pace and power, killing the music and deafening the listeners, is to be strongly deprecated. Too many of our churches are now over-organized.

We may close with some explanation of words and phrases used in connection with the organ. The name in the plural (*organa*) is often found in the early records and was evidently employed to denote the complex structure of the instrument and also to distinguish it from the word *organum* applied to the practice of rendering the plain-song in fourths, fifths, and octaves. A "double organ" is an instrument with a keyboard compass descending to 8-foot *C* or 12-foot *G*, which were denoted under the old English nomenclature as *CC* and *GG* respectively. A "single organ" descends only to 4-foot *c* or 6-foot *G* (English *C* or *G*). "A pair of organs" is a conventional phrase denoting a compound unit, and applied also to regals and virginals (Chordophones, i.B.a.).

The means of increasing or diminishing the volume of sound, known as the swell, was invented by Jordan in 1712, though in some form or other it must have been used in the *Claviorganum Piano e Forte* (*c.* 1598) described under Chordophones, ii.B.a. It consisted of a shutter pulled up or down by a rope attached to a pedal and placed over the echo organ. This "Nag's head" swell was not adopted, however, on the Continent; for in 1771 Dr. Burney could find no organ with a swell in France, Italy, or Germany. At the close of the century Shudi's "Venetian" swell with narrow louvres· was adapted from the harpsichord for this purpose by Green, the famous English builder.

Besides the large organs there were in medieval times small instruments. The "Portative" (Plate IX, 2), also called in Italy *Rigabello* and *Nimfali*, had only a limited compass, but it could be carried, suspended by a strap over the shoulder, and played at the same time by one person, his right hand fingering the keys and his left hand on the bellows at the back of the pipes. The "Positive" organ (Plate IX, 3, and *Frontispiece*) was somewhat larger in size and was placed on a table or stand when in use: it afterwards became the chamber organ. An instrument introduced by Baduel of Paris in 1876 and called the *Flautophone* reverted to the primitive practice of supplying the wind for the little stopt pipes from the mouth: the keys, like piston-valves, were placed above a small wind reservoir and gave a compass of two and a half octaves. It reminds us of the Muristus pneumatic organ described in an Arabic MS. of the ninth century, and fully explained by Dr. Farmer in *The Organ of the Ancients from Eastern Sources* (1931). Here the air reservoir, which consisted of an inflated skin, was filled by the breath of four or twelve men, who blew "with violence." Labour was no doubt under compulsion in those days.

BARREL ORGANS

i.B.b. The application of automatic mechanism to the organ is by no means confined to Europe. Drawing their ideas from Philo's and Hero's works the Arabs in the ninth century constructed "the instrument which plays by itself." This combined hydraulic power with a revolving and shifting barrel provided with small pegs or pins; by these means the air was compressed within the wind-chest and the little pallets communicating with the pipes were opened. Kircher (1650) illustrates many devices of this kind, moved by weights or by springs. In the last century the *Apolionicon*, built by Flight and Robson in 1818, was considered the masterpiece of such productions. It not only had five manuals available for separate players, but could be entirely controlled by automatic machinery through three shifting cylinders, which revolved at the same time under steam power. Sundry instruments of percussion were sounded in the same way, adding to the orchestral effect.

A humbler form of instrument was the *Orgue de Barbarie*, so named from its maker, Barberi, and not from the little ape which usually accompanied the player. The use of these barrel organs in churches followed the departure of the earlier church bands, and under the auspices of the clerk discoursed their somewhat limited repertoire of music. Of their doings and misdoings much has been written; but as musicians skilled on the keyboard were not always at hand in the village communities, the happy combination of keyboard and barrel, which appeared later, was by no means out of place. Orchestrions, for reproducing orchestral compositions, were much in vogue in the latter half of the last century and, with their tubular pneumatic action, great, swell, and pedal organs, their automatic stop control and full percussion effects, were able to render music which was then impossible for individual performers.

The artistic little organs called *Serinettes*, which contained a pricked barrel worked by a handle, were frequently used for teaching singing birds or for providing merry tunes for home entertainment.

ii. REED-VOICED TYPE

ii.A. Whereas in the previous sub-class the idea of the sound production appears to have been derived from Nature's music, in the reed-voiced instruments, now to be considered, the method of producing the necessary "flutter" suggests human artifice and inventiveness. For the reed principle consists in the rapid vibration of a tongue of wood or metal against or within a frame, or of two such tongues beating against each other. There are various forms this method may assume:

(1) The single-beating reed, striking against a wooden "lay," as used on the clarinet or against a metal frame, as employed in the organ.

(2) The double-beating reed, in which two reed tongues

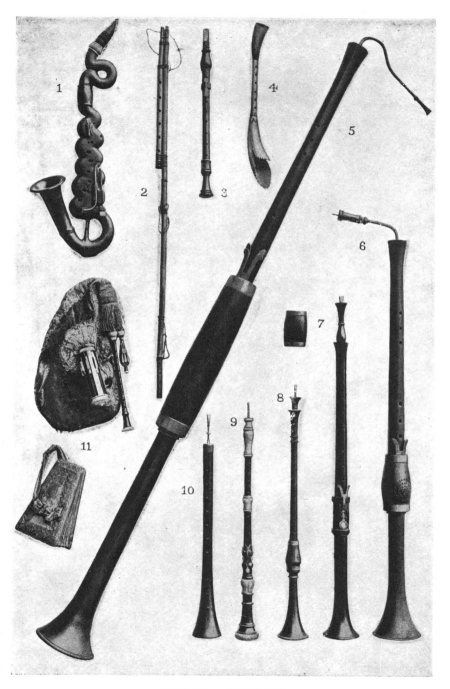

PLATE VIII.   AEROPHONES

PLATE VIII

vibrate against each other, as required for the oboe and bassoon.

(3) The retreating reed, or inverted double reed, in which the two plates normally in contact with each other are, by air pressure, opened for vibration. Certain forms of organ reeds, known as *Diaphones*, have been made in this way. It is also found in frequent use amongst the American Indians of the north-west coast; also in Morocco and in Japan amongst the Ainos.

(4) The ribbon reed, wherein a strip of thin membrane is tightly fixed at each end and stretched across a narrow opening edgewise. On blowing through the slit the edge of the membrane pulsates. This, too, is found amongst the coast Indians of America, and in Europe produces the nasal tones of Mr. Punch under the name *Voix de polichinelle*.

(5) The free reed, which on an entirely different principle allows the tongue to vibrate freely within its frame instead of striking against it. It is the reed of the mouth harmonica and harmonium, and brought from China.

For our present purpose, as will be observed, we may omit the third and fourth forms of reed and concentrate, so far as European instruments are concerned, on the single-beating reed, the double-beating reed, and the free reed.

CLARINET

ii.A.a¹. The single-beating reed accompanied by a cylindrical tube is of very ancient invention. It was in use as early as the beginning of the third millennium B.C. in Egypt, which may have been the country of its origin. It is one of the "squeakers" easily constructed by country children by cutting a small tongue in a hollow rush or corn stalk. These reeds were used for some of the double pipes which have been discovered in Egyptian tombs, and are now represented by the *Arghool* (Plate VIII, 2) and *Zummarah*, so common in that country and the eastern Mediterranean districts. It seems certain that one kind, at any rate, of the ancient Greek *Aulos* (a pipe so wrongly called a flute) employed this form of reed; for Theophrastus in the fourth century B.C. describes the making of such reeds in his *Historia Plantarum* (IV, II, 4) and distinctly asserts that the knob of the natural reed was left at one end. It is known, however, that the very slender pipes made use of a double-beating reed, as we shall explain in the next section.

Throughout the Middle Ages the single-beating reed appears to have been chiefly confined to peasant folk. It is still commonly found on the hornpipes and bagpipe "chanters" of the Greek islands and shows itself, not only on the *Launeddas* of Sardinia (a triple pipe), the *Alboquea* of the Basques, the *Brielka* and *Galeika* of Russia (the latter a double pipe), the *Duda* of Poland and the *Piva* of Dalmatia, but on the old-world *Pibgorn* of Wales (Plate VIII, 4) and the *Stock-horn* of Scotland, where the pipe is also found in the double form. In Italy it appears in the popular "trumpets" made at Florentine fairs, and in France it was known as the *Chalumeau*, a word derived from the Latin *calamellus*, "a little reed," or from the Greek *calamaulos*, "a pipe of reed." As a folk instrument it has been confused with the *Chalemie*, a conical pipe with a double-beating reed, described below (ii.A.b²). Towards the close of the seventeenth century J. C. Denner of Nuremberg, while endeavouring to improve its meagre resources (for it had only attained to one key for a^1 as an extra note in its upper compass), discovered that by adding a second key for b^1 flat or b^1 natural he could extend the compass to the first overtones (Plate VIII, 3). As the cylindrical tube is practically closed by the beating reed at one end it follows the harmonic series of a stopt pipe, and the first overtone is the twelfth. John Denner, his son, affixed an open bell to the lower end about the year 1720, and on it placed a long key for b^1 natural or c natural. This was the clarinet, so named as at first it was considered a substitute for the high-pitched trumpet called the *Clarino* (iii.A.b^1), the tone of which in the upper register it closely resembled. An early use of the instrument under its new name is found in the MS. score of an *Overture* in Handel's own handwriting, preserved in the Fitzwilliam Museum at Cambridge, and composed about the year 1740. The title "Overture" was in those days frequently given to an orchestral work consisting of various movements in concerto style, and in this case there is in it a *Concertino* for two clarinets in *D* and a *Corno da caccia* in *D*. The compass of the clarinet parts ranges from a to d^3 (actual sounds); they are very like trumpet parts, though the use of the complete scale throughout their compass belies that instrument. In those early days, too, the clarinet was frequently made in the *D* key rather than in the *C, B* flat, or *A* pitches. The original set of the score is interesting. The work, in five movements, has never been published and will be found under *MSS. and Sketches by G. F. Handel*, No. 264 (Mann and Maitland, *Fitzwilliam Music*, 1893). By the middle of the eighteenth century the value of the clarinet began to be appreciated, though it was often still scored for under the name *Chalumeau*, as by Gluck in his *Orpheo* and *Alceste* (1767). Its first appearance in the theatre orchestra was probably in Rameau's *Zoroastre* (1749), though, as the *Chalumeau*, it is found in Keiser's *Croesus* (1711) and Telemann's works.

For the further development of the instrument f sharp

g sharp keys were added about the year 1750 by Fritz of Brunswick. A sixth key (lower c^1 sharp) was placed on it by Stadler or Lefèvre *c*. 1789; hitherto the low *f* hole and the c^1 hole had been pierced in duplicate. Müller of Paris, the eminent performer, raised the number of keys to thirteen in 1810, and about the year 1842 Klosé, in conjunction with Buffet, remodelled the whole system with rings, following the lines which Boehm had already adopted for the flute. This system, with a few additional improvements added in later years, is now generally adopted by modern clarinettists. The so-called "speaker" key, which ensures the production of twelfth or first overtone, was carried round to the front of the instrument by Wehl (*c*. 1845). In 1867 Romero of Madrid produced a clarinet with twenty-eight holes and elaborate mechanism which, although it removed certain difficulties of execution, caused others by an alteration of fingering. Albert of Brussels placed two open rings on the lower joint to correct the intonation automatically, and Barret added two rings to the upper joint, which simplified the fingering. Schaffner of Paris, following the system adopted by him for the flute to ensure the correct geometrical and acoustical division of the tube (i.A.a^1.), produced an instrument which, however theoretically correct, demanded the perfect closing of twenty holes covered by small metal plates.

Apart from the small clarinets in *F* and *E* flat, which are generally confined to the use of military bands, the employment of instruments in different pitch was due to technical difficulties of fingering which arose in certain keys, although there is also a variation in tone quality, a fact which composers were not slow to recognize. Beethoven appears to have preferred the *B* flat instrument for solo work, and Mozart the quieter-toned clarinet in *A*. Frequent attempts have been made to construct an instrument which can combine by the use of sliding tubes these changes of pitch, but they have hitherto proved ineffective. The advanced mechanism, however, and the high artistic ability of the present-day performers, both in tone and execution, practically enable the use of one instrument for all purposes, viz. the *B* flat clarinet with an extension to *e* flat at the bottom of the compass.

The *Clarinette d'amour* (*Liebes Klarinette*) is an alto instrument with a pear-shaped bell similar to that of the *Cor anglais*. It was introduced at the close of the eighteenth century, mainly by Tuerlinck of Malines, and has been made in *A* flat, *G* and *F* keys. The latter pitch is also that of the tenor clarinet used in military bands, an instrument which must not be confused with the basset horn (*Corno di bassetto*), made generally in the same pitch. This is a much older form of instrument, dating from about 1770 and fitted with additional keys—either diatonically or chromatically arranged—to extend its downward compass by an additional third. It possesses a peculiarly rich tone, which appealed strongly to Mozart as seen in his *Clemenza di Tito*, *Requiem*, and other works. Beethoven employed it in his score of *Prometheus*, and Strauss included it in that of *Electra* (1909). The earlier model adopted for the instrument assumed an angular shape, like that of the older *Cor anglais*, but now it is usually made with a straight tube. A *Contra-Basset Horn*, an octave lower in pitch, was introduced in the first half of the last century.

Bass clarinets, too, have been made during the past one hundred and fifty years, beginning with that by Grenser of Dresden (1793). Streitwolf of Göttingen in 1828 produced such an instrument in bassoon shape descending to B_1 flat, and others have been made with straight tube and recurved bell. Papalini of Pavia, about 1820, constructed it in serpentine form with five keys, the tube being formed by two pieces of wood joined together with brass rivets (Plate VIII, 1). In 1838 Catterini of Bologna produced the *Glicibarifono*, an instrument with parallel tubes in upright form, and in 1839 Wieprecht of Berlin followed on the same lines with the *Batyphone*, a contra-bass clarinet two octaves below the ordinary instrument. An earlier attempt, known as the *Contrebasse Guerrière*, had appeared in 1808. In 1890 Besson's model, with a threefold tube and elaborate mechanism, provided a new and organ-like tone for the orchestra, combining as it did both cylindrical and conical tubing. In 1909 Heckel of Biebrich-am-Rhein introduced a somewhat similar instrument with improved mechanism for obtaining the correct intonation of the higher register. Though frequently used by composers, such as Meyerbeer (1836), Liszt, and Wagner, the tone of the bass and contra-bass clarinets lacks quality.

Amongst the freaks of the clarinet type made during the last century we may mention a French double-clarinet with parallel tubes in one block of wood. The holes were covered by metal plates raised by little keys similar to those of the piano, and the whole was contained in a rectangular case. Two tubes, each carrying a clarinet mouthpiece, served for sounding this ultra-modern revival of the classical double pipe. Clarinets, too, in the shape of walking-sticks commended themselves to the dilettanti of the early nineteenth century.

SORDONI AND KRUMHORN

ii.A.a². We have dealt with the clarinet as the result of the combination of a cylindrical tube with a *single*-beating reed; but it is possible to combine the cylindrical tube with the *double*-beating reed; in fact, the clarinet itself can be sounded with a bassoon reed, while it still retains the properties of a stopt pipe. But the double-beating reed prefers a much smaller bore than that found on the clarinet, and in this form the combination became the popular principle of some of the most admired wind instruments of classical and medieval days.

In its primitive form the double-beating reed is quite as ancient, perhaps even more ancient, than the single-beating reed, for it is another of the "squeakers" easily constructed by simple folk by compressing the end of a hollow straw or rush stem. In this way it was used in Egypt in the fourth millennium B.C. for those slender double pipes so frequently portrayed in the wall-paintings, and remains of both pipes and reeds have been discovered in the ancient tombs. Unknown, however, in China in early times it was taken there from the West during the first millennium of our era as the *Kuan* (*Pi-li*) or "Tartar Horn"; but, as this possesses a cylindrical tube and is often played in pairs like the double pipes, it is more probably due to Greek influence from Bactria rather than to any Tartar origin.

Throughout the Middle Ages the same type of instrument with a deep quiet tone was popular in Europe. The *Sordoni* and *Doppioni*, described by Praetorius (1618), with two parallel cylindrical tubes in one block, were of this class, and their low humming was much admired. The French *Courtaut*, mentioned by Mersenne (1635), was similar but with little tubes (*tetines*) placed on each side, for right- or left-handed players, to enable them to control the holes placed in the main tube at the back. The *Racket* (*Cervelas*, *Wurst-fagott*) was much shorter owing to the ninefold reflexion of the inner bore. The *Cromorne* or *Tournebout*, *Krumhorn* (*Frontispiece*), with a straight bore and the end of the instrument recurved, was generally sounded with the reed beneath a perforated cap; while the *Cornamuse, Rauschpfeife*, and *Bassanelli*, with straight tubes throughout and yet softer tone, were similarly played. For all these Praetorius gives complete family groups in four parts; and useful as they may have been for "still music," their lack of resonance has relegated them to the museum case in this more boisterous age.

A very quaint instrument called the *Tartöld*, with a cylindrical metal tube wound in spiral form and concealed beneath a leather covering, is found in the sixteenth century and a complete set of five instruments is included in the Ambras Collection, now preserved at the Kunsthistorisches Museum in Vienna. In outward appearance they resemble snarling dragons with protruding tongues; the finger-holes are placed on the back of the "animal" and the reed attached to the tip of its tail. They may have been constructed for merry use at carnival-times.

It is interesting to notice that this combination of the cylindrical tube with the double-beating reed is maintained in the "chanter" of certain forms of bagpipe, and also in the little cylindrical box containing the drones of the *Musette*, a French bagpipe very fashionable in the seventeenth and eighteenth centuries (ii.B.a.).

SAXOPHONE

ii.A.b[1]. Passing to the reed instruments with conical tubes, the use of the single-beating reed is primitive in so far as it is found on some of the small signal-horns made from the natural animal-horn, or now more usually in metal. The earliest example, however, of such a type for instrumental purposes is the *Caledonica* invented by a Scottish bandmaster named Meikle about the year 1820. It appears to have been improved by the London maker Wood, and became known in England as the *Alto Fagotto*, miscalled by later writers the Tenoroon, as explained by Mr. Rendall (*Musical Times*, 1932). Meikle's original instrument is preserved at Edinburgh University, and has been described with illustrations by Mr. Langwill in *The Musical Progress* (April 1934). In shape like a small bassoon, it was played with a clarinet reed, and bearing a conical bore sounded the octave as its first overtone. A reputed predecessor, made by Desfontenelles of Lisieux in 1807, is a clarinet-type instrument sounding the twelfth as the overtone. In 1840 Sax of Brussels produced his family of saxophones, which, notwithstanding their hollow tone, have found a definite place in the military music of the present day, and in such orchestral works as Strauss' *Sinfonia Domestica*. As a perquisite of the dance band it is hardly done justice. Sax is reputed to have discovered the instrument while attempting to alter the overtones of the clarinet; but the use of a small clarinet mouthpiece on the ordinary bassoon, introduced in the last century for practice purposes, may have assisted his efforts. Saxophones have been made in numerous pitches from the high *F* to the sub-contra-bass, but the favourite instruments for solo work are the alto or tenor. Another form of the instrument is the *Heckelclarind*, named after the inventor. It corresponds to the pitch of the *Cor anglais*, but is played with a single-beating reed. It is used for the shepherd's air in Wagner's *Tristan und Isolde*.

In Hungary there had long existed a national instrument called the *Tarogato*, with a conical bore and played with a double-beating reed. This has recently been improved by Schunda of Budapest, who has substituted a single-beating reed and made it available for orchestral purposes by adding fourteen keys.

OBOE AND BASSOON

ii.A.b². The resonator *par excellence*, however, of the double-beating reed is the conical tube. In the second millennium B.C. a new instrument appeared in Mesopotamia called the *Imbubu*. Under this name we can recognize the Syrian *Anbub*, associated in Asia Minor, as the *Gingras*, with the orgiastic rites of Cybele, the Mother-goddess, whose worship flourished in Phrygia and the Taurus. It is described by the classical writers as of high pitch and plaintive tone, or as a little pipe with the voice of a cackling goose. It must, therefore, have been an "octave" instrument with a conical bore. We find it also at the same period in Egypt. Assyrian sculptured slabs show it used in pairs for processional purposes, whilst illustrations of the Roman *tibia* frequently depict its open trumpet-shaped bell. This is the instrument which in medieval Europe was known as the *Schalmei*, *Chalemie*, *Chirimia*, *Cialamella*, or *Shawm* (Plate VIII, 5–8), though with the conical tube considerably lengthened. By inverting the conical bore, as in the *Schrierpfeife* of the sixteenth and seventeenth centuries, the effect of a stopt pipe was obtained, though, according to Praetorius, the tone was still "strong and bright" as compared with cylindrical-tubed instruments (ii.A.a².).

It is, however, with the *Schalmei*—another word derived from *calamus*, a reed—that we are principally concerned, for it became the parent of the *Hautbois* or Oboe of the modern orchestra. Though its vibratory principle was well known in Europe before the Christian era, the instrument received an increased popularity and more marked recognition by its employment in the armies of the victorious Moslems, to whom the sound of the *Zamr* (Plate VIII, 10) was an incentive to bravery. The association of Western nations with Orientalism during the Crusades also left its impress on its development.

The reed of the Oriental oboe is not placed between the lips but thrust entirely into the mouth, the lips pressing against a metal disc attached to the reed-tube. The tone is therefore very raucous and uncertain; though the instrument, used in this way, is still found in Turkey and the Dalmatian districts as the *Zurna* or in Greece as the *Zurnas*. In the European form of medieval times the reed is controlled by the lips, but the metal disc lingers in the *pirouette* or funnel-shaped block of wood against which the lips are placed. According to the practice of the time the Schalms or Shawms were grouped in a complete family from the high treble instrument, about 17 inches in length, to the great bass *Pommer* over 10 feet from reed to bell and a compass from F_1 to f. The smaller instrument is now represented by the *Musette*, a little pastoral pipe which must not be mistaken for the French bagpipe of the same name. It is also known in Italy amongst the Abruzzes as the *Piffero*, in Spain as the Galician pipe (*Gaita Gallega*), and in Catalonia as the *Gralla*. In Brittany it retains the older name *Bombarde*, derived from the German *Bomhart* (*Pommer*), which is given to this family by Agricola (1528). When the reed of the pipe is covered with a cap, so that it cannot be controlled by the lips, the instrument appears as the *Hautbois de Poitou*, which is still played in French country districts. Mersenne (1635) describes it under three different sizes. The so-called practice chanter of the bagpipe resembles it in this particular. It was also known to Praetorius under the name *Nicolo*.

As all these instruments were made with straight tubes,

i.e. not reflexed as in the bassoon, the difficulty of managing the deeper-toned members must have been great. The alto *Pommer* was furnished with one key (for the lowest note) of somewhat primitive construction and hidden beneath a perforated cover. The larger instruments had four keys under similar coverings. The chromatic scale was obtained by the system of "cross-fingering." In the sixteenth century the *Discant Schalmei* became known in France as the *Haulxbois*, and in England as the *Howeboie* (Plate VIII, 9). The name implied that it was a high-pitched wooden instrument as contrasted with the larger and deeper *Bomhart* or *Pommer*. In England during the thirteenth century it had also received the name *Wayte* pipe, because it was the recognized appurtenance of the watchmen. Besides the flutes or recorders called "pilgrims' staves" possessed by King Henry VIII, he also had in his collection shalmes bearing the same name. Mersenne informs us that reed pipes of slender form were so described, and that they were used by the pilgrims who visited the shrine of St. James at Compostella to while away the weariness of the journey. Perhaps they were a kind of *Stockpfeife* available also as a staff.

In the sixteenth century the hautboy or oboe, as it is now called according to the German and Italian designation, had already its lowest key, and in the following century another key for e^1 flat was added, very often duplicated for right- or left-handed players. In 1727 the g^1 sharp key appeared, replacing the double-hole, and also the b^1 flat key. By the opening of the nineteenth century it had at least nine keys with an octave "speaker" key. By this time, too, the heavy build of the old shawm, with its trumpet-like bell, had given way to the graceful lines and rounded bell now associated with this delicate-toned instrument. A new form, of high pitch, has recently appeared in the *Piccolo-Heckelphone*. Its narrow bore gives it a penetrating but controllable effect, and as it is a fifth above the ordinary oboe it is useful in supporting the upper register of that instrument. To the perfection of the oboe many French makers have contributed, such as Bizey (early eighteenth century), Delusse (late eighteenth century), Brod, Triebert, and Buffet in the last century. Like the clarinet, by the adoption of the Boehm system and Barret's improvements, its fingering has been greatly simplified.

The alto oboe or *Hautbois d'amour*, a fourth lower in pitch than the treble instrument, was the favourite of Bach; its incurved bell adds a softness to its delicate timbre. It has now taken its place again in the orchestra.

The tenor oboe has assumed various forms. In Italy the tube was at first curved almost in a semicircle, and it retained for some time the wide and open bell of the shawm. The name *Oboe da caccia*, "hunting oboe," may have been given to it because its shape was convenient for playing on horseback or from the fact that its pitch was identical with the ordinary hunting-horn in *F*. Bach, in his Leipzig music, wrote frequently for the tenor instrument under this name. In the middle of the eighteenth century, however, its tube was bent angle-wise at the middle joint, and possibly the name *Cor anglais* then given to it, and used by Gluck in his score of *Alceste* (1767), may have been a confusion with *Cor anglé*. In England the instrument appears always to have been made with a straight tube, and it continued in use in English wind bands when it had been superseded on the Continent by the horn. It was the "tenor hoboy" of Purcell's score in *Dioclesian* (1690), and its rich, plaintive tone-colour is admirably displayed in Dvořák's *New World Symphony* and Wagner's *Tristan*.

The baritone or bass oboe—an octave below the treble—was improved by Triebert for the oboist Vogt, and has been more recently perfected by Heckel of Biebrich, and also by Evette and Schaeffer of Paris. A baritone oboe of Swiss or Tyrolese origin, known as the *Basse de Musette*, which appeared in the eighteenth century, retained the large size and heavy appearance of the earlier *Schalmei*. In 1863 a metal instrument of the oboe type was invented for military bands by Sarrus of Paris. It is of stronger and harder tone, and has been constructed as a complete family from the soprano *Sarrusophone* in straight form to the contra-bass *Sarrusophone* in multifold shape and as a substitute for the *Contra Fagotto*. The *Heckelphone*, which also takes the name of its inventor, is a baritone oboe with a wide conical bore; it has a full, rich tone which is much admired, capturing the approval of Strauss in his *Salome* (1905) and of Schillings in his *Mona Lisa* (1915).

We have already alluded to the cumbersome shape of the deeper-pitched instruments of the *Schalmei* class. To whose mind occurred the brilliant idea of reflexing or doubling the tube so as to render the form more compact we do not know. But it created a new series of sound-producers culminating in that most attractive and sensitive instrument the bassoon (*Fagotto*). As was natural, the first efforts in this direction would have been made with instruments possessing a cylindrical bore, and, so far as present details are obtainable, the *Phagotum* of the Italian Canon, Afranio, constructed before the year 1521, was the earliest attempt. This interesting instrument will be described more fully under its proper heading, viz., that of the bagpipes (ii.B.a); but the fact remains that the two columns of wood which were attached in parallel to form the *Phagotum* were, each of them, bored with two small cylindrical tubes united by a short cross or U-shaped channel. In the detailed descriptions and illustrations of Virdung (1511) and Agricola (1528 and 1545) we find no hint of such a device; but by the time Zacconi (1592), Cerone (1610), and Praetorius (1618) wrote the full principle is developed, beginning with the *Sordoni, Doblados, Doppioni,* and probably the *Dulceuses* of Henry VIII (1547) or the *Dulȝaine* with cylindrical bores, and ending with the conical-tubed *Fagotti* or *Dolciani.* We may, therefore, legitimately conclude that this device of Afranio, though his instrument failed, was welcomed at once, and that by the second half of the sixteenth century the bassoon was *un fait accompli.* The name *Fagotto* may have been taken from the original invention, for the worthy Canon's instrument looks more like a "bundle of sticks" than do the first forms of the bassoon, which were constructed in one block. A famous maker towards the end of the sixteenth century was Schnitzer of Nuremberg, and as early as 1578 Philippe van Ranst was Court fagottist at Brussels. These first essays were of two kinds; the open *Fagott* had the usual spreading bell, but the tube-end of the stopt *Fagott* was covered by a perforated block of wood to soften the sound. In the seventeenth century the instrument, however, assumed its present shape, the two tubes being outwardly separated except in the lowest joint. In 1659 it appears with the oboe in Cambert's *Pomone.* The French word *Basson,* adopted in England, signifies its valued position as the foundation-tone of the wind instruments in the orchestra.

In the seventeenth century the name *Curtal* was given to it in England; the tenor instrument, descending only to *G,* being a single curtal or corthol, and the bass instrument, descending to *CC* (according to the English nomenclature of the period), a fifth lower. The German name *Kortholt* (*Kurzholz*) is given to the shorter instrument of the sixteenth and seventeenth centuries by Praetorius; on the other hand, Mersenne's *Courtaut*, described under ii.A.a², though also a short instrument, had a cylindrical bore.

Like other instruments of the sixteenth and early seventeenth centuries, the bassoon was made as a complete family, from the *Discant Fagott* ($g–c^2$) to the *Doppell Fagott* ($F_1–g$); but the *Chorist Fagott* ($C–g^1$) became the favourite pitch though the tenor instrument, called in England the tenoroon, is occasionally used. At the beginning of the seventeenth century the bassoon had but two keys for *D* and *F*, but by the middle of that century a third for B_1 flat was added and the instrument lengthened to receive it. In the second quarter of the eighteenth century the *G* sharp key appears, and in the latter half the *D* sharp and the *F* sharp keys. At the opening of the nineteenth century the keys were eight in number, as well as two keys for the higher overtones. Towards its ultimate perfection the names of Almenräder, Savari, and Boehm stand out pre-eminent, while later makers, especially Heckel of Biebrich-am-Rhein, have simplified its fingering and improved its intonation.

The *Fagottino*, or octave bassoon, is no longer made, having been superseded by the *Cor anglais*. Praetorius in 1618 mentions the construction of a true *Contra-Fagott* by Hans Schreiber of Berlin; it was an octave below the ordinary bassoon. In the early years of the eighteenth century Stanesby Junior, the famous English maker, constructed a similar instrument for use in Handel's oratorios. It is now preserved in the National Museum in Dublin, and is 8 feet 4 inches in height, with four keys, and descending to the 32-foot B_2 flat. For an instrument of similar pitch Haydn wrote in his

Creation (1798), and Beethoven used it freely. The *Tritonicon,* or Universal-contrebass, invented by Schöllnast of Presburg (1839), had five conical brass tubes placed in parallel and fifteen keys; the compass was over two octaves from D_1, and it is still used in military bands on the Continent in place of the *Sarrusophone.* Moritz of Berlin (1856) constructed a metal *Contrafagotto* for military use on the same lines, with a keyboard somewhat similarly arranged as that of the pianoforte, which was attached to the side of the instrument. It was called the *Klavier Kontra-fagott.*

Towards the close of the nineteenth century Haseneier of Coblenz, in his *Contra-Bassophon,* produced a shorter but stouter form of the instrument, with four parallel tubes, nineteen keys, and a compass from C_1. The original design was made by Dr. Stone of London. Though possessed of great power, it was rather rough in tone, and it has now been superseded by Heckel's model with its more characteristic bore and even tone; it descends to B_2 flat. Mahillon of Brussels produced a *Contra-Basson* in brass, with fifteen lever keys, opening the lateral holes at intervals acoustically correct. Owing to its large bore it is fitted with two octave keys and has a rich, broad tone. In 1873 a *Sub-Kontra-fagott* was constructed by Cerveny of Koniggratz, descending to 64-foot B_3 flat.

MOUTH HARMONICA

ii.A.c. The free reed, in which the tongue vibrates within its frame instead of on it as with the clarinet reed, is a production of Eastern Asia. From distant ages the Chinese have used it for their primitive mouth-organ, the *Shêng.* In earliest days the tongue was cut out of a thin slip of bamboo; now it is made of metal. The principle is recognized in Malaysia and is embodied in the *Phan* of Indo-China. Mersenne (1635) gives an illustration of this latter instrument, but the peculiar action of its reed seems to have remained unnoticed in Western Europe until a Chinese missionary, named Amiot, sent specimens of the *Shêng* to the Minister of Arts at Paris in 1777. About the same time it gained attention in Denmark and Russia. In 1792 it was incorporated in the organ, and became in 1810 the characteristic principle of the accordion and harmonium, described under ii.B.b.

At the beginning of the nineteenth century the reed was blown directly in various forms of mouth harmonicas, known as the *Aura* or *Mundäoline*. A very early example of German make, and probably one of the inventions of Buschmann of Berlin, consists of a small cone of ivory into which, for portability, a smaller and similar cone is fitted. Each bears at its truncated end a metal plate with four free reeds. By blowing through one set the tonic chord is sounded, on the other the dominant chord, the conical tubes acting a resonators. The whole instrument, when closed, is but $2\frac{1}{4}$ inches in length. In Wheatstone's *Symphonium Regal*, though blown from the mouth, touches are added for the fingers, thus anticipating the concertina of 1829. The simplicity of construction which underlies the free reed—somewhat similar to that of the Jew's harp—has suggested its use for various forms of children's toys, such as humming-tops and small trumpets. The *Psall-melodicon* of Weinrich (1828) was a wooden tubular instrument with a bell and small keys, rather like those of the clarinet; the opening of them allowed the breath of the player to pass through the reed. The *Harmonicor*, made in trumpet shape, with a series of pistons each containing a reed, enabled the player to obtain a compass of two chromatic octaves. Its self-contained tonal power, however, has prevented the application of the free reed to tubes provided with finger-holes and designed to form a scale, the strength of the reed overpowering any sound waves set up by the tube. Even this, nevertheless, has been attempted in the *Keluri* of Borneo, but with small success.

BAGPIPES

ii.B.a. The invention of the bagpipe, on which, though the wind is supplied either by the mouth or by small bellows, the pressure is sustained by a collapsible reservoir, takes us back to very distant days. The earliest form of such an instrument would have been found in something like the medieval *Platerspiel* or bladder-pipe. Here an elastic bag is inserted between the mouthpiece and the body of the pipe which holds the reed. The player, by keeping the bag distended with his breath, can prolong the sound even while momentarily inhaling. Illustrations of this instrument, under the name of *Chorus*, appear in the twelfth century of our era, but the idea—save for the elasticity of the air reservoir—is contained in the gourd-pipes of pre-Christian times. A terra-cotta figurine from Susa, dating to the eighth century B.C., is supposed to represent the earliest example of the true bagpipe, though, either through accidental breakage or for artistic purposes, a mouth-tube is not shown. It is also very doubtful whether the *Symphonia* mentioned in the Book of Daniel (chap. iii) and translated "dulcimer" was really a bagpipe, as such a name for it does not appear till the end of the first century of our era.

In some form or other, however, it was known to the Greeks in the fifth century B.C. under the name *Physallis*, probably the "bladder-pipe" form; and in India the Sanskrit name *Nagabaddha* was given to it. It is presumably of Asiatic origin, if inference may be drawn from the simple forms of the instrument still in use on that continent. It travelled westward, partly through roving gipsy bands and partly by commercial intercourse with Central Europe. Probably the Romans, who knew it as the *Tibia utricularis*, rather than the Celts, introduced it into Britain; and the Arab invasion of Spain popularized it still further. In that country the common title, *Gaita*, given to it is derived from the Arabian word *ghaida* associated with wind instruments. The names applied to bagpipes in Europe are various and denote some special characteristic. Some instruments have bellows for supplying the wind, as well as the compressible bag for sustaining the sound; and, as a general rule, the Eastern European type uses a cylindrical chanter with a single-beating reed, whilst the Western type prefers a chanter with a double-beating reed.

It is interesting to observe the traces of these two types as they exist to-day. The Eastern type is found in the Turkish, Bulgarian, and Polish *Gajda*, with two parallel cylindrical tubes both having single-beating reeds, the one serving as a chanter, the other as a drone. The Dalmatian *Piva* is similar, but the two tubes are sometimes pierced through a solid block of wood and the lower end is terminated with a curved piece of horn, a general way of adornment in the Greek islands. But these characteristics also appear in Russia on the *Volynka* and *Shabur*, used by Finnish tribes on the Volga. In Spain during the thirteenth century, as depicted in the illustrations to the *Cantigas de Santa Maria*, the Eastern type, represented by the Arabian *Zuqqara*, was in use; but the present bagpipe there found, called *Gaita gallega*, approximates to the Western type. As instruments of this latter type, i.e. with a double-beating reed on the chanter, we may mention the *Biniou*, used in Brittany, with a conical or a cylindrical chanter and one drone with a single-beating reed. The *Cornemuse* or *Chalemie* of France, in the Auvergne form, has one conical chanter and one drone; but in the Nivernais form it possesses one chanter and two drones. The Calabrian *Zampogna* or *Cornemusa* of the Abruzzi possesses two conical chanters and two drones, all with double-beating reeds. The great Highland pipes of Scotland display one chanter with a double-beating reed and three drones with single-beating reeds; the Lowland pipes are a small representative of it. The German *Bock*, which Praetorius tells us was the largest form of bagpipe in that country, has one chanter and one drone; whilst the *Schäfferpfeife* or shepherd's pipe and the *Hümmelchen* ("little buzzer"), though smaller, had two drones, and the *Dudey*, smallest of all, three drones. These are all mouth-blown pipes; but at some period, probably during the earlier part of the sixteenth century in Italy, bellows such as we find with the *Phagotum*, shortly to be considered, were brought to the aid of the performer and, placed under his right elbow, furnished the wind supply. In France they appear with the *Musette* (Plate VIII, 11) in the early part of the seventeenth century, a dainty instrument, at first with only a single chanter and four drones included in a little cylindrical box, pierced with small tubes and regulated by slides. Double-beating reeds were used throughout, and (*c.* 1650) a small, flat-shaped chanter with six keys to give additional notes below the compass of the long chanter was placed at its side by Martin Hotterre. Sometimes the *Cornemuse* in Auvergne is furnished with these bellows. In the Neapolitan *Surdelina*, described by Mersenne (1635), we have two chanters and two drones, the latter covered with an elaborate system of keys and all with double-beating reeds—a veritable portable organ in that writer's opinion. The same idea is embodied in the Irish union or *Uillean* (elbow) pipes, which appeared in the eighteenth century. Here there is, however, but one chanter with a chromatic scale of two octaves and two or three drones, which are technically called "regulators," and on which the keys, when depressed by the hand or wrist of the player,

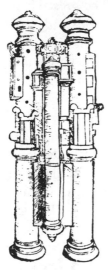

FIG. 7.—PHAGOTUM

produce a crude harmony of tonic and dominant chords. The Northumbrian or Border pipe, an artistic little instrument of the eighteenth century, has a chanter and four drones, the latter mounted on one stock.

As for the derivation of these various names, the word *Musette* is a diminutive derived from *Muse* (the Latin *Musa*), a reed pipe, and it has been suggested that the horn bell, so common in the East and familiarized by the Crusades to Europeans, produced the name *Cornemuse*. The horn bell frequently appears in the illuminations of the thirteenth- and fourteenth-century Psalters. The German *Bock* takes its name from the goatskin from which its bag is made, and the *Hornbock* from its horn-tipped drones. The Italian *Zampogna* is a corruption of the late Latin and Greek *Symphonia*, denoting an instrument of many simultaneous sounds. The modern German name, *Dudelsack*, is derived from the Polish *Dudy* (i.e. pipes).

A particularly interesting instrument of the bagpipe class is the *Phagotum* or *Il Phatogus* of Afranio, to which allusion has been made under previous sections. The inventor, who lived at Pavia in the first part of the sixteenth century, by employing the orthodox skin-bag pressed under the left arm and small bellows beneath the right elbow, constructed a melodic instrument by means of parallel chanters each pierced with a double cylindrical tube and amply provided with keys. On it music in one or two parts could be played at will. Its key mechanism was wonderful and far in advance of any similar work of its period. Afranio for many years found great difficulty in controlling the reeds placed with the caps of his chanters; but, by using two single-beating reeds, one of silver and the other of brass, for the respective tubes, he perfected it sufficiently to enable him to perform on it at a banquet in 1532. This ingenious invention, which we believe gave the idea for the parallel tubes of the bassoon, is mentioned and illustrated by his nephew Ambrosio in his work on the Chaldean language (1539). A full description of it, together with a reproduction of the original designs, will be found in Grove's *Dictionary of Music* (1927). Ambrosio's magnificent illustrations notwithstanding, the *Phagotum* was by no means a large instrument. With its two pillar-like chanters, connected somewhat like the letter H, it was only 16 inches in height; it was suspended by a cord from the neck of the seated performer and rested on his knees. In some manuscript instructions for the instrument (dated 1565) it is called a *Fagotto*, as it is also in the programme of the banquet. "No vain or amatory melodies" issued from it; only "divine hymns and songs." The left tube or chanter had a diatonic compass of ten notes (c–e^1), and that on the right hand also had ten notes (G–b).

Ambrosio informs us that he had seen a *Phagotum* with three tubes and that it could be made to descend to G_1, which was the downward compass of its successor, the contra-bass *Sordino*, so that it was "no mean little organ." And such, as we have seen, was the bagpipe considered. Not only did it add merriment to rural feasts and marriage processions, but even in the churches it was employed to supplement the larger organs and add a picturesque touch to the celebrations of Christmastide. In France during the seventeenth and eighteenth centuries the *Musette* was in the highest esteem for the pastoral plays and *fêtes champêtres* so popular at the Court. It served as the natural accompaniment of the *Ballets* of Lulli, and its music, in what is termed *Musette*-form, supplied some of the finest opportunities for the skill of our great classical composers. The artistic embellishments lavished on its construction and decoration, the handsome needlework of its bag-cover, show the estimation in which it was held in the days of its glory—a glory still reflected in the admiration of collectors. But the bagpipe has also its sterner side, for to Greeks and Romans, as now for our Irish and Scottish regiments, the sound of the pipes roused the army to warlike prowess and inspired them on the march.

REED ORGAN

ii.B.b. Whether the musicians of the old world employed the principle of the beating-reed in their water-organs (i.B.a) is uncertain. From the remains of these and the pneumatic organs still extant it appears probable that they did not, although early in our era the instruments of the Arabian musicians possessed reeds. The first notice we have of the use of the single-beating reed in organ work, that is, with a keyboard, is given us by Praetorius, who in 1618 states that in the second half of the fifteenth century Traxdorff of Mainz constructed an organ which had the sound of a *Schalmei*, a reed pipe, for a church in Nuremberg. This was evidently

PLATE IX. AEROPHONES

PLATE IX

1   BIBLE REGAL (*c.* 1700)

2   PORTATIVE ORGAN (as used *c.* 1500)

3   POSITIVE ORGAN (J. Loosemore, 1650)

the beginning of the little instrument known as the *Regal* (*Regol* or *Rigol*). The name is popularly derived from the supposition that it was first made for or used by royal personages; but more probably it arose from the fact that it was employed in regulating (*regolare*) the singing of the Plain Chant, for which, being portable, it was well suited. The name *Regales*, we must remember, was also given to the wooden xylophones struck with little hammers (Autophones, i.A.c.). Two bellows, raised alternately, supplied the wind, and the little pipes lay immediately behind the keys. A still more portable form appeared in the sixteenth century and was called the Bible-Regal; the bellows were in the shape of a hinged book, into which the instrument could be placed when not in use. King Henry VIII possessed seventeen regals, both double and single (i.e. of 8-foot and 4-foot pitch), and provided with two to four stops, for by this time ranks of flue-pipes had been added to the original reeds.

In the large organs, meanwhile, the *Regal-werke* had assumed an important place. The "open" reedwork included tone reproductions of the *Schalmei, Trompete, Posaune* (trombone), *Zincken* (cornets), and *Krumhorner*; and the covered or capped reedwork represented the *Sordun, Racket, Bärpfeife, Bombard, Fagott,* and *Dolcian,* besides varieties of the original *Regal.* Great attention has since been given to the "voicing" of the reed-stops, as the tone largely depends on the alignment of the curve of the metal tongue. The names of Cavaillé-Coll and Willis are pre-eminent in this respect. The weighting of the tip of the tongue has enabled sounds of low pitch to be produced from shorter reeds, even for the 64-foot trombone stop at Sydney, Australia. Reed-pipes have also been made with double tongues, i.e. with a single-beating reed on either side of a wooden or metal frame. They have also been formed as retreating reeds with the tongue beating on the inner side of the frame. The tubes or bodies attached to organ reed-pipes are not so much for determining the pitch as for qualifying the tone by reinforcing through shape and size certain series of the overtones. Among the more recently invented tone qualities that of the *Diaphone* (Hope Jones, 1893) may be mentioned. The action consists of a fluttering pallet or valve connected with the usual resonating tube, and it is very efficient on a low wind pressure. By altering the tension of the spring of the valve the tone can be varied, as well as by giving a different shape or size to the resonator. The diaphonic horn more closely resembles the beating-reed in its construction, a vibrating disc being attached to the tip of a spring. With regard to the wind supply, the mechanical action required for sounding the reed-pipes of an organ is, of course, the same as that necessary for the flue-pipes, which has been described under i.B.a.

The application of a separate keyboard to the free-reed type dates from the beginning of the last century. It has been attributed to several different makers. Grenié of Paris (1810) in his *Orgue Expressif* applied it to free reeds, with tubes acting as resonators, and showed that by varying the wind-pressure expression could be obtained without altering the pitch of the sounds. But Eschenbach in Bavaria, with his *Aeoline* (1816), and Häckel of Vienna, in his *Physharmonica* (1818), first presented the idea of using the free reed without a tube, as in the harmonium. The *Hand-Aeoline* of Busch-mann (1822), the *Accordéon* of Buffet (1827) or Demian (1829), and the Concertina of Wheatstone (1829) were attempts to render the new instrument more portable, of which the American rocking-melodeon of the middle of that century, blown by pressing down the left side of diagonal-shaped bellows, was another instance. In this, as in most of the other instruments mentioned, finger-touches were substituted for the more normal keys.

The *Accordéon* (called in Russia the *Garmonnaia*) has now been developed into an instrument of considerable size and importance. The earlier "touches" have been replaced by a keyboard similar to that of the piano, with a compass of three octaves or more and with an octave-coupler slide. For the fingers of the left hand, which actuate the bellows, some one hundred and twenty "touches" or studs are provided for supplying basses and chords, and the larger instruments possess four or five sets of reeds.

The *Apollo-Lyra* or *Lyre enchantée* (1830) resembled the classical lyre in shape, but upon it forty-four small keys admitted wind to free reeds placed in the interior; as in the *Harmoniflute* by Pâris of Dijon (1837), the necessary wind was supplied by the mouth of the player through a tube to the air-reservoir. The name *Harmoniflute* has also been given to a form of accordéon or accordion.

In 1837 also Leclere of Paris produced the *Mélophone*, its body being modelled after the guitar and containing the bellows; the neck was fitted with seven rows of twelve "touches" each, giving a succession of semitones from B to e^4. The "touches" pulled open, by small wire connections, the spring valves which permitted the wind to pass through the reeds. Its appearance was greeted in France with much enthusiasm, and Halévy introduced it into one of his operas.

An instrument on the same principle was the *Mélophone-harpe*. This was made in harp shape, the "touches" of the finger-board being placed just below the curve of the neck and the reeds concealed within a short sound-box. The bellows, worked by a foot-treadle, were placed in the pedestal upon which the instrument stood. As the harp portion was strung with fifteen strings, an accompaniment could be played with the right hand, while the left hand executed the melody on the *Mélophone*. Yet another form was the *Cécilium* (1861), which was constructed in the shape of a violoncello, the two bellows being actuated by a handle something like a bow and the "touches" being placed on the neck of the instrument as on the *Mélophone*. The French inventor created a family of the *Cécilium* type—treble, tenor, and bass—the first named having a chromatic compass from A to e^4, and bass instrument descending to E_1.

Green of London in 1833 produced the *Seraphine*, which attained a popular vogue in this country notwithstanding its rather harsh tone. Samuel Wesley introduced it to the public notice. In 1834 Cavaillé-Coll's *Poikilorgue* appeared; it was so called because the wind pressure could be "varied" (and therefore the expression) by means of a pedal. In 1838 Fourneaux constructed an instrument with two keyboards, the upper of 8-foot tone and the lower of 16-foot tone, which could be coupled together, an effect which is now produced by means of stops.

In 1841 the "percussion" action was invented, a small hammer striking the reed and setting it immediately in vibration; by this means instantaneous response was obtained, and Alexandre of Paris adopted it in 1849. Debain, however, was the first to produce the instrument under the name *Harmonium* (1840), and to his subsequent improvements, together with those of Mustel and Dawes, the free-reed keyboard instrument has attained its perfection, both in variety of tone and capability of expression. The "American organ," originally known as the *Melodeon*, was introduced about 1860. On it the reeds are vibrated by suction instead of by propulsion, whereby, it is claimed, a softer and more organ-like sound is produced. It has appeared under various titles.

At the close of the last century a small free-reed instrument, called the *Orchestrina*, was made in London. It represented the tones not only of the different reed instruments used in the orchestra, but also those of the cornet, horn, and trombone. Each *Orchestrina*, with its expressive row of reeds and transposing keyboard, could, if necessary, supply the place of its orchestral prototype.

Free reeds, when incorporated in the large organs, are commonly registered as the *Cor anglais*, *Musette*, etc., but owing to the perfection attained in voicing the beating reed, their use is generally discontinued. In small organs, however, a 16-foot free reed as a pedal-stop for soft combinations has been found useful.

REED-ORGAN PLAYERS

ii.B.c. Automatic mechanism has been applied for several centuries to organs with beating reeds, but neither so early nor so elaborately as to the pipe organs. To the latter alone does Kircher devote himself in his *Musurgia* (1650). The handle-organ with reeds has the usual pinned barrel. The *Ariston* (c. 1890) is played on the pneumatic principle with a perforated roll of paper or a circular plate; and the "pianola" system (Chordophones, ii.B.b) has been applied to the *Orchestrelle* and *Eolian* reed-organs.

Under this heading may also be included such an automatic device as the *Antiphonel* of Debain (1846), for attachment to the organ or harmonium. Small points, short or prolonged, actuated levers which touched the keys of the instrument, before which the *Antiphonel* was placed, the action being moved by a handle.

The *Organette*, which is on the American organ system, automatically reproduces orchestral works by a perforated paper band. The perforations, as they pass over the ends of the air-tubes connected with the reeds, allow the wind to be drawn in, thus setting them in vibration. A similar instrument, under the name *Cartonium*, appeared in 1861. Electricity has now supplanted these earlier devices.

iii. LIP-VOICED TYPE

iii.A. When man first learned to sound the cheerful horn is shrouded in the mists of antiquity. Yet we may infer, from the manner of its sound-production, that it arose after the discovery of the flue-blown tube, suggested by Nature, and before the application of the vibrating reed, which implies a certain amount of human ingenuity. It has been suggested that the method of raising the sound waves by the vibration of the lips—in reality a primitive form of the retreating reed—was discovered by our forefathers' preprandial requirements or postprandial satisfaction. One of the earliest forms of lip-voiced instruments is the spiral shell, found as the *Čank* or conch-trumpet in Asia and as the *Biou* in Europe. Now, in order to get at the fish concealed within it, it was necessary to break off the tip of the shell and either to push it or blow it out. With the final blast that heralded the meal the vibration of the lips was discovered. Or, it may be, that the same process was required to clear the marrow-bone; for bone-trumpets—even human—are still in use in some parts of the world.

The earliest record, however, of the making of a trumpet
or horn which we have been able to discover is contained
in a very ancient description of the labours of the Sumerian
hero, Gilgamesh, dated from the fourth or third millennium
B.C. In this instance the instrument was constructed of wood;
in fact, made out of the hollow branch of a tree, with the
added refinement of a somewhat larger portion attached to
the end to augment the sound. In our description of *The Music
of the Sumerians, Babylonians, and Assyrians* (1937) we have
given the text of this interesting account. The Kirghis and
Kalmuck folk of nearer Asia still use this early form. It is
very probable, too, that inland peoples first employed lip-
vibration on the large hollow river-reeds; for, in the story
as related on the cuneiform tablet, the word used for the
tube of the instrument means also "a reed." To this elementary
instrument would soon have been added by experience a
resonator of gourd, wood, or horn, serving as a bell. This
type of trumpet or horn still exists in the Abyssinian *Malakat*
and in many of the African and Asiatic specimens. That this
principle of sound production must have been recognized in
very early days is shown by the carefully constructed mouthpieces found on the metal horns and *Lurs* of the Bronze Age
in Europe (*c.* 1500 B.C.), and discovered in Denmark, Sweden,
and Ireland. Probably it is to these Alpine and Nordic races,
settled originally in the central regions of Western Asia, that
we owe the horn and the trumpet. In Egypt the latter instrument, for state or military purposes, appears about 1500 B.C.
in a completed form. The idea passed into Africa through
the traders of the Eastern Mediterranean, and it is in this
connection that the side-blown metal horns, found in Ireland,
can best be explained. For they are similar in this respect to
the elephant and other animal horn-trumpets found still in

Africa. In this latter case the side-hole is born of necessity, as with primitive tools the cutting and boring of the solid horn-tip was wellnigh impossible. On the metal horns there was no such compelling need, but they followed the archaic design.

The use made of horns and trumpets in the dim ages of their history was to cause fright or fear. There was no such "soft cooing" to attract as in the present day. For this purpose they were employed in ritual to scare the demons, who were the cause of human ills, and in war to strike terror into the approaching foe. Even the sturdy Romans quailed before the din of the Celtic horn-blowers. Whether these untutored musicians sounded any such thing as a trumpet call is very doubtful. The Romans themselves puffed out their cheeks when they blew the large circular *Bucina* or the crescent-shaped *Cornu* or the straight *Tuba*; if so, the production of the overtones or upper notes would be difficult. Signals, when given, were no doubt rhythmic, like the trumpet *Tara-tantara* of Ennius' poem and the signals blown on the Jewish *Shophar* or ram's horn trumpet.

Having mentioned the subject of overtones or harmonic notes, we may here appropriately deal with this innate peculiarity of all these lip-voiced instruments, and upon which their due classification depends. For musical purposes, let us admit at once, they are by nature incomplete, as no sort of regular scale can be produced on them, except in the very extreme register.

For several centuries, therefore, efforts have been directed towards constructing a perfect scale throughout the series, and the history of the trumpet and horn is bound up with the various devices employed for this purpose. But, before entering into these details, we may illustrate this particular point in the following way.

Taking the double octave from c^1 to c^3, on instruments pitched in the key of *C*, for convenient comparison, there are three ways in which the harmonic notes may present themselves:

(1) The straight little hunting-horn, about 2 feet in length of tube and giving as its fundamental note c^1, provides the following series:

(2) The cornet, of 4-foot length with the fundamental *c*, provides the following:

(3) The trumpet, of 8-foot length with the fundamental *C*, provides the following:

It is evident, then, that the nearest approach to a scale is found in No. 3, so the trumpet became the principal treble lip-voiced instrument in the orchestras of the seventeenth and eighteenth centuries, with the horn following it an octave lower.

But, still earlier, it had been made possible to fill up the gaps diatonically in No. 1 by the use of finger-holes, bored in the tube and six or seven in number, the chromatic intervals being obtained by cross-fingering. Such were the *Zinken*

(*Cornetti,* cornets) of the sixteenth and early seventeenth centuries.

In dealing with No. 2 fewer holes were required for the diatonic scale, as the harmonics are closer. So keys were added, closing the open holes, three being sufficient to yield a diatonic scale and seven being required for the chromatic. Such were the keyed bugles of the early nineteenth century. Moreover, with a sliding tube, moving from its natural position into six extended positions, the same result could be obtained. Such was the trombone of the fifteenth century. The general principle of the "valve" action, which has ousted the finger-holes and the keys, since it appeared at the opening of the last century, is that it automatically adds to the main tube the necessary lengths of tubing to lower the pitch of the harmonic series a semitone, two semitones, or three semitones, as required to fill the gaps.

No. 3 type remained unaltered until the close of the seventeenth century, when its scale also was completed and attuned by a single sliding tube as used on the *Zug-trompete*, which was employed by the waits or watchmen for the playing of the *Chorales* or hymn tunes, which meet us so frequently in Bach's scores.

At the opening of the nineteenth century a twin-slide trumpet was produced by Hyde of London, which became the recognized instrument of the English orchestras for more than half a century.

Such, in brief, were the principal devices adopted to obtain the complete scale on these lip-voiced tubes; and to them perhaps we should add the use of the hand, placed within the bell of the horn, a method attempted even on the trumpet.

As these gaps have thus all been filled, in the three instances of the double octave (c^1–c^3) which we have given, it may perhaps be supposed that it is immaterial which of the three groups of harmonic overtones is employed. But this is an entire misconception, and has led to unfortunate results. For, apart from the questions of mouthpiece and tubing, each of these groups has its own peculiar and characteristic tone. No. 1 (now but little used) is barbaric and hard, even in its lower-pitched representatives, the Serpent and the *Ophicleide*. No. 2 is full-bodied but uninspiring. No. 3 is brilliant and assertive. It was, therefore, an ill-conceived step to convert the royal tone of the 8-foot trumpet into the commonplace scale of a 4-foot instrument by halving the length of its tube, even though a more or less cylindrical bore is maintained; but such are the so-called high *B* flat and *A* trumpets used in some of our orchestras. Such 4-foot instruments may have their proper and useful place, like the cornet and discant trombone; but the substitution of the lower range of harmonics for the trumpet is not art.

In dealing with our scheme of classification we observed that if yet further sub-groups were desired beyond classes and divisions, we might add sections; and if it is wished to arrange the lip-voiced instruments according to the range of harmonics normally employed, we can do so in this way:

§ *Lower Harmonical,* i.e. instruments using the two lower octaves of the harmonic series, such as the medieval cornetts, the serpent, bass horn, ophicleide, and heavy tubas.

§§ *Middle Harmonical,* i.e. instruments with a general range in the second and third octaves of the harmonic series, such as the bugle, flügel-horn, modern cornet, sax-horns, and trombones.

§§§ *Upper Harmonical,* i.e. instruments finding their mean scale in the third and fourth octaves of the harmonic series, such as the trumpet and horn.

A division, too, of these instruments into *Ganz-instrumente* (complete) and *Halb-instrumente* (incomplete) is popular in Germany, but such terms must not be used capriciously. A "complete" instrument is one which employs the lower octaves of harmonics and has its scale diatonically and chromatically perfected by mechanical means—finger-holes, keys, or valves. The cornetts and ophicleide group are therefore *Ganz-instrumente*, and also the deep tubas with four valves and the seven-cylinder trombones. The bugles, horns, and trumpets are *Halb-instrumente*, because they are not complete in the scale of the lower harmonics. It is misleading to define a *Ganz-instrument* as one that will produce more easily its fundamental harmonic, for that largely depends on the shape and size of the mouthpiece and the ability of the performer. With a tenor trombone in our collection made by Neuschel of Nürnberg in 1557 there are two old ivory mouthpieces, apparently original; one is similar in size and cup to that usually found on a tenor trombone; the other has a deeply conical cup and a broad rim. With the former the fundamental note is treacherous; with the other it speaks at once. But we should not call it therefore a *Ganz-instrument*, because its lowest octave is still incomplete.

The ·curious trick of producing chords on the horn has frequently captivated popular imagination, and even such a classical composer as Weber has employed it in the *cadenza* of his *Concertino for Horn and Orchestra* (1815). To obtain the effect a low note is sounded on the instrument, and the performer hums a consonant note of higher pitch. A third note is formed as a resultant. It is said that Tartini was the first to observe this phenomenon upon the violin in 1714. Mr. Blandford, in the *Musical Times* (1926), states that the effect of the succession of such chords on the horn reminds him of that produced by the toy humming-top, fitted with reeds and changing its notes when touched.

Whereas the flue and reed types of instruments have received but few alterations in their bore and general outline during the past century, the lip-voiced type has obtained a remarkable addition to its numbers owing to the invention of the valve system. Their respective tone colours depend, too, not only on the shape of the mouthpiece but on the form of the resonating tube. The cylindrical-tubed trumpets and trombones practically remain unaltered, but the conical-tubed instruments vary considerably. They may, for instance, be grouped as:

(i) *Sub-conical*, i.e. a mixed combination of cylindrical and conical tubing, as on the cornet and some of the sax-horns.

(ii) *Conical*, i.e. a gradually increasing conical bore throughout, as on the orchestral horn, the French *Clairon*, and the bugle.

(iii) *Super-conical*, i.e. with a markedly increasing conical bore, as on the bass tuba, whence its ponderous tone in the lowest register of its scale.

SIMPLE HORNS

iii.A.a[1]. We have already mentioned some of the simplest forms of horns, and these types still exist in Europe. The primitive wooden instrument, generally bound with strips of bast or bark to keep the two halves of the tube together and to prevent leakage, is still to be found amongst mountain folk. The Russian *Rojok*, the Norwegian *Luur*, the Rumanian *Bucium*, and the Swiss alp-horns are recognized examples, the last-named, in their straight form, resembling the *Holzern*

Trommet of Praetorius (1618): they are now, however, frequently made like a trumpet in threefold shape. Somewhat more perfect in finish is the leather-covered French *Huchet* and the metal German *Hifthorn* and military *Halbmond*. Early types, too, are the straight little *Hirschrufhörner* used for signalling in the chase and the horns of the Flemish tower watchmen with one turn. The *Oliphant* or Roland horn, made of ivory and often finely carved, is quite an ancient form, and, as a cylindrical tube is often found at the smaller end, a scale of lip-formed notes can be played upon it, as is practised for producing the lowest notes of the orchestral horn. Still larger and in circular shape was the *Trompe de chasse* (*Waldhorn*), of which Raoux of Paris was so famous a maker in the late seventeenth century. The largest type of this kind was known as the *Parforce Horn,* and encircled the body of the player, being used for hunting fanfares. A similarly large hunting-horn is called in Germany the *Fürst Pless Horn.* As the *Oliphant* was the emblem of knightly rank and prowess, so the *Shophar* of ram's horn was and still is the ritual horn of the Jews. The Bugle, too, probably takes us back in its name to the primitive horn of the wild ox; or it may be another form of the Swiss name *büchel* for a horn; if so, it carries us still further into the past to the old Aryan word *buk* "to blow" or "puff," derived probably from the general effect of the performer's efforts; the ancient Sumerian horn was called *pukku.* The straight glass trumpets made for the Epiphany celebrations in Rome and Florence are on the lines of the old Roman *Tuba.*

A simple type of horn, originally straight but in later times turned almost at a right angle at its smaller end, played an important part in the musical establishment of the Empress Elizabeth of Russia. A band of thirty-seven members, entirely provided with these instruments, was formed by Maresch in 1751. Each horn represented one particular note as it was blown by the player, and the whole gave a chromatic compass of three octaves. Russian horn bands became the fashion for almost a century, and by assiduous practice quick passages could be executed with precision. In 1788 the band at St. Petersburg consisted of eighty performers.

A curious *Cor de chasse* (*Jagdhorn*), known as the *Trompe de Lorraine*, was introduced by Gregoire of Nancy in 1867. Although barely 18 inches in length it commanded the scale of the large hunting-horn, the tube being wound twenty times round the bell in spirals like a shell.

When the *Waldhorn* entered the orchestra at the close of the seventeenth century it was found necessary to alter its normal pitch to the key of the composition played in order to obtain as many of the harmonic notes as possible. This was effected by *tons de réchange* or crooks (*Krummbügel*), consisting of various lengths of tubing inserted into the small end of the instrument. Sax of Brussels, in his *Cor omnitonique*, placed them all on the instrument, the required length being added by means of a graduated sliding-tube. It rendered the horn, however, very heavy. In early days, too, the horn was played with the bell end aloft; but about 1753 Hampel of Dresden, by adopting the practice of holding the instrument downwards, found that on placing his hand within the bell he could flatten the open harmonics, and thus partially complete the scale. It was for the time a useful makeshift, but fatal to equality of tone.

CORNETTO AND OPHICLEIDE

iii.A.a². As already said, the first attempt to construct a complete scale on the lip-voiced instruments took the form of finger-holes. Even on the very primitive shell-horn a hole is sometimes found, enabling the player to produce a second sound of different pitch from his main blast. So, too, in Africa horns are used with two or three holes. In the Slav countries of Europe as well as among the Finns and Scandinavians animal horns are pierced with two to five holes for the fingers. Their *Bukke-horn* is in fact a step towards the more perfect instrument. This is found in the medieval cornett (*Zink, Cornetto*), a name derived from its similarity to the small animal-horn; for in its main form the curved cornett or *Krummer Zink, Cornetto curvo* (Plate X, 1, 2), which dates at any rate from the tenth century of our era, has still preserved the natural shape of its progenitor. The instrument, first outlined in wood and then split in half, was hollowed out with a conical bore and bound together again with a covering of leather. Six finger-holes were placed on the front and one hole at the back. Another form, known as the straight cornett or *Gerader Zink, Cornetto diritto* (*Frontispiece*), closely resembled the wooden tubular horns frequently employed by pastoral peoples. In the mute cornett or *Stiller Zink, Cornetto muto*, similar in shape (Plate X, 4, 5), the mouthpiece was an integral part of the instrument and not an attachment. According to seventeenth-century writers there were three sizes of the curved cornett—the high cornett (*Cornettino*) in e^1 or d^1, the ordinary cornett in *a* or *g*, and the *Cornon* or tenor cornett in *d* with a *c* key. Each instrument had a scale of two octaves; and there was also a bass cornett in *G*. But, as Mersenne remarks, the true bass instrument was the serpent (Plate X, 6), descending to *C* and taking its name from the fact that it was bent in serpentine form to enable the player to reach the distant finger-holes. It seems that the tenor cornett (Plate X, 3), which had just a wavy outline, was called in

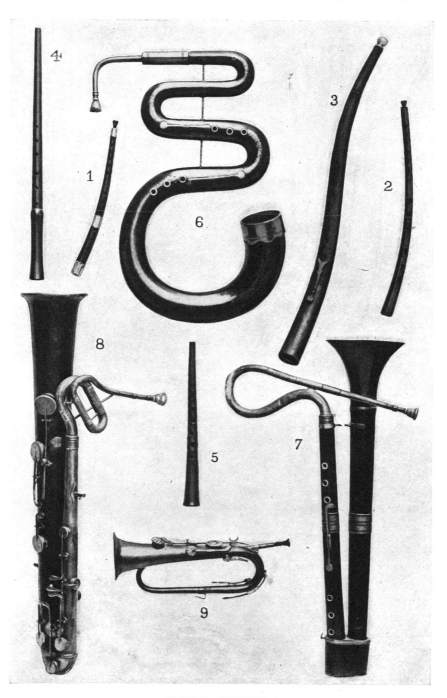

PLATE X. AEROPHONES

PLATE X

1   HIGH TREBLE CORNETT (1518)

2   TREBLE CORNETT (*c.* 1600)

3   CORNON or TENOR CORNETT (*c.* 1600)

4, 5   MUTE CORNETTS (seventeenth century)

6   SERPENT (*c.* 1780)

7   MILITARY BASS HORN (*c.* 1800)

8   OPHICLEIDE (*c.* 1825)

9   KEYED or KENT BUGLE (*c.* 1820)

England the Lyzard. The serpent is said to have been first constructed by Canon Guillaume of Auxerre (*c.* 1590). In the inventory of musical instruments kept at the Castle of Ambras in the Tyrol (1596) there is an entry of wind instruments called *Schlangen* ("serpents"), viz. a bass, two tenors, and two discants. These may be identical with Guillaume's so-called invention; on the other hand the cornetts, especially those of lower pitch, were sometimes ornamented with a snake's head as a bell. The serpent formed the popular bass instrument of the wind bands in the church orchestras of France and England for more than two centuries, only yielding to its own offspring, the bass horn and the ophicleide. The *Cornetti* appear in Monteverdi's *Orfeo* (1607), and were employed by Bach to support the upper part of his *Chorales*, a position particularly suited to them. Their last appearance seems to have been in Gluck's *Orfeo* (1762). The serpent, too, found a place in Mendelssohn's *Meeresstille Overture* (1832) and *St. Paul* (1836). Beethoven scored for it in his March in *D* for Military Band (*c.* 1816), and it also played its part in Wagner's *Rienzi* (1842) and Bennett's *May Queen* (1858). It was not beloved by Berlioz, who considered it more suitable for the *Dies Irae* and Masses for the Dead.

Serpents a fifth lower than the ordinary bass instrument have been made, and a contra-bass serpent, an octave below the bass, was constructed by two mechanics in the last century and included in musical performances held at York Minster. It is now in the Municipal Museum at Huddersfield—a monster unto many. Improvements were attempted on the original form to render it more adaptable for military bands on the march; even King George III of England directed that for this purpose it should be held horizontally instead of vertically. The French maker, Coeffet, produced in 1828 an *Ophimono-*

P

cléide, which is described as a kind of serpent with only one key, yet producing a complete chromatic scale! About 1789, however, Regibo of Lille had altered the serpentine shape into that of the bassoon with an upright bell (*Serpent droit*). The *Ophi-barytone* or *Serpent Forvielle* (1823), the *Serpentone*, and the Russian bassoon were the result, and several of these forms were decorated with a serpent's head instead of the normal bell. Frichot's bass horn (Plate X, 7), which appeared in London at the beginning of the nineteenth century, was made also in metal for military use; it found a place in Mendelssohn's *Funeral March* for Burgmüller (1836) and in Spohr's *Ninth Symphony* (1849).

The difficulty of fingering and the uncertainty of intonation owing to the unequal distribution of the finger-holes led to the application of keys, which closed much larger openings placed at their true positions on the tube of the instrument. The *Ophicleide*, or keyed serpent (Plate X, 8), invented by Halary of Paris in 1817, was the result, and it was included in the scores of Spontini's *Olympia* (1817), Mendelssohn's *Midsummer Night's Dream* (1832), and *Elijah* (1846), and Schumann's *Paradise and the Peri* (1843). In 1820 Streitwolf of Göttingen improved upon it with his chromatic bass horn. Until the introduction of the valve tubas the *Ophicleide* bore a prominent place in orchestral compositions; it was usually constructed in metal, but specimens are found wholly or partially in wood. Its compass of over three octaves, with all chromatic notes, offered great resources, and its wild barbaric tone, consequent on the harmonic register from which its sounds were produced, was appreciated by Mendelssohn in the Baal scenes of his oratorio *Elijah*. Alto or tenor instruments in *F* and *E* flat were made, and also a contra-bass *Ophicleide*. Berlioz informs us that the latter required an amount of breath which would exhaust the lungs of the most robust man. All these instruments of the *Cornetto* type had the distinction of being *ganz-instrumente*, for their scale was perfect from the fundamental harmonic.

Another type of keyed instrument belonging to this division is the keyed bugle (*Klappenhorn, Cor à clefs*). In 1760 Kölbel of St. Petersburg produced a horn with one or two keys called the *Amorschall*, for the use of postilions or for signalling; and in 1791 Weidinger of Vienna applied four to six keys to the trumpet. Such attempts led to the keyed bugle, introduced by the English bandmaster, Halliday (1810), with five to seven keys and called also the Kent bugle in honour of the Royal Regent, the Duke of Kent, then Commander-in-Chief of the British Army (Plate X, 9). This instrument gained great popularity until it was eclipsed by the valve cornopean, and the mail coaches sped over the highways to its merry notes. Unfortunately for its respectability it was only a *Halb-instrument*, the lower octave of its compass being represented by a solitary *b* natural. Upon its analogy, however, the valve *Flügelhorn* was made on the Continent, the name being derived from the fact that the player marched on the right-hand "wing" of the military band. The tenor *Flügelhorn* (*Alt-horn*) was sometimes made in crescent shape. A shake-key was added at one time to the modern cornet and a single key placed also on the orchestral horn to obviate some of the very "closed" notes, formed by the hand within the bell. In 1859 Sax of Paris gave three keys to the cornet, in order to facilitate the production of the highest notes by raising their pitch; but the whole resonance and proportions of the instrument were affected by the addition.

SLIDE HORN

iii.A.a3. An interesting experiment of attaching a slide to the orchestral horn was made in 1812 by Dikhuth of Mannheim. It was another device intended to replace the closed sounds made by the hand. The action was simple, the slide being actuated by a spring, so that when the right-hand thumb of the player released the little crook attached to it, it moved outward and, on pressing the crook, the slide returned. It lowered the pitch of the instrument by a semitone, and also corrected some of the faulty harmonics. The action may have been suggested by Hyde's slide trumpet (*c.* 1808). Unfortunately it was not generally accepted, and the incoming of the valve system banished it. The so-called *Inventions-horn*, introduced by Hampel of Dresden (*c.* 1753), had slides, but they were merely substitutes for the crooks usually inserted into the small end of the instrument: a similar attachment was made on the trumpet by Wögel (1748).

We may here mention the vexed question of the *Corno da tirarsi*, or slide horn, for which Bach in his cantatas has scored some of his *Chorales*. In our opinion it was identical in form, scale, and compass with the *Zug-trompete* (described later under iii.A.b3). It was also of the same pitch, and only differed in tone through the use of a mouthpiece with a deep conical-shaped cup, as made for the horn, in place of the shallow cup characteristic of the trumpet mouthpiece. Mr. Blandford (*Musical Times*, 1936) questions whether the deep conical cup was in use in the late seventeenth and eighteenth centuries; but a horn by William Bull of London, dated 1699, in our collection, has its original ivory mouthpiece made in this way; and also the ivory mouthpiece of the trombone, dated 1557, previously mentioned, is constructed in the like manner. By changing the mouthpiece it was possible to produce on the *Zug-trompete* the trumpet tone or the horn tone. A fuller explanation of this subject is given by Dr. Sandford Terry in his work on *Bach's Orchestra* (1932).

VALVE HORN

iii.A.a⁴. It is somewhat strange that the application of the valve principle to the lip-voiced instruments, in order to obtain the missing notes of the harmonic scale, should have

FIG. 8.—CHROMATIC TRUMPET

"The notes produced from the patent trumpets and horns are always in the natural tone of the instruments, which are proved capable of regular harmony and fine tune, in all keys, minor as well as major; and without the assistance of crooks, or any change whatever in the instrument." (CLAGGET.)

been so long delayed. At the close of the fifteenth century the invention of the slide for the *Posaune*, or trombone, showed that by the addition of certain lengths of tubing to the main tube the desired result could be obtained. In the early seventeenth century too, if not before, the tuning-bit (*Krummbügel*) was in use for the trumpet in order to alter its pitch. It was not, however, until the closing years of the eighteenth century that the idea of a valve or tap, switching on to the main instrument an extra length, was recognized as a practical proposition.

To Charles Clagget, an Irishman resident in Long Acre, London, we owe the introduction of the valve, though the method he adopted on his chromatic trumpet and chromatic horn is elementary compared with modern developments. He realized, as he tells us in his *Musical Phenomena*, No. 1 (1793), wherein he gives an illustration of it (Fig. 8), that by combining tubes of different lengths, properly proportioned, and by applying such a machine as should give the performer an absolute command over either at his pleasure, he would remove some of the defects in the trumpet and horn scale; and by a machine with a "tempering" power he would perfect them. So he combined two trumpets, one in *D* and the other in *E* flat; and at the small end of their united tubes was placed a cylinder, into which the one common mouthpiece was fitted. The cylinder or machine, which he also calls a "valve," not only enabled one or other of the trumpets to be sounded at will, but also lowered the pitch of either instrument by a whole tone and flattened or "tempered" any note of the scale as required. The finger, placed on a small pin projecting from the cylinder, controlled the action of the valve, but whether it was of the rotary type or of the piston type he does not tell us. In fact, in his pamphlet and in the official specification of his instrument he is very reticent as regards the actual mechanism; but informs us that it had received the highest commendation of Dr. Burney as well as leading musicians and singers, and that he had rejected every offer made to him from the Continent in connection with his patent (1788). A compass of all chromatic notes throughout two octaves and a minor third is given for these instruments, and Clagget adds "practice and attention will enable good musicians to increase the number." Public performances were given in London and Bath, consisting of solos and duets on his patent horns, which were also recommended for use in military bands.

It has been thought necessary to enter into these details

because the invention of the valve action has been claimed for Viennese or for German mechanics. The earliest example of any such device on the Continent, however, is in connection with a valve trumpet made by Kerner of Vienna in 1806. In 1818 Blühmel and Stölzel patented in Berlin a two-piston valve action for the horn, lowering the pitch by a semitone or a whole tone (in combination by three semitones), all that was necessary to complete the usual compass of the instrument chromatically. These early valves were made in the shape of square boxes, and the pistons themselves were constructed of square blocks of solid brass. The windways were bored in them in the same horizontal plane, and they were actuated by long slender rods with finger touches.

In 1825 Stölzel introduced a tubular piston with a more rapid movement, but owing to the many angles necessary for the tubing the sound was not so good from the point of resonance. The wind entered by the bottom of the first valve and left by the bottom of the second valve, as seen on some of the earliest cornets, then called *Cornopeans*. The practice survived until about 1846. A third valve, lowering the pitch three semitones, was used by Stölzel on his trombones. In 1824 Shaw patented in London his transverse spring slides with double tubes in U-shape. By depressing the touchpiece the movable tubing was added to the main instrument. The idea appears to have been taken from the trombone or the trumpet slide, and was developed both in an "ascending" and "descending" action. It was improved at a later date and became known as the *Wiener Ventil*; even now it is to be found on some Belgian instruments. In 1827 Blühmel designed the rotary valve action (*Dreh-Ventil*); the rapidity of its movement is greatly in its favour for quick execution, but the mechanism is rather more elaborate than that of the piston valve (*Pump-Ventil*). In 1833 appeared the *Berliner Pumpen*, with short pistons of large diameter. They were evidently based on the rotatory action, though converted into a straight movement, and were improved in 1839 by Perinet of Paris, who gave to the pistons greater length and less diameter.

Shaw patented a disc-valve action in 1835, which was afterwards adopted by the French maker, Halary. The discs were made in pairs, one being attached to the additional tube lengths with suitable windways, and the other revolving on it under the action of a lever provided with a touchpiece. The action removed the sharp angles hitherto so detrimental to tone, but the great difficulty of keeping the faces of the two discs wind-tight was against its adoption. To an English doctor, J. P. Oates, must be attributed many of the ideas which have since been employed by various makers; for he did not patent them. The objection to the piston valve was the angular position of the windways; and in 1859 the French maker, Besson, secured direct passages with the same diameter of bore preserved throughout in every combination of the pistons. Courtois followed with another application of Dr. Oates's improvements, and Distin of London in 1864, using a tube with windways soldered into it, produced the light-valve action which has since become general.

It is, however, to the celebrated firms of Sax (Brussels and Paris) that the progress of the valve instruments is largely due, and the sax-horns, saxo-trombas, sax-tubas will stand as a lasting memorial of their ingenuity and skill. The sax-horns (1845), known in France as *Bugles à pistons*, form a complete family, though the soprano and high soprano parts are now taken by cornets. These differ from the sax-horns in having tubing of a smaller diameter, and therefore possessing a slightly brighter tone. *Sopranino* instruments, an octave above the ordinary cornet in *B* flat, have been made. The *Cornet* (by Courtois, *c.* 1828) became popular in France as a dilettante instrument, probably on account of its frequent use by Rossini, as for instance in *William Tell* (1829). Berlioz, writing in 1843, realized the danger of its indiscriminate use; for he says "melodies will always have to fear from this instrument a loss of a portion of their nobleness, if they have any, or, if they have none, an additional triviality." Valve tenor horns such as the *Primhorn* (Cerveny, 1873) and the *Cor alto* and *Tenor Cor* (Besson, 1890) are devices to replace the orchestral horn by instruments playing in the middle-harmonic register, a change almost as questionable as the substitute for the trumpet. Their usefulness in military bands, especially on the march, is, however, evident.

A baritone *Bugle à piston* was sometimes called in France the *Clavi-cor* (1838), presumably because it was introduced to replace the alto *Ophicleide*. With a large bore it appeared as the *Euphonium*. Instead of the upright model the larger instruments of the sax-horn type frequently adopted the circular form; such were the *Sonorophones* (1858) and the *Helicons* (1845), the latter assuming in Prussia even a quadrangular shape. The circular form is very convenient for carriage, but the tone is more round and less telling. The size of some of the deeper-pitched instruments in the upright model is magnificent: a double *E* flat bass—called sometimes the *Contra-Bombardon*, or, if with very large bore, the *Sousaphone*—will stand more than 5 feet in height with a bell diameter of 3 feet. The scale is complete from A_2 with three valves; if, as a tuba, with four valves, from E_2 flat.

The outstanding difficulty in the valve system has been hitherto the inability of keeping the very low notes of the instrument in tune. Owing to the incorrect proportion of the additional tubing, the valve-formed notes are too sharp and the necessary flattening has to be done by the lips of the player. Instruments have been constructed with six valves, corresponding to the "positions" on the trombone slide, or with a lever adding extra tubing. But the first efficient device was invented in 1874 by Blaikley of London; by an automatic method a loop of tubing is added to the length of the instrument when one or other or both of the first two valves are used in conjunction with the third valve. Mahillon of Brussels in 1886 produced the same result in his "regulating pistons," the use of the first and third valves in combination bringing into use additional tubing. Such improvements as these have enabled the valve action on the large tubas of Sax to produce the lowest notes of their fundamental octave in perfect tune, even when a fourth valve is added to prolong the chromatic series throughout the whole compass.

TRUMPET

iii.A.b.[1] In dealing with the lip-voiced instruments with cylindrical tubes, we are reminded of the early origin of the trumpet and trombone type, of which they are characteristic. As the conical shape of the tube was derived from the natural animal·horn, so the cylindrical tube is the counterpart of the river-reed, which, with the attachment of a gourd or a short horn, provided for primitive man another efficient sound-producer.

We have already alluded to the old Sumerian legend of Gilgamesh in connection with the conical horns; but it would be a mistake to imagine that these ancient peoples distinguished, as clearly as we do, between the conical and the cylindrical shapes of the tubing; the effect was to them more important than the cause. The truly cylindrical instrument of the Romans was called the *Lituus*, which retained many of the earlier characteristics in its narrow tube (at times over 4 feet in length) and its small upturned bell. As the circular *Bucina* was the signalling instrument of the Roman infantry, though it was also employed for civil purposes, so the *Lituus* was allotted to the cavalry. Its similarity to the augur's wand for taking omens may have been accidental; but, by the association of this shape of trumpet, as shown in the Jewish *Shophar*, with ritualistic practices, it is possible that the shape of the wand was due to its having been originally a wind instrument for summoning the attention of the gods. Closely resembling the *Lituus* is the ancient Celtic *Karnyx*, a war-horn with a conical bore.

In a wall-painting at Pompeii of the first century A.D. there is apparently the representation of a true trumpet, not merely in the shape of its bore but in having the long tube bent by a short turn in parallel, as in the modern instrument. If so, the type was not generally adopted in Europe until twelve or thirteen centuries later. The popular trumpet of the Middle Ages was the *Busine*, the Spanish *Anafil*, from the Arabic *al nafir* (trumpet). It was included under the general title of *Cors Sarrazinois* or Saracen horns.

The short, straight *Trompe* or *Trompette* was restricted to military purposes, but the longer instrument, of nobler proportions, was admitted into civil functions and associated with the shawms, flutes, and stringed instruments. From the *Busine*, however, came the trumpet of to-day by the folding of the tube. This innovation, or perhaps we should say re-introduction, appeared about the year 1300 in Northern Italy; its attribution to the French trumpeter Maurin (*c.* 1498) must therefore be corrected. At first the tube was simply folded twice in one plane, as illustrated by Virdung (1511), who calls it the *Thurner Horn* or tower-watchman's horn. It was necessarily, by its zigzag form, weak in construction, but far more portable than the 6-foot length of the *Busine*. In the middle of the fifteenth century, however, the third length was turned over on the first length, as shown by Virdung for the *Felt-trumet* and *Clareta*, the two lengths being kept rigid and apart by a grooved block of wood. In this same form it existed till almost the end of the seventeenth century. The difference between the field trumpet (a military instrument) and the *Clareta* or clarion seems to have consisted mainly in the diameter of the cylindrical bore, and may account for the seventeenth-century distinction between the *Clarino* for the high trumpet part and the *Tromba* for the lower part. A curious trumpet with a double tube is figured by Virdung and dated A.D. 1150. He gives it the name of *Chorus*, which, as we have seen, was also bestowed on an early form of bagpipe. It is said that, although there is but one mouthpiece and one bell at either end of the two oviform tubes, the tone (as given by a reproduction) is not much affected by the double column of air issuing from it. Praetorius (1618) describes another interesting development as the *Jäger Trommet*, an instrument with the cylindrical tubing wound in many turns, like the post-horn. It was known in the late seventeenth century as the Italian trumpet, and is the instrument shown in the famous painting of Reiche, the trumpeter of Bach's day, whose great artistic skill has been described by Dr. Sandford Terry (*Bach's Orchestra*, 1932).

The closing years of the sixteenth century saw the admission of the trumpet into the orchestra, for hitherto it had been the pre-eminent adornment of royal and warlike pageantry; in 1581 a ballet, composed for the marriage of

Margaret of Lorraine, placed together two *Trombe*, two *Viole da braccio*, and a *Fagotto.*

In Monteverdi's orchestra (1619) parts were scored not only for harpsichords, viols, lutes, trombones, organs, cornetti, and a piccolo-flute, but also for one *Clarino* and three *Trombe.* Besides these two names for the instrument, we find, in the classical scores of the seventeenth and eighteenth centuries, that the *Tromba* was also called *Principale*, forming, as it did, the main body of the group. If it was used to replace the kettledrums it was called *Toccato* (*Touquet*, Tucket), and merely sounded the tonic and dominant in its low register.

The masterly control which the musicians of the seventeenth and early eighteenth centuries acquired over their instruments is well known. Artists, such as Fantini and Reiche, seem to have almost attained the impossible both in compass, execution, and even chromatic intonation, which in their day was wholly dependent upon the practised embouchure of the performer.

Unfortunately for most performers, the harsh harmonics of the upper register remained, and it was said that such discordant notes, "when the trumpet shall sound," could not fail to raise the dead. Efforts were made to counteract these glaring defects, and the hand or stopt-trumpet was produced about the year 1753 in imitation of the practice adopted by Hampel for the horn. The instrument was altered into a crescent shape (*Trompette à demi-lune*), which brought the bell within reach of the player's hand placed over it. But the muffled effect of the *sons bouchés*—even indifferent on the horn—were entirely out of keeping with the brilliancy of the trumpet, and the experiment failed. An *Inventions-Trompette* was also tried, with the necessary crooks attached to the instrument, which was of the Italian or circular shape. Bass trumpets, an octave below the ordinary pitch, are still used; but the model adopted by Wagner for *Der Ring des Nibelungen*, which was nearly 23 feet in total length, proved unmanageable.

KEYED TRUMPET

iii.A.b². In 1760 Kölbel had placed a key on the horn to avoid some of the "closed" sounds, and soon afterwards it was applied also to the trumpet. This was followed in 1801 by Weidinger's keyed-trumpet, its five keys enabling the player to obtain the complete chromatic scale. It continued in use in Italian and Austrian bands till the latter part of the last century, but the inequality of tone was against its general adoption.

SLIDE TRUMPET

iii.A.b³. Since the fifteenth century the perfect method for scale production has been the slide for instruments with cylindrical tubing. Why it was not adapted to the requirements of the trumpet until the close of the seventeenth century is difficult to understand; but until that century the trumpet had stood outside orchestral use and was united with the kettledrums in military and state functions.

We have already mentioned the *Tromba da tirarsi*, of which we find the name in the scores of Bach, in dealing with the horn. This instrument "to draw out," known also as the *Zug-trompete* or slide trumpet, appears in the middle of the seventeenth century; a specimen by Veit of Naumberg, dated 1651, is preserved in the Instrumenten Museum at Berlin. The slide consists of a single tube inserted in the first

length of the tubing, and the body of the instrument is pushed
out or drawn in over it. As this is rather a cumbersome con-
trivance, the *Zug-trompete* was held somewhat downwards,
and Altenburg, in his *Trompeter und Pauken-Kunst* (1793),
likens it to the alto trombone. No such long "positions,"
however, are required for its slide, as the instrument is on an
upper-harmonical basis. It was generally employed for playing
the chorales by the tower watchmen, and it is for this purpose
Bach uses it, leaving still the *bravura* work to the natural
Clarino or high trumpet. Further details are given in Dr.
Terry's *Bach's Orchestra.*

In 1695 Purcell wrote a *canzona* for the funeral of Queen
Mary; it is for "flat trumpets," whereas the ordinary harmonics
sounded on the instrument suggest the major key. The instruments used may have been of the *Zug-trompete* type, or
perhaps discant trombones, of which we speak presently.
On the other hand, it is known that the English trumpeters
had contrived a method of playing in the minor key, perhaps
in *G* minor with lip adjustment for passing notes.

A more convenient slide trumpet was introduced at the
beginning of the last century by the celebrated English player,
Hyde. A twin slide, attached to the middle of the tubing,
was pushed out by the fingers towards the player and returned
by means of an elastic band. An improvement was effected
by Woodham of London, who made Hyde's trumpets, in
which coil springs and a gut cord supplanted the perishable
elastic. The Harpers, father and son, were the great performers
on this instrument during the nineteenth century in England,
for the model was not adopted on the Continent and the valve
action has now displaced it.

TROMBONE

The early history of the trombone is, fortunately, less doubtful. We may dismiss at once the mythical Roman trombone (*Tuba ductilis*), for the Latin name merely informs us that the metal, of which the tube was made, was "drawn or hammered out," instead of being cast in a mould. The story, too, of the trombone found at Herculaneum in 1738, with a tube of bronze and a mouthpiece of gold, will not bear examination. The name given to it, *Trombone*, simply means "a large trumpet," and the proper title of the slide instrument in Italian is *Tromba spezzata*, or "the broken (separated) trumpet," the French *Trompette rompue*. We are told there were several of these *Tromboni* found; if so, certainly some would have survived in our museums. There is an account given by the late Roman writer, Apuleius, of a procession in which it is said "trombones" were used. Fortunately Apuleius knew better, and he called his musicians "tibicines"; but an Italian writer of the early seventeenth century substituted "tubicines" for the original word, and the trick was done. The instruments really used were the *Plagi-auloi* or cross-blown reed-pipes, described under ii.A.a¹.

The first reliable illustration occurs in the fifteenth century, although on a Burgundian ivory carving of the previous century something like a large *Zug-trompete* is shown. In the fourteenth century it is mentioned by Spanish writers under the name *Sacabuche* or *Saquebute*, that is, "draw-trumpet." From this name comes the French *Saquebute* and the Old English *Sagbut* or *Sackbut*. In Germany it retains the ancient title of its progenitor, the long and straight *Busine* or *Pusine*, whence the more modern *Buzaun* or *Posaune*. This derivation accounts for the German tradition that the Trumpet of

Judgment is the trombone ("*es wird die Posaune schallen*," Luther); and it is said that the *obbligato* to Handel's famous aria in the *Messiah* was played on an alto trombone. It is interesting in this connection to note that Bonanni (1722) records the use of the straight trumpet with a slide amongst country folk in Italy, which he dignifies by the name *Tromba dritta spezzata*. An illustration of such an instrument occurs in the Psalter of René II of Lorraine (1451–1508), and an early Trombone will be seen in our frontispiece.

In the sixteenth century the trombone, under one name or another, was in high esteem and general use, being associated with the *Schalmes* in the wind band. In Monteverdi's *Orfeo* (1607) we find the family complete except for the discant instrument, a fact which Praetorius mentions. Attempts were made to shorten the unwieldy length of the deeper models by making a turn in the tube between the slide and the bell. But the double-slide trombone, designed by Halary in 1830, solved the difficulty, for by duplicating the tubes on both sides the "positions" of the contra-bass instrument were practically the same as on the tenor in the octave above. Wagner used the contra-bass trombone in *Der Ring des Nibelungen*, but the difficulty of keeping the double tubes airtight militates against its efficiency.

Mersenne (1635) calls the trombone the *Trompette harmonique*, and although few alterations have been made in its simple construction, various liberties have been taken with its appearance. In the eighteenth century the bell was made in imitation of a serpent's head, tongue and all; for a time the approach of the military band, with these formidable-looking instruments in the front rank, must have had an awe-inspiring effect; but the tone suffered, notwithstanding their classical name of *Buccin*. Another device consisted in turning the bell over the shoulder of the player in order to throw the sound backward and to prevent the pressure of air on the march, a method adopted in America for several other military instruments.

The discant trombone appeared at last, for it was made in Germany in the later seventeenth century, and was one of the instruments which the *Stadtpfeifer* was required to learn, as it was employed, like the earlier cornetts or *Zinken*, for chorale playing. It was, until lately, confused with the *Zug-trompete*, but lacks its resonance, owing to the short length of tubing required for playing in the middle harmonical register. In this respect it is identical with the modern B flat trumpets. It is practically unknown in France, but has obtained some appreciation amongst the votaries of the jazz band.

VALVE TROMBONE

iii.A.b4. The addition of valves to this very perfect form of sound-producer, on which by its slide every shade of intonation can be produced as on the bowed stringed instrument, has been rightly questioned. For ease in tuition and speedy transference of valve-instrument players from the sax-horns or euphonium to the valve-trombone it is, of course, useful, and for mounted bands it is necessary. But in the orchestra it is out of place except in one particular, viz. for the extension and completion of the downward compass to the fundamental note. One valve to lower the whole pitch of the tenor trombone by a fourth is sufficient to enable the slide to fill up the missing chromatic notes in the lowest register; thus it becomes a *Ganz-instrument* like the four-valve euphoniums and tubas. Seven cylinder valves have sometimes been placed on the instrument; these dispense with the slide entirely and overcome some of the difficulties of intonation and correct pitch in the lowest octave. In fact, most of the usual forms of valve action, already described, have been from time to time applied to the trombone. The Viennese cylinder action, very popular in Belgium, is the least likely to affect the pure tone. Absolutely true intonation was claimed by Sax for a trombone with six piston valves and seven distinct bells! Besson added a single valve, in order to avoid the more extended and awkward "positions" of the slide; and some French instruments are provided with a "shake" valve.

VALVE TRUMPET

On the trumpet the valve action assumes one or other of the methods already mentioned. A new model, suitable for Bach's demands, has recently been introduced by Menke of Leipzig. Whilst retaining the old dimensions, both as to length and size of bell, and thicker metal to produce a softer tone, it is fitted with two rotary valves to supplant the use of the dissonant harmonics.

The so-called Bach trumpet used by Kosleck of Berlin, which was very efficient under so skilful a player, had but little in common with the seventeenth-century instrument. It was a treble octave trumpet in *A* with a straight tube, similar to that of some coach-horns, and two or three piston-valves; the mouthpiece with a conical cup was made of soldered metal and not cast.

Even yet higher-pitched trumpets in *C*, *D*, and *F* have been used, but in all these substitutes tone is sacrificed to ease of execution.

An attempt, too, was made to combine the cylindrical tubes of the trumpet or trombone with the conical bore of the horn in one instrument. Besson, at the beginning of the century, produced the *Doublophone*, a union of euphonium and trombone, with a fourth piston-valve to effect a quick change from one to the other. It might be useful where players are few and variety of tone is desired. One mouthpiece serves the two purposes; the bells are separate and of different shapes.

A final word may be added about the mute or *Sourdine*, mentioned by Mersenne in 1635. The old device consisted in almost closing the bell of the instrument with a plug; in the case of the orchestra horn the hand is employed, and, if the wind pressure is raised, a *cuivré* or brassy effect is obtained. In the modern echo attachment the column of air is diverted from the resonant bell into an inverted conical chamber pierced with a small orifice for its emission.

V

ELECTROPHONIC INSTRUMENTS

including

THE AETHEROPHON, ELECTRONDE, TRAUTONIUM,
HELLERTION WITH KEYBOARD AMPLIFICATIONS,
SUCH AS THE PIPELESS ORGAN

INSPIRED by the remarkable achievements of radio-telephony, electrophonic or, as some call it, electronic music is the outcome of researches made during the past ten or twelve years. A careful distinction, however, must be drawn between this new and fundamental use of electricity for sound-production and that described under preceding classes, in which the initial vibrations are mechanically produced either by the reverberations of a sonorous substance or by the pulsations of air or by the vibrations of a string. In such cases electricity plays but a secondary part.

Avoiding, as far as possible, highly technical terms, pure electrophonic music is effected in the following way:

i.A.a. The property of the thermionic radio valve to produce electrical oscillations is well known, and corresponds with the "flutter" already mentioned in connection with wind instruments (Aerophones, i.A.a). Their very high frequency usually renders them inaudible, but if two valves are made to oscillate with slightly different frequencies the resultant oscillations will have the frequency of their difference. This phenomenon is termed *heterodyning*, and the *heterodyne* frequency, brought within audible pitch, can be amplified and reproduced in a loud-speaker.

The fundamental frequency of the valves may be altered by introducing a variable condenser in the valve circuit. Turning the index of the condenser, as in "tuning in," changes the frequency of the valves concerned. If the two valves are oscillating with precisely the same frequency, no sound is produced; but a very slight alteration in the frequency of one of them results in a steady throb, like the beating of a drum. Further movement of the condenser index increases the *heterodyne* frequency to a deep musical note, the pitch of which can be raised at will through about nine octaves, until, owing to its extreme height, it is again inaudible. The effect, however, is a *glissando*, otherwise a "howl," upwards or downwards, unless the movement is taken in steps.

Jong Mager, in his *Sphaerophon*, obtained this result by marking the condenser with definite gradations for the chromatic scale; but, even with the quickest movement, objectionable "slurring" between the notes still occurred. In the *Aetherophon*, Professor Theremin has employed a different method of control. The valve circuit is connected to a vertical rod projecting from the instrument; the operator's hand and this rod form a condenser with an earthed circuit. The approach or withdrawal of the hand to or from the .rod alters the capacity of this "hand-condenser" and so raises or lowers the pitch of the note produced. With the hand some three feet away from the rod only deep throbbing occurs, but as it approaches the rod the whole gamut of the scale is heard. The difficulty of definite "attack" is still, however, in evidence. Martin Taubmann, nevertheless, has overcome this defect in his self-contained *Electronde* by the use of a small switch held in the left hand. On pressing it simultaneously with the movement of the hand a sharp "attack"—even a staccato—is obtained. By a quickly graded action of the fingers of the right hand in a line with the rod, rapid passages can be played; and, with a slight quivering of the hand, a *vibrato* can be obtained. The artistic execution, however, of this music "on the air" demands patient practice, correct judgment, and a keen musical ear.

i.A.b. That some guide should be devised for those not so gifted was only natural, and so-called "manuals" or elementary keyboards were introduced. Dr. Trautwein of Berlin, on his *Trautonium*, has placed a metal string over a metal rail, and added marks to show where the finger should be placed to press the string on the rail for the correct scale. He uses, too, the impulse variations of a neon lamp; and, by adding subsidiary oscillating circuits to this basic circuit, is able to control the tone-colour of the sound produced, through the action of small studs. On the *Hellertion* of Helberger and Lertes a closer approach is made towards a keyboard. There are, it is true, no actual keys, but a strip of wood, coloured to represent the ordinary piano keyboard, is placed above a rod-like "manual" and acts as a guide to show the proper position of the finger upon it for any required note, while pressure of the finger on the "manual" increases the volume of sound. By combining three or four of these instruments and placing their manuals in parallel beneath the guide, polyphony is possible in combining their sounds. The later developments made by M. Martenot on Theremin's original system also possess a so-called keyboard; but the more difficult and more artistic method of performance is also provided for, the player wearing on his finger a ring attached to a cord, while the actual production of sound is controlled by means of a key to prevent slurring.

All these instruments are purely melodic, that is, like the wind instruments, only one note can be produced at a time, though rapid *arpeggios* are sometimes played which may deceive the ear. Not only is orchestral imitation possible, but they also have the power to produce new shades of tone; great range of volume, too, can be obtained by the use of an amplifying switch or pedal.

PIPELESS ORGANS

i.B.a. The appearance of a true keyboard, and with it the free use of chords, is seen in the pipeless organs now in use on the Continent as the result of this electrophonic music. We may mention the *Givelet-Coupleux Organ*, installed in a French church, and also in one of the Parisian broadcasting stations (PTT). The church organ has thirty-four stops, varying in tone and register, beside couplers. There are three manuals, of five chromatic octaves each, and a full pedal-board. The principle of sound-production is practically the same as that already described; but in the organ there is a separate valve for each note, made to oscillate at an audible frequency immediately the electrical current is passed through it on depressing the key. Each valve is tuned to a definite pitch in the ordinary musical scale. The response is rapid, and the "swell," by an amplifying pedal, most effective.

Among the merits claimed for this latest form of organ are that it is less expensive than the normal instrument and that the valves can be placed anywhere in the church or in the vestry, while the loud-speakers can be concealed in any spot, giving the best acoustical result for choir and congregation.

In the Welte Phototone (Berlin) light produces the sound, being registered on a photo-electric cell. Each rotating disc carries one tone and each oscillating line on the disc has a different tone character. The tone can be recorded in part from original organ-pipes or synthetically constructed by adding overtones to the basic sound.

ii.B.a. Electro-magnetic methods have not, so far as the writer is aware, been employed as yet for the "direct" production of sound, and there is accordingly a gap where Subdivision A of this section should be. Whether this gap will be filled remains for the ingenuity of inventors. Indirect sound production, however, that is, through keyboards or other mechanism, shows great promise. In the electro-magnetic method, as distinct from the oscillatory method which we have just examined, radio valves are not used for producing the sound (although they may be employed to amplify it) but notched discs revolving before magnets. A portable example of this type is the Hammond organ, an American invention of very recent date. It has two manuals of five octaves, each with a pedal-board, tremulant, and an amplifying swell of great power. The stops are arranged in a line over the upper keyboard, and each can be drawn in eight degrees of sound-intensity. To the left of the manuals are a series of black-coloured keys, arranged keyboard fashion. They form pre-set combinations of the various stops and are designed to give different varieties of tone, thus superseding composition-pistons or pedals. It has been mathematically calculated that by combining with the eight intensity-degrees the subsidiary circuits, which, like those on the *Trautonium*, add portions of the harmonic series to the basic sound, twenty-five million varieties of tone-colour are at the player's disposal!

ii.B.b. An instance of automatic sound-production on this

system is seen in the Electric Gramophone now superseding the mechanical instrument.

iii.B.a. An electro-static method—for which also direct application (A) is as yet wanting—has been developed by Mr. Leslie Bourn (Messrs. John Compton, London) and offers several advantages over the electro-magnetic system. Sound-attack and sustained or echo effects may be emphasized or modified to any desired extent. Each stop is complete in itself and can be combined with any other stop in the usual way and without any such deficiencies as would be due to "extension." The added tone-harmonics being true (i.e. untempered), the blend of sound is perfect and the tone-colours distinct. Twelve discs give as many as thirty independent tones each, so that pitches from 32 to 2 feet and any mutations are easily obtainable. In fact, the whole organ with its manuals, pedals, and swell behaves exactly as if it were furnished with ranks of pipes in any orthodox groupings.

For the Electrones used by the firm in cinema instruments each disc has on it forty-eight notes of the tempered scale.

iii.B.b. This system can be employed automatically for the production of Bell-tones for churches and clocks, etc. Clang, ring, and hum-note are accurately reproduced with any desired amplification. Even the effect of the swing of a large bell, or its muffling and half-muffling, can be given, and chimes or automatic change-ringing fitted.

Other ways of producing Electrophonic music will no doubt be tried, but these have already been satisfactorily tested for churches, halls, opera-houses, and for home use also.

So dawns a new Art, and already many composers, such as Honneger, Ibert, and Milhaud, have recognized its possibilities in scoring for it. Undoubtedly it is yet in its infancy; but the unknown tonal effects and the mysterious charm which lie hidden within its unexplored realm may in the years to come place this latest form of sound production in the forefront of our musical instruments.

INDEX

Accordion 210, 211
Acetabula 39
Aelyau 63
Aeolian Harp 156; keyboard 157
Aeolsklavier 59
Aerophonic instruments 30, 35, 159–244; Plates VII–X
Aetherophone 246
Aiuton 50, 58, 59
Amorschall 227
Archi-cistre 99; Archlute 94
Arci-cembalo 113; Arci-viola 142
Arpeggione 142
Aulos 169 f., 186, 191, 240
Aura (*Jew's Harp*) 53; (*Harmonica*) 202, 210
Autophonic instruments 29, 32, 37–59; Plate I

Bagpipes; ancient forms 203; Eastern types 204; Western types 205 f.; popular use 208
Balalaika 92, 102
Banjo 101
Barrel Organ 183; Spinet 114
Baryton 141
Basset Horn 189
Bassoon (*Fagotto*); mediaeval forms 198; open and stopt 199; development and makers 200 f.; octave Bassoon 200; tenor 200; double 200–201; orchestral use 199–201
Bells 42–47; keyboard 48, 49; machine 117; automatic 51, 52; electrophonic 250
Bibliography 17 f.
Blockflöte; see Recorder
Bombarde (*Bomhart*, *Pommer*) 195 f.
Bow; origin 133–135; development 139
Bow Harp (*Bogen-harfe*) 78, 79
Busine (*Pusine*, *Posaune*) 235, 240

Caledonica (*Alto Fagotto*) 193
Carillons and Chimes 46, 48 f., 51 f., 250
Chalemie (*reed-pipe*) 186, 194; (*bagpipe*) 205
Chalumeau 186 f.; (*eunuque*) 74
Chekker 103 f., 119
Cherubine minor 50
Chitarrone 94
Chordophonic instruments 30, 34, 77–157; Plates II–VI
Chorus (*bagpipe*) 201; (*trumpet*) 236
Chromatic Trumpet (Clagget) 229 f., Fig. 8
Cithara 80, 82, 84, 87, 97, 99, 138
Cither (*Citole*) 97 f.; keyed 118
Clappers 38 f.
Clarinet; primitive 185; allied forms 186; development and makers 187 f.; alto and tenor 189; bass and contrabass 190; orchestral use 187, 189, 190
Classifications; early 25, 27; medieval 26; modern 27 f.; adopted 29–36; horns, etc. 219, 221
Clavichord; origin 119; action 120; fretted and fret-free 120–122; d'amour 128. Fig. 2
Clavicylindre 58
Clavicymbalum 105, 107 f., 121
Clavicytherium 107, 109; later types 108
Claviola (*tongued*) 54; (*keyed-viol*) 154
Claviorganum 114, 122, 182
Clock-jacks 51
Colascione (*Colachon*) 92 f., 94
Collection of instruments 15 f.
Cor anglais 197
Cornamuse (*reed-pipe*) 192; (*bagpipe*) 205, 206
Cornet 217, 219, 233

253